Paul, the Founder
of Christianity

Paul, the Founder of Christianity

YOSEOP RA

RESOURCE *Publications* • Eugene, Oregon

PAUL, THE FOUNDER OF CHRISTIANITY

Copyright © 2021 Yoseop Ra. All rights reserved. Except for brief quotations in critical publications or reviews, no part of this book may be reproduced in any manner without prior written permission from the publisher. Write: Permissions, Wipf and Stock Publishers, 199 W. 8th Ave., Suite 3, Eugene, OR 97401.

Resource Publications
An Imprint of Wipf and Stock Publishers
199 W. 8th Ave., Suite 3
Eugene, OR 97401

www.wipfandstock.com

PAPERBACK ISBN: 978-1-6667-1703-7
HARDCOVER ISBN: 978-1-6667-1704-4
EBOOK ISBN: 978-1-6667-1705-1

NOVEMBER 4, 2021

Unless otherwise noted, Scripture quotations contained herein are from the Holy Bible, New International Version®, NIV,® copyright © 1973, 1978, 1984, 2011 by Biblica, Inc.™ Used by permission. All rights reserved worldwide.

Dedicated to

Dr. Daniel SungYul Kim, DDS, and Mrs. Hooja Chon Kim

With thanks in Jesus Christ

Contents

Preface | ix

PROLOGUE | 1

1 THE RECONSTRUCTED LIFE AND LETTERS OF PAUL | 11

2 THE LORD JESUS CHRIST SON OF GOD | 57

3 THE DEATH OF JESUS CHRIST | 95

4 REDEMPTION AND SALVATION | 124

5 THE LAW | 153

6 THE END OF WORLD | 174

7 THE SPIRIT OF GOD | 199

8 THE CHURCH OF GOD | 227

EPILOGUE | 251

Bibliography | 255

Ancient Documents Index | 259

Preface

MANY BIBLICAL SCHOLARS HAVE studied the theology of Paul. Thus, I was doubtful whether there was a need to write another book about it. However, I reached the conclusion that there are still many things that can be reinterpreted. Having judged from a perspective of redaction and the history of ideas, there are still many instructions to be uncovered about how Paul developed his theology in response to the changing circumstances of the recipients of his letters.

I have been pursuing the nature of Christian faith. Initially, I studied Q based on the Synoptic Gospels and published a book titled *Q, the First Writing about Jesus* in Korean in 2002 and then in English in 2016. However, I came to the conclusion that this is a pre-Christian faith. Nevertheless, this study is a good source for tracing the transition from the Jesus movement to Christianity. Therefore, I was forced to study Paul's epistles. As a result, a couple of books could have been published in Korean: *A Commentary on Galatians: The Gospel of Cross, Paul's Six Letters for the Corinthians, Paul's Four Letters for the Romans,* and *The Formation of Paul's Theology*. Now, putting them together, I can present my view that Paul was the founder of Christianity. Inasmuch as almost twenty years have interrupted the study on Q and the eventual publication of Paul's Christianity, I have expanded my theological study in order to know the nature of Christian faith.

My study of Paul's life and theology may be shocking. This will be different from the relationship between Paul and the apostles of Jerusalem as we have known so far. In particular, there will be many things that differ from those reflected in the book of Acts. It will be revealed that the theological controversy over the Gentile table in Antioch was a watershed in Paul's life and theology. The conflict between Paul and the apostles of Jerusalem was the motive that gave birth to Christianity.

This will be revealed in the process of how Paul developed the theological thoughts on various topics embedded in the sixteen letters subdivided from the seven genuine epistles.

I have been helped by many people in publishing this book. I would like to thank Dr. Jae Hyung Cho, from whom I received tremendous academic insight. While I traced the nature of Christianity, he provided generous critiques and encouragement. I think of Professor Gerd Lüdemann, whose work on *Paul the Founder of Christianity* gave me considerable stimulus. Above all, I would like to show my gratitude to Dr. Daniel SungYul Kim, DDS, and Mrs. Hooja Chon Kim, to whom this book is dedicated. Their financial support and encouragement made it possible for this book to be published in English in the USA. Finally, I would like to thank Mr. Jim Tedrick, Managing Editor of Wipf and Stock Publishers, for allowing my manuscript published.

Yoseop Ra
May 16, 2021

Prologue

THIS PROLOGUE PROVIDES BASIC information to understand how I trace the formation of Paul's theology. It is inevitable to examine his genuine epistles from a perspective of fragmentary theory in order to show that some of them have been compiled with short letters. They will be separated into two, three, or even four short letters. Then, sixteen letters will be defined and can be listed according to the chronological order in terms of their composition.

The sixteen letters will provide readers with a foundation upon which the life of Paul could be reconstructed. The important events can be listed as follows: persecution of church, reception of revelation about the Son of God, inheritance of the tradition of Christ in Damascus, acknowledgement of Jesus on the basis of Q in Jerusalem, first missionary trip, apostolic meeting in Jerusalem, theological controversy over the Gentile table in Antioch, second missionary trip, challenge of some Gentiles against Paul under the sponsorship of the apostles of Jerusalem, and third missionary trip. In the meantime, Christianity was born to the Gentiles and grew as time passed.

I will use the sixteen letters as the primary sources that show how Paul developed his theological thought. For this, the following topics will be studied: the Lord Jesus Christ Son of God, his death, the concept of redemption and salvation, the Law, the end of world, the spirit of God, and the church of God. Each theological topic will be described against the backdrop of the life of Paul. Then, it will be revealed that Paul founded Christianity in the middle of the second missionary trip.

My study is completely new to Pauline scholars and students. Accordingly, I would like to focus on describing what I found anew. For understandable reasons, the discussion of secondary literature had to be kept to a minimum. Then, my study will make readers see the reconstructed life of Paul and the process of how he changed and developed his thought on theological topics in response to the changing circumstances of the recipients of his letters as time went by.

THE COMPILED EPISTLES OF PAUL

Paul left the greatest number of epistles in the Christian Scriptures. While conservative scholars have considered the thirteen epistles to have been written by him, critical scholars accept only seven of them as genuine.[1] To them belong Romans, 1 Corinthians, 2 Corinthians, Galatians, Philippians, 1 Thessalonians, and Philemon. I would follow the critical stance on the matter of Paul's genuine epistles; as a result, it will not be discussed anymore here because its discussion is beyond the scope of argument in this book.

What matters is that some of Paul's genuine epistles seem to have been compiled as well. An appropriate reconstruction of them constitutes one of the perennial conundrums of studies about how Paul changed and developed his theological thought over time. Above all, 1 Thessalonians and Philippians deserve our attention because they are supposed to have been composed of two short letters. For instance, in 1 Thessalonians the word "finally" appears with an implication of ending part of the epistle (1 Thess 4:1); however, the text of 4:1—5:28 is too long to be an ending of a letter. This makes critical scholars conclude that two different letters are interwoven in 4:1—5:28. A break is found in 4:9 with a customary phrase of περὶ δὲ, which refers to the answer to the question raised by the Thessalonians after reading the previous letter or hearing a lecture. This paves the way to the conclusion that 1 Thessalonians consists of two short letters at least.[2] In similar manner, the word "finally" appears two times in Philippians (Phil 3:1; 4:8). This also reveals the fact that Philippians is combined with two letters at least.[3] It is noteworthy that 1 Thessalonians

---

1. Lüdemann, *Paul*, loc. 66 of 3299.

2. Brown says, "That two letters have been combined to make up 1 Thess has been suggested by a small number of respected scholars (e.g., W. Schmithals), but unity is overwhelmingly asserted" (Brown, *Introduction*, 457). However, he does not discuss the matter in any further detail. For the fragmentary theory of First Thessalonians, see Schmithals, "Historical Situation," 123–218; and Richard, *Jesus*, 248–52.

3. According to Brown, "That two or three letters have been combined to make up Philippians is widely suggested, but a respectable case can be made for unity" (Brown, *Introduction*, 484, 497-98). There are many scholars who argue for the unity

and Philippians, as short epistles, are composed of two different letters at least.

Second, 1 Corinthians is supposed to be a combination of three different letters. There are too many places that show the clue for this compilation. From a redactional perspective, sudden change of content provides an evidence of edition; for instance, 1:18–31 follows 1:10–17 by the connecting word "cross"; however, it seems that they deal with something different from each other. Whereas the division among the Corinthians caused by baptism is the main topic in 1:10–17, the message of the cross for salvation is delineated in 1:18–31. This shows that 1:10–17 and 1:18–31 originated in two different letters. Another example is found among the texts of idols. For instance, the issue of idol offerings is dealt with in 8:1–13, and the controversy over apostolate is suddenly treated in the following text of 9:1–27. Then, Paul focused on the issue of idol worship in 10:1–22. And finally, the issue of idol offerings returns in 10:23—11:1. Then, the texts of 8:1–13 and 10:23—11:1 are likely to originate from the same letter and are interrupted by 9:1–27 and 10:1–22. From the fact that the issue of the apostolate does not go well with that of idol worship, it can be inferred that the texts of 9:1–27 and 10:1–22 were derived from two different letters. There is another case that shows the interpolation between the two texts of same theme. As many scholars have pointed out, chapter 13, dealing with the issue of love, seems to be interpolated in between chapters 12 and 14, which treat the spiritual gifts.[4] It is then believed that chapters 12–14 are composed of two different letters at least. A similar phenomenon is found in chapter 15, which discusses the issue of resurrection. While the resurrection of Christ is mentioned for a moment in 15:1–11, the resurrection of Christ as well as the saints is believed in 15:12–28; on the other hand, the transformation of the resurrected body is discussed in 15:29–58. The three texts listed above show different focuses from each other. Thus, a temporary conclusion can be drawn that 1 Corinthians is composed of three different letters at least.

To strengthen the temporary conclusion drawn above, it is necessary to see a subtle change of content in a couple more cases. First, there

---

of Philippians; see Garland, "Composition," 141–73; Schnelle, *History and Theology*, 135–37; and Standhartinger, "Join," 418–26. Some scholars argue for the composition of Philippians with short letters; for instance, Reuman, Osiek, and Marxsen belong to them.

4. Lüdemann *Paul*, loc. 1175 of 3299.

are two texts that do not fit with the context of chapter 12; for instance, the issue of confession in 12:2–3 and that of baptism in 12:13 interrupt the flow of content that deals with the spiritual gifts. It is possible that they were located in the present places with a certain intention. Second, a subtle difference is found in 14:20-22. When it is eliminated, the literary flow is natural from 14:18-19 to 14:23-25 in terms of theme, that is the preference of prophecy to tongues. Third, 14:33b-38 interrupts the flow from 14:26-33a to 14:39-40 in terms of the difference of theme. The examples listed above show that chapters 12 and 14 are composed of two different letters at least. A delicate difference is found between 16:5-6 and 16:7-9 in that whereas the former was written prior to Paul's visit to the Macedonian region, the latter was written after the visit. Although there are more places that show the combination of three different letters, I will not deal with them anymore on account of lack of space. It is, then, logical to conclude that 1 Corinthians consists of three different letters at least so far.[5]

Third, 2 Corinthians is the typical case that reveals the compilation clearly.[6] Critical scholars have observed the natural flow from 1:1—2:13 to 7:5-16 with regard to the meeting with Titus in Troas. This shows the possibility that the text of 2:14—7:4 is a part of another letter interpolated in between 1:1—2:13 and 7:5-16. Thus, the text of 6:14—7:1 is often considered a special case written earlier than any other texts in 2 Corinthians.[7] In addition, chapters 10-13 show a stronger tone than that embedded in chapters 1-9. This informs that chapters 10-13 originated in a letter different from those to which chapters 1-9 belonged. Thus, it can be said that 2 Corinthians has been also composed of three or four different letters. In consequence, Paul seems to have sent six letters at least to the Corinthians.[8]

---

5. Hurd lists the opinions of scholars on how First Corinthians was composed of three shorter letters (*Origin*, 45). His study is based on those of scholars such as Johannes Weiss, Alfred Loisy, Paul-Louis Couchoud, Maurice Goguel, Johannes Zwaan, Walter Schmithals, and Erich Dinkler.

6. It seems that Second Corinthians is composed of at least three or four letters. Bornkamm, "Vorgeschichte," 179–90, 192–94.

7. See Thrall, "Problem," 132–48.

8. Brown says that some scholars recognized two or more separate letters interwoven in First Corinthians but that the majority of scholars favored its unity. As for Second Corinthians, Brown acknowledges that two or three letters are combined (*Introduction*, 512, 542). See also Furnish, *II Corinthians*, 30–48. In addition, Jewett insists that seven letters are found in First and Second Corinthians ("Redaction,"

It seems that Romans consists of four different letters.⁹ This is detected from the observation that there are several particles according to topics. They are literary blocks among 1:1–17; 1:18—3:31; 4:1—5:11; 5:12—8:30; 8:31-39; and 9:1—11:36. It seems that the texts of 1:1–17; 4:1—5:11; and 8:31-39 originate in a letter in the sense of dealing with the issue of "being righteous by faith"; in other words, the text of 1:18—3:31 was interpolated in between 1:1-17 and 4:1—5:11 at the time of the compilation of Romans. And then, the texts of 5:12—8:30 and 9:1—11:36 were added in sequence. The compilation of 12:1—16:27 seems a bit complicated because ethical teachings are intertwined. To make the long analysis short, it seems that Romans has been composed of four different letters because there are abundant cases that hint at the compilation among texts.

The discussion above makes it possible that some epistles of Paul can be divided into short letters. As mentioned before, the unnatural flow of content is the most plausible evidence for the division into short letters. It seems that 1 Thessalonians is to be divided into two letters, Thess(A) (1 Thess 1:1—2:16; 4:1-8; 5:26-27) and Thess(B) (2:17—3:13; 4:9—5:25, 28). In similar manner, Philippians seems to be a combination of two short letters, Phil(A) (Phil 3:1b—4:3; 4:8-9) and Phil(B) (1:1—3:1a; 4:4-7, 10-23). Then, it seems that Paul sent at least six letters to the Corinthians.¹⁰ I would claim that 1 Corinthians consists of three letters at least: Cor(A) (1 Cor 1:4-9; 3:16-17; 6:9-20; 10:1-22; 11:2-16; 12:31b—14:1a; 14:20-22, 33b-38; 16:5-6, 10-11, 13-14; 2 Cor 6:14—7:1), Cor(B) (1 Cor 1:10-17; 5:1-5, 9-13; 6:1-8; 7:1-17, 25-40; 8:1-13; 10:23—11:1; 11:17-29, 33-34; 12:1, 4-12, 14-31a; 14:1b-19, 23-33a, 39-40; 15:12-28; 16:1-4, 12, 15-18), and Cor(C) (1:1-3; 1:18—3:15; 3:18—4:21; 5:6-8; 7:18-24; 9:1-27; 11:30-32; 12:2-3, 13; 15:1-11, 29-58; 16:7-9, 19-24). In the same vein, 2 Corinthians is also supposed to be a compilation of at least three letters: Cor(D) (2 Cor 1:1—2:13; 7:5—8:24; 13:11-13), Cor(E) (2:14—6:13; 7:2-4; 9:1-15), and Cor(F) (10:1—13:10). In similar manner, Romans can be divided into four letters.¹¹ They are supposed

---

398-444). See also Yeo, *Rhetorical*, 81-82.

9. Brown says, "A very small minority posits the joining of two separate letters; a larger minority maintains that chap. 16 was added later" (Brown, *Introduction*, 560, cf. 575-76). However, he does not discuss how two letters are joined in Romans. It is likely that he is referring to the opinion that chapters 9-11 were added later.

10. Ra, *Corinthians*, 9-338.

11. Ra, *Romans*, 5-272.

to be Rom(A) (1:1–17; 4:1—5:11; 8:31–39; 12:3–13; 14:1–12; 15:22–29; 16:1–16, 21–27), Rom(B) (1:18—3:31; 12:14—13:7; 14:13–23; 15:30–33), Rom(C) (5:12—8:30; 13:8–10; 15:1–13; 16:17–20), and Rom(D) (9:1—12:2; 13:11–14; 15:14–21). Finally, having added Galatians and Philemon, considered an integral letter, it can be said that Paul sent sixteen letters to the Gentiles churches. There may be other conclusions based on different approaches to the compilation of Paul's seven epistles. However, such an attempt has not yet been made by any scholar. Thus, I would like to discuss the process of how Paul changed and developed his theological thought on the basis of the divisions listed above.

It is then necessary to list the sixteen letters of Paul according to the chronological order of composition. For this, the issue of setting reasonable standards comes to the fore. I would suggest the intensity of challenge against Paul. As shown in Galatians, after the apostolic meeting in Jerusalem, Cephas was invited to the Antiochene church (Gal 2:1–14).[12] However, there he was rebuked by Paul for his withdrawal from the Gentile table. Then the Galatians seriously challenged Paul. If so, it should be filled in with what happened in between. It seems that the reaction of the apostles of the Jerusalem church was important. More realistically, Cephas returned to Jerusalem and reported to the apostles of Jerusalem what happened in Antioch. In turn, having been annoyed with Paul, they seem to have decided to send representatives to the churches in the region of Gentiles in order to make them keep the Law and be circumcised. As a result, some Gentiles who followed the Jewish instructions challenged Paul. Accordingly, Paul had to reflect his response in his letter.

Then, it should be examined how much each of sixteen letters reflects the conflict and challenge. Above all, Thess(A) and Cor(A) are supposed to have been written earlier than any other letters because they do not reflect the challenge against him. Then, the intensity of conflict gets stronger in Cor(B), Thess(B), Phil(A), Cor(C), Galatians, and Cor(F) according to their present order. This reflects the fact that, having been sponsored by the apostles of Jerusalem, some Gentiles began to challenge Paul against the gospel and his authority. On the other hand, there was

---

12. The theological controversy over the Gentile table in Antioch is not mentioned in the book of Acts. Its author did not want to write a story about the shameful conflict. Lüdemann believes that it should be dated before the apostolic meeting, although Paul placed it after the apostolic conference (*Paul*, loc. 425–40 of 3299). To my judgment, there is no reason to change the order between the apostolic meeting and the theological controversy in Antioch because Paul wrote various events from a biographical viewpoint.

a certain period of time without the notion of conflict and challenge; for instance, Paul comforted the Corinthians to restore the relationship as reflected in Cor(D) and to be reconciled with them as reflected in Cor(E). Finally, Romans, supposed to have been written at the end of Paul's life, does not reflect the conflict with those sent by the apostles of Jerusalem. No representative was sent to the Roman church because Paul did not establish her. However, it turns out that the Jewish members of the Roman church raised questions about his negative view on the Law. They even criticized him for his answers. Then, it can be said that Rom(A), Rom(B), Rom(C), Rom(D), Phil(B), and Philemon were written in sequence.

The sixteen letters can be listed chronologically according to the criterion suggested above. They would be as follows: Thess(A), Cor(A), Cor(B), Thess(B), Phil(A), Cor(C), Galatians, Cor(D), Cor(E), Cor(F), Rom(A), Rom(B), Rom(C), Rom(D), Phil(B), and Philemon. There could be other ways of listing them according to other criteria. However, I believe that the order listed above would be acceptable because the motive of conflict appears to be evident in response to the changing circumstances of the recipients of his letters. It is undeniable that some Gentiles were sponsored by the apostles of Jerusalem and that they challenged Paul.

THEOLOGICAL TOPICS

Paul dealt with various topics from a theological perspective. Each of them will be addressed according to the chronological order of sixteen letters starting from Thess(A) to Philemon. When we trace how Paul changed and developed his theological view, it turns out that the challenge of some Gentiles against him played the role of a watershed.

It is necessary to briefly describe the changes in Paul's interpretation of theological topics to be addressed. With regard to the Lord Jesus Christ Son of God, it will be manifested that Paul began to describe him as the redemptive savior after he had acknowledged the challenge of those sent by the apostles of Jerusalem. His view on the death of Jesus Christ changed from being compulsory to being spontaneous and sacrificial for the redemption and salvation of people. Paul changed his view on the Law from positive to negative at the time of being challenged by some Gentiles. He stopped explaining the end of world when the challenge against him reached its peak. The spirit of God was increasingly defined as an entity for the salvation of people, and the church of God began to be associated with Christ. In this way, the relationship with the apostles of Jerusalem had a profound influence on Paul in terms of theological interpretation.

There could be a critique against the hypothesis that Paul changed and developed his thoughts on various issues as time passed. For instance, J. Christiaan Beker cast doubt about the linear developmental process of Paul's theology as follows:

> However, it is problematic whether a developmental process can be demonstrated in Paul's career in such linear fashion, especially when we realize that the total pauline correspondence took place within the spans of no more than six years (A.D. 50–56) and that the letter period was preceded by almost fifteen years of nonliterary, apostolic activity (Gal 2,1). Thus, there is no clear evidence for a maturing in Paul during his letter-writing period. . . . Yet, it exhibits a crucial failure in that it employs the situational variety to construct a developmental scheme, Paul's evolutionary growth as a thinker. The relation between "situation" and "thought" is not explored in its integrity, because the situation is viewed in terms of Paul's greater or less mature development, as the case may be.[13]

Beker's insistence seems to be quite persuasive to deny the linear development of Paul's theology. The reason that Beker would not accept it is because he was too much confident in his hermeneutical presupposition that consists of coherence and contingency in regard to Paul's theology. Beker believed that Paul's authoritative instruction on the triumph of God through the death and resurrection of Christ is to be understood against the backdrop of an apocalyptic perspective while it was differently expressed in each occasion of Gentile churches.

Beker is not free from some critiques. It is dubious whether Paul regarded the death and resurrection of Christ as the core theology as soon as he had received the revelation about the Son of God. To my judgment, they were not very important topics in the early days of Paul's mission to the Gentiles. In addition, Beker's hermeneutical presupposition consisting of coherence and contingency should be criticized because, as we

---

13. Beker, *Paul*, 32–33. Lüdemann says that if "all of Paul's letters would have been composed within a period of about five years . . . little room would be left for any theory regarding the development of Paul's thought reflected in the letters"(*Paul*, loc. 178 of 3299).

shall see, Paul developed his view in response to the changing circumstances of the recipients of his letters. Beker should have analyzed Paul's genuine epistles from a literary as well as historical perspective more in detail for the appropriated reconstruction of Paul's life and thought. This indicates that my analysis on the chronological approach to the sixteen letters will make readers see how Paul developed his theological thought as time went by.

Paul developed theological interpretations on various topics. I believe that even if his letters had been written in the short period of six years, it was long enough for him to change and develop his views in response to the challenge initiated by the apostles of Jerusalem against the gospel and his authority. When the sixteen letters are arranged in chronological order, the trajectory of his thoughts and theology will certainly be revealed.

METHODOLOGY

It is necessary to discuss the methodology for the study of how Paul changed and developed the theological interpretation. I would like to choose a methodology with a focus on isolating the original letters from the compiled epistles and listing them according to chronological order. In this regard, redaction criticism and the history of ideas can be recommended.

Redaction criticism will be used to distinguish the short letters compiled into each epistle of Paul. This was born while studying the Synoptic Gospels; however, it can be applied to the Pauline epistles. Above all, it is important to pay attention to the unnatural flow of content, which implies that someone else has applied the treatment later. In addition, it is necessary to pay attention to the different literary forms, term, grammatical changes, changes of tone, theological themes, intended readers, compositional purposes, etc.[14] Then, they will provide the logical foundation upon which readers can notice how and why the later redactor combined a couple of letters into a compiled epistle. If we can find an independent letter, we will be able to find a consistency of logic in it.

A chronological approach is needed to trace the development of each theological topic. The history of ideas is a good methodology to

---

14. Mack, *Lost Gospel*, 108.

trace it.[15] This is a methodology that studies the development of a concept and aims to trace its origin by looking at the process of expressing, preserving, and changing certain ideas or thoughts in history. In other words, it identifies the characteristics of the units of interest and makes them into a new combination, based on the existence of ideas shared by each generation, whether implicit or explicit. In doing so, the researcher must carefully look at the effect that a particular subject has on people. At this time, the possibility of ideas unfolding contrary to thoughts and expectations should be considered.

I believe that the two approaches presented above are sufficient to trace how Paul changed and developed his theological ideas and thought on various topics. When they are applied to the study on his theological topics, it will be revealed that Paul brought new theological interpretations to the Gentiles as an alternative to the Jewish instruction of those sponsored by the apostles of Jerusalem. In the meantime, it will become apparent that Christianity was born among the Gentiles.

---

15. Lovejoy, *Great Chain*, 3–20.

1

The Reconstructed Life and Letters of Paul

PAUL'S LIFE CAN BE reconstructed on the basis of the sixteen letters sent to the churches in the region of Gentiles. When they have been arranged in chronological order, they will show that Paul received the revelation about the Son of God, inherited the tradition about Christ in Damascus, and learned more about Jesus from Cephas in Jerusalem. Later, he developed his theological interpretation on various topics during the missionary trips.[1] His life can be divided into three parts according to his relationship with the apostles of Jerusalem. The first one starts with the event of revelation about the Son of God in Damascus and finishes with his return to Jerusalem to meet the apostles after the first missionary trip. The second part includes Paul's second trip after the theological controversy over the Gentile table in Antioch. The apostles of Jerusalem sent representatives to make the Gentiles challenge Paul against the gospel that he had proclaimed. Having faced their challenge, Paul developed his theological interpretation on various topics. And the third part consists

1. Someone could raise the question of whether it is necessary to reconstruct Paul's life because it is narrated in the book of Acts. Acts, however, is supposed to have been written at the beginning of the second century CE in order to harmonize the ministries of Peter and Paul. It is clear that Paul's genuine letters and the book of Acts reveal lots of differences in the description of his life and thought. The book of Acts is not free from criticism with regard to its historicity. Thus, when a discrepancy is found between Paul's letters and the book of Acts with regard to his life and thought, we have to rely upon his epistles because they were written by Paul. His biographical description is more reliable than that written by the third party, the author of Acts.

of Paul's trip to Rome and stay there. Among the three different parts, the second one is to be paid attention most because, having faced the challenge of some Gentiles sponsored by the apostles of Jerusalem, Paul drastically developed his theological view on how the Gentiles could be the true people of God. He got through the harsh situation with new interpretations of various topics. At that time, having unfolded his view on the crucifixion of Christ as the means of redemption and salvation, he sublimated the theology to the gospel of Christ. This is a breakthrough that made Paul able to win the Thessalonians and the Philippians, but he failed to win the Corinthians and the Galatians. In the meantime, having been independent from the Jerusalem church, Christianity was born among the Gentiles.[2]

A. THE FIRST MISSIONARY TRIP

It is necessary to look at what Paul achieved at the beginning of his mission to the Gentiles. A certain amount of information has been known about his life from the time of receiving the revelation about the Son of God to the second visit to Jerusalem for the apostolic meeting. In the meantime, the first missionary trip took place with a great achievement among the Gentiles. It seems that Paul was subordinate to the apostolic authority at that time. Paul relied upon the Jewish tradition on various topics.

A Persecutor of Church

A certain amount of information has been known about Paul before the event of revelation. The most typical feature is that he was a persecutor of the church of God. This is due to his zeal for the Law.

---

2. Lüdemann claims that Christianity was a third group separated from Judaism and Hellenists. According to him, "Therefore Jew and Gentile are equally qualified and eligible to join the people of God, and in joining, both became members of a third group, as separate from Judaim as it was from Hellenist.... Be that as it may, it was clear that Paul did create a new and separate socioreligious reality" (*Paul*, loc. 1727–30 of 3299). The issue of becoming the people of God comes to the fore. However, it is dubious whether Christiany stemmed from the Hellenists which derived from the group of Judaism in Jerusalem. In addition, he does not point out the moment that Christianity was born among the Gentiles from a theological point of view. This will be discussed in the following chapters.

The earliest part of Paul's biography is absent. His birthplace, birthdate, and parents are not mentioned in his epistles.[3] It is, however, definite that he was a Jew as known from the description that he was circumcised on the eighth day of birth and born as a man of the tribe of Benjamin (Phil 3:5). In addition, Paul identified himself as a Hebrew, an Israelite, and a descendant of Abraham (2 Cor 11:22). From a religious perspective, he was advancing in Judaism beyond many Jews of his own age (Gal 1:14).[4] Moreover, as a Pharisee, Paul insisted on his faithfulness to the Law and faultlessness in front of other people (Phil 3:5–6).[5] This means that he was accustomed to the tradition of ancestors. In this way, a certain amount of information about his origin and status has been known.

Paul defined himself as a persecutor of church before he had received a revelation from God. His zeal for Judaism was enormous (Phil 3:6). He was eager to persecute the church of God; he even attempted to destroy her (Gal 1:13). His persecution of the disciples of Jesus indicates that the basic elements of their preaching had a powerfully disturbing effect on him.[6] Later, he confessed that he was the least of the apostles and did not even deserve to be called an apostle since he had persecuted the church of God (1 Cor 15:9).[7] It should not be denied that his persecution of church occupied an important place in his religious life.

The reason that Paul persecuted the church of God has not been known exactly. According to Beker, "Paul's persecution of the church was motivated by his Pharisaic conviction that by definition a Messiah who suffered death could not be the Messiah but had to be an impostor."[8] His interpretation is not to be denied; however, Paul did not mention this kind of conviction in his epistles. Rather, it is likely that the different

---

3. According to the author of Acts, Paul was born a Diaspora Jew in Tarsus of Cilicia and educated under the family of Gamaril (Acts 22:3).

4. It is described in the book of Acts that Paul spent his youth in Jerusalem and studied under Gamaliel (Acts 22:3; 26:4). However, Paul did not give any hint at his educational background in his letters.

5. According to the book of Acts, Paul was zealous for the Judaism as a Jew and Pharisee (Acts 26:5). This kind of description is accordant with Paul's own biographical description.

6. Lüdemann, *Paul*, loc. 2142 of 3299.

7. It is told in the book of Acts that Paul took part in persecuting the disciples of Jesus and killing Stephen (Acts 7:54–60; 22:20). It is, however, to be noted that Paul did not mention this kind of execution at all in his letters.

8. Beker, *Paul*, 182.

stance on the Law as well as the critique against the Pharisees made Paul persecute the church of God, composed of the disciples of Jesus. This will be soon verified when we study the first three redactions of Q. In any case, Paul persecuted them because they preached a teaching different from the ordinary Judaism he had been in.

It seems that Paul persecuted the church of God in Galilee.[9] According to him, the churches of God in Judea were persecuted by fellow Jews (1 Thess 2:14), but his face had not been known to them (Gal 1:22). This means that Paul was not personally known to the members of churches in Judea. In other words, there was no personal relationship with them. Then, Paul was not one of those who had actively persecuted the disciples of Jesus in the region of Judea, including Jerusalem. Rather, it seems that Paul had persecuted them before they advanced to Judea, whose center was Jerusalem, and established churches there.[10] In consequence, it can be said that he was active in Galilee, where the disciples of Jesus had started preaching his instruction as reflected in the formation of the first three redactions of Q, which will be discussed later in this chapter.

The Revelation of God about the Son

God revealed his Son to Paul in or near Damascus. Since he did not elaborate a description on the event of revelation, only a small amount of information has been known about it. It was, however, a turning point that made Paul a minister for the Gentiles after being a persecutor of church.

Paul briefly described his experience of revelation. According to Paul, God was pleased to reveal [ἀποκαλύψαι] the Son to him, so that he might proclaim the Son of God to the Gentiles (Gal 1:16). It was a personal experience that happened regardless of his intention or wish.[11]

---

9. Lüdemann believes that the persecution happened in Damascus on the basis of the principle that people return to a place where they have been before as reflected in Gal 1:17 (*Paul*, loc. 269 of 3299). It is likely that he looked for a harmony with the description in Acts 9:1–19.

10. According to the book of Acts, the church started with 120 people in an attic of unknown person in Jerusalem (Acts 1:12–15). It seems that number 120, the multiple of number 12, was chosen for a theological purpose by the author of Acts. On the other hand, Paul knew nothing about the allegation that the Christian church started in Jerusalem. Rather, as we shall see in Q, a community of the disciples of Jesus started in Galilee and advanced to Jerusalem probably via Judea.

11. It is said in the book of Acts that Paul went to Damascus to arrest the disciples

It was definitely initiated by God. The revelation was given to him in Damascus, as the phrase "and later returned to Damascus" implies (1:17).[12] Then, Damascus was a meaningful place to Paul in his religious life. However, Paul did not mention whether the Son of God was related to Jesus or not. It is unfortunate that Paul said nothing more about the event of revelation in his epistles.[13]

Paul left a clue as to when he received the revelation. It seems that the revelation was given to him around 35 CE, fourteen years before the meeting with the apostles in Jerusalem, supposedly held in 49 CE (Gal 1:18; 2:1; cf. Acts 15:1–21).[14] Otherwise, there is no clue to identify when Paul received the revelation. Without doubt, the revelation would have had a great influence on him later. The event of revelation was a turning point to Paul in his religious life. In consequence, there are still many things to be researched in regard to the event of revelation.

The Damascus Tradition

It is inevitable to discuss what happened in Damascus after Paul received the revelation. Although there is no direct mention of it, it seems that he had a chance to inherit the tradition about Christ defined as the gospel (1 Cor 15:1–5). Although Paul did not describe how the gospel of Christ had been handed down to him, it is plausiable that he received it in Damascus.

---

of Jesus (Acts 9:1–2). It is, however, dubious whether the high priest had the authority to allow Paul to seize them in the foreign land. It is also suspicious whether the disciples already expanded to Damascus within five years after the death of Jesus. At any rate, the reason that Paul had gone to Damascus was not written at all in his epistles.

12. It is said in the book of Acts that Paul saw a heavenly vision on the way to Damascus (Acts 9:3). This is described against the backdrop of Jesus' baptism written in Luke's Gospel (Luke 3:21–22).

13. Lüdemann argues that Paul reflected his experience of revelation in the following texts: 1 Cor 9:1; 15:8; Phil 3:8a; 2 Cor 4:6 (*Paul*, loc. 1892–1964 of 3299). The event of revelation Paul received is described in detail in the book of Acts (Acts 9:1–19). Paul met Jesus of Nazareth in a vision on his way to Damascus. It is, however, to be noted that it was composed by the author of Acts in order to fill up the historical gap resulted from Paul's silence about what had really happened.

14. There are some scholars who believe that God gave the revelation to Paul seventeen years ahead of the apostolic meeting. According to Lüdemann, opinion differs as to whether the term "then" used in Gal 2:1 refers to the event of conversion or to the first trip of Paul to Jerusalem in order to visit Cephas (*Paul*, loc. 283 of 3299). He believes that the revelation was given to Paul around 31–32 CE.

Damascus was a meaningful place to Paul. Having spent a certain period of time in Arabia after the event of revelation, Paul returned to Damascus (Gal 1:17). Since nothing resulted from his visit to Arabia, he could not help but return to Damascus. However, the reason that he went to Arabia and returned to Damascus has been unknown. In addition, no information has been given with regard to what happened to Paul there. However, it seems that Paul was exposed to the tradition about Christ there. Otherwise, there is no reason that he mentioned the revisit to Damascus even if there were no concrete evidence.[15]

The gospel Paul possibly received in Damascus is simple. It can be summarized as follows (1 Cor 15:3–5):[16]

> Christ died according to the Scriptures,[17] was buried,
> was raised on the third day according to the Scriptures, and appeared.[18]

The gospel of Christ is composed of four elements. To them belong the death, burial, resurrection, and appearance of Christ without theological interpretation.

It is not easy to interpret the gospel of Christ. First, the title "Christ" did not exclusively refer to the historical Jesus.[19] It seems that the gospel of Christ was created on the basis of various traditions of the Hebrew

---

15. Beker believes that Paul received the gospel about the death and resurrection of Christ in Antioch (*Paul*, 130). However, this is nothing more than an interpretation based on speculation. It is described in the book of Acts that Paul proclaimed Jesus as the Son of God in the synagogue of Damascus immediately after he had heard the voice of Jesus of Nazareth on his way there (Acts 9:19–22). This indirectly supports the fact that Paul identified the Son of God as Christ, whom he had learned about there.

16. There have been many hypotheses with regard to the range of tradition that Paul received. For the examination of 1 Cor 15:3–5, refer to Conzelmann, "Analysis," 15–25; and idem, *I Corinthians*, 251–54. He believes that 1 Cor 15:5 is the end of the tradition. On the other hand, Jeremias thinks that the tradition ends in 1 Cor 15:4 (*Eucharistic*, 101–2).

17. Having been dependent upon Hooker, Barrett argues the phrase "our sins" was inserted by Paul to the tradition of the gospel (*First Letter*, 339; cf. Hooker, *Jesus*, 119).

18. For more detailed analysis, refer to Ra, *Origin*, 14–17.

19. At the time of Jesus, Jews had various perspectives on Christ "the Messiah." For instance, the political Messiah was expected since the Maccabees had recovered the Jerusalem temple from the hand of Syria in 164 BCE. On the other hand, the aspiration for the priestly Messiah did not extinguish as written in the *Testament of Levi* (*T. Levi* 18:1–9). Especially, the Teacher of Righteousness was to be understood against the backdrop of the highest priest. It is, however, important to observe that the Christ whom Paul received from his religious predecessors was related with neither the political nor priestly one.

Scriptures. The phrase "Christ died according to the Scriptures" reminds readers of various servants of God who suffered during the mission. Among them, the best candidate is "the Suffering Servant of YHWH" (Isa 53:10). Then, the phrase "he was raised on the third day according to the Scriptures" seems to have been written against the backdrop of Hosea (Hos 6:2). This is the only text that mentions revived life on the third day. Therefore, "Christ" may not necessarily refer to the historical "Jesus." It is quite possible that Paul linked Christ with the Son of God known to him through the revelation.

The identity of those who handed the gospel of Christ over to Paul can be revealed to some extent from the context. Paul left some hints about them in his epistles. First, they seem to be the Greek-speaking members of Jewish-Christian community because the tradition reflected in 1 Cor 15:3–5 echoes the Septuagint (*LXX*). In this respect, they probably were among the Diaspora—that is, in Gentile areas outside of Israel.[20] Second, they seem to inherit the Pharisaic tradition. This is possible on the assumption that they communicated the issue of resurrection to Paul. Paul was able to accept the gospel of Christ without hesitation as a former Pharisee. Third, they seem to be those who helped Paul to escape through the window in the wall under the governance of King Aretas in Damascus (2 Cor 11:32–33; cf. Acts 9:23–25).[21] From the fact that he rose to the reign in 37–39 CE, it can be said that Paul escaped there in between 37 and 39.[22] This indicates that Paul received the gospel of Christ from those whom he had met in Damascus. Otherwise, there is no place that can be connected with those who transmitted the gospel to Paul. In consequence, the above discussion provides readers with a clue that those who handed the tradition about Christ over to Paul can be called the "religious predecessors" or the "first Christians." They were the first group of people who had faith in Christ. In addition, the gospel of Christ

---

20. Conzelmann, *1 Corinthians*, 252. It is described in the book of Acts that Paul became blind after receiving the revelation on his way to Damascus and then met Ananias (Acts 9:10–19a). If so, Ananias could be presented as one of those who passed on the tradition of Christ. On the contrary, Lüdemann claims that the Hellenists of the Jerusalem church later passed on the tradition of Christ to Paul (*Paul*, loc. 2519–21 of 3299). However, this kind of interpretation was due to efforts to harmonize the descriptions between Paul and the author of Acts.

21. Since the Jews tried to kill Paul, a certain number of people helped him to escape from Damascus (Acts 9:23–25). This is to some extent different from what Paul described in Second Corinthians (2 Cor 11:32–33).

22. Barrett, *Second Epistle*, 303; cf. Strack and Billerbeck, *Kommentar*, 3:530.

can be called the "Damascus tradition" because it was handed over to Paul in Damascus.

The Jerusalem Tradition

It is inevitable to study what Paul learned from Cephas in Jerusalem. He seems to learn more about Jesus and his instruction on the basis of the first three redactions of Q. It is, however, noteworthy that Paul maintained the Jewish tradition while identifying the Son of God with the historical Jesus.

Paul went up to Jerusalem after the escape from Damascus. It was probably in 38 CE, three years after the event of revelation (Gal 1:18).[23] Paul probably knew to some extent that the Son of God revealed to him had been associated with Jesus from the moment of receiving the revelation. This is why Paul talked about his decision not to meet the apostles before him just after the experience of revelation (1:17). It seems that Paul was confused about meeting with the disciples of Jesus, whom he had persecuted. Paul wanted to take time to think about the Son of God revealed to him. Thus, he went to Arabia and then returned to Damascus. Otherwise, there is no reason that Paul went up to Jerusalem to meet Cephas immediately after he had left Damascus.

The first stay of Paul in Jerusalem was short. It was no longer than fifteen days, visiting Cephas and an accidental meeting with James, the Lord's brother (Gal 1:19). It is definite that they were afraid of Paul, who had persecuted them (1:13, 22). At any rate, Paul visited them in order to know whether the Son of God revealed to him could be related with Jesus. The reason that Paul wanted to know more about Jesus is because he had somewhat heard about him during the time of persecuting the church of God. Probably, he "had only a passing acquaintance and strained relationship with Jesus' immediate disciples."[24] The Greek term ἱστορέω, from which the English word "history" originated, informs readers of

---

23. According to the book of Acts, Paul went up to Jerusalem several days after he had met Jesus of Nazareth in vision (Acts 9:23-27). It is, however, noteworthy that the author did not mention how long it took between his escape from Damascus and visit to Jerusalem. Nevertheless, it cannot be denied that the author seems to tell that Paul's visit to Jerusalem did not take a long time, in contrast with what is described in Galatians (Gal 1:18).

24. Lüdemann, "Paul," lines 13-14.

Paul's effort to know more about Jesus. Paul would have tried to learn as much as possible from Cephas.

It seems that Cephas delivered the instruction of Jesus on the basis of the first three redactions of Q. To my judgment, they were completed in Galilee no later than the death of Herod Antipas in 39 CE.[25] The texts of the first three redactions of Q would be as follows:

I. John the Baptist and Jesus

A. John

Q^1 3:2–4 (Luke 3:2–4 / Matt 3:1–3, 5–6)[26]

Q^1 3:7–8a (Luke 3:7–8a / Matt 3:7–9a)

Q^1 3:9 (Luke 3:9 / Matt 3:10)

Q^3 3:16–17 (Luke 3:16–17 / Matt 3:11–12)

Q^3 3:21–22 (Luke 3:21–22 / Matt 3:16–17)

B. Jesus

1. The Sermon

Q^1 6:20b (Luke 6:20b / Matt 5:2b–3)

Q^2 6:21 (Luke 6:21 / Matt 5:4, 6)

Q^3 6:22–23b (Luke 6:22–23b / Matt 5:11–12b)

Q^1 6:27 (Luke 6:27 / Matt 5:44a)

Q^3 6:28 (Luke 6:28 / Matt 5:44b)

Q^1 6:29–38 (Luke 6:29–38 / Matt 5:39–40, 42, 45–48; 7:1–2, 12)

Q^3 6:39–42 (Luke 6:39–42 / Matt 15:14; 10:24–25; 7:3–5)

Q^3 6:43–45 (Luke 6:43–45 / Matt 7:16, 18; 12:33–35)

Q^3 6:46–49 (Luke 6:46–49 / Matt 7:21, 24–27)

---

25. Herod Antipas had a nickname of "Swaying Reed" (Q^3 7:24). It seems that the third redaction of Q was being composed during his reign over the Galileans. Cf. Theissen, *Gospels*, 26–42. Having insisted that references to Jerusalem appear in religious symbols or in apocalyptic situations, Arnal concludes that Q was written in Capernaum of Galilee (*Jesus*, 159–64). In this regard, I think that, while the first three redactions of Q were possibly composed in Capernaum of Galilee, the fourth one was completed in Jerusalem. As for this, refer to my book titled *Q*, 21–242.

26. The superscript added to Q refers to the redactional stage to which the text belongs.

    2. The Activity
       Q^3 7:1–10 (Luke 7:1–10 / Matt 8:5–10, 13)
  C. Jesus and John
       Q^3 7:18–27 (Luke 7:18–27 / Matt 11:2–10)

       Q^1 7:29–30 (Luke 7:29–30 / Matt 21:31–32)

       Q^3 7:31–34 (Luke 7:31–34 / Matt 11:16–19a)

II. **Jesus' Commission of Disciples and Their Mission**
  A. The Followers of Jesus
       Q^2 9:57–58 (Luke 9:57–58 / Matt 8:19–20)
  B. The Manual for Ministry
       Q^3 10:2 (Luke 10:2 / Matt 9:37–38)

       Q^2 10:4–12 (Luke 10:4–12 / Matt 10:7–15 (11:24))

       Q^3 10:13-16 (Luke 10:13–16 / Matt 11:21–23; 10:40)

       Q^3 10:21–24 (Luke 10:21–24 / Matt 11:25–27; 13:16–17)
  C. The Lord's Prayer and Its Application
    1. The Lord's Prayer
       Q^2 11:2–4 (Luke 11:2–4 / Matt 6:9–13)
    2. The Confidence in the Prayer
       Q^2 11:9–10 (Luke 11:9–10 / Matt 7:7–8)
    3. The Confidence in the Father: The Vocative of God
       Q^2 11:11–13 (Luke 11:11–13 / Matt 7:9–11)
    4. The Kingdom of God: The Second Petition
       Q^2 11:14–15, 17–20 (Luke 11:14–15, 17–20 / Matt 12:22–28)

       Q^3 11:21–23 (Luke 11:21–23 / Matt 12:29–30)
    5. The Temptation: The Fifth Petition
       Q^2 11:16, 29–30 (Luke 11:16, 29–30 / Matt 12:38–40)

       Q^3 11:31–32 (Luke 11:31–32 / Matt 12:41–42)

       Q^3 11:33–35 (Luke 11:33–35 / Matt 5:15; 6:22–23)

       Q^3 11:39–46 (Luke 11:39–46 / Matt 23:4, 6–7, 23, 25–28)

       Q^3 11:52 (Luke 11:52 / Matt 23:13)

       Q^3 12:2–3 (Luke 12:2–3 / Matt 10:26–27)
    6. The Fear of God: The First Petition

Q^2 12:6-7 (Luke 12:6-7 / Matt 10:29-31)

Q^3 12:8-9 (Luke 12:8-9 / Matt 10:32-33)

7. The Daily Bread: The Third Petition
Q^2 12:22-31 (Luke 12:22-31 / Matt 6:25-33)

Q^3 12:33-34 (Luke 12:33-34 / Matt 6:19-21)

8. The Forgiveness: The Forth Petition
Q^2 17:3-4 (Luke 17:3-4 / Matt 18:15, 21-22

III. The Coming of the Son of Man and the Kingdom of God

A. The Preparation for the Son of Man
Q^3 12:39-40 (Luke 12:39-40 / Matt 24:43-44)

Q^3 12:42-46 (Luke 12:42-46 / Matt 24:45-51)

B. The kingdom of God
Q^3 13:18-21 (Luke 13:18-21 / Matt 13:31-33)

Q^3 13:24-27 (Luke 13:24-27 / Matt 7:13-14, 22-23; 25:10-12)

C. The Coming of the Son of Man
Q^3 17:23-24 (Luke 17:23-24 / Matt 24:26-27)

Q^3 17:26-27, 30 (Luke 17:26-27, 30 / Matt 24:37-39)

Q^3 17:34-35 (Luke 17:34-35 / Matt 24:40-41)

The texts listed above show a well-organized redaction of Q. The first three redactions of Q show the progress of the Jesus movement that started with unknown disciples in Galilee.

It seems that Paul learned about Jesus from Cephas on the basis of three redactions of Q. The divine sonship appears in association with Jesus in Q (Q^3 3:22; 10:22).[27] As shown before, Paul had a new view on the Son of God revealed to him (Gal 1:16) and connected him with Christ as learned from the religious predecessor in Damascus (1 Cor 15:3-5; Gal 1:17). Then, he was finally able to identify the Son of God with Jesus as learned from Cephas. There was no difficulty for Paul to identify the Son of God with Jesus, because he had a certain kind of knowledge about him at the time of persecuting his disciples. This made Paul able to use the title "Jesus Christ the Son of God" after he had met Cephas in Jerusalem.

27. Lüdemann believes that "Paul was familiar with traditions about Jesus' teaching and knew certain specific elements of that teaching" (*Paul*, loc. 2240-345 of 3299). Without doubt, they are from Q.

Paul seems to share the faith with Cephas at the beginning of mission to the Gentiles. The faith was also shared with the Jewish members of churches in Judea, to whom Paul was unknown by face, as reflected in Galatians: "The man who formerly persecuted us is now preaching the faith he once tried to destroy" (Gal 1:22–23). This means that there was a time when Paul communicated the same faith with the Jewish congregation. If so, this is probably a Q-based faith. In this regard, what Paul learned about Jesus from Cephas on the basis of Q can be defined as the "Jerusalem tradition."

The third redaction of Q seems to provide readers with the reason that Paul persecuted the disciples of Jesus. First of all, the issue of persecution is mentioned in the third redaction of Q (Q³ 6:22–23b; 11:21–23; 12:8–9). It is, however, unfortunate that the persecutor is not described in detail. Without doubt, they were the fellow Jews belonging to the same society with the disciples of Jesus in Galilee. Second, new interpretations of the Law are listed (Q³ 11:39–46, 52). They were a little new to ordinary Jews, including the Pharisees and the lawyer. It is plausible that the new interpretation of the Law made Paul annoyed and that he persecuted the disciples of Jesus because he was a Pharisee zealous for the Law.[28] In addition, the woes against the Pharisees would have been added as a factor in Paul's persecution of the church of God, composed of the disciples of Jesus. At this moment, it is necessary to see that the death of Jesus is not mentioned in Q; thus, there was no resurrection, either. This implies that Paul did not persecute the disciples of Jesus for the unclaimed death and resurrection. Thus, it can be said that Paul was one of those who persecuted the disciples of Jesus in Galilee as reflected in the third redaction of Q.

No more information is given with regard to the first visit of Paul to Jerusalem. It has not been known whom Paul went up to Jerusalem with and whether the disciples of Jesus had fellowship with the religious predecessors of Damascus.[29] I believe there was no communication among them because the Christ reflected in the Damascus tradition is completely different from Jesus embedded in the Jerusalem tradition.

---

28. Lüdemann, *Paul*, loc. 1090 of 3299.

29. In the book of Acts, Barnabas is presented as the one leading Paul to Jerusalem after the event of revelation (Acts 9:27). It can be then assumed that Barnabas was one of those whom Paul had met in Damascus. Barnabas could be one of the religious predecessors who handed the gospel over to Paul. However, it must not be overlooked that Paul never talked about where he had met Barnabas in his epistles.

Either way, Paul tried to claim that his first visit to Jerusalem had little effect on him at the time of writing Galatians on account of the challenge of the Galatians sponsored by the apostles of Jerusalem. On the contrary, this reflects the fact that it was significantly effective.

Paul received the tradition about the Lord's Supper. It is evident in the statement that "I received from the Lord what I also passed on to you" (1 Cor 11:23). Hereby, it seems that "the Lord" refers to Jesus. Then, the Lord's Supper is recorded far more theologically than the Lord's Table (10:16–17; 11:23–26). The difference between them informs us that Paul changed and developed the tradition as time passed. When we think of Paul having no chance to meet the Lord Jesus and receive the tradition of supper directly, we are urged to trace how it was handed down to Paul.[30] Even if it is possible that the tradition was transmitted by Cephas, I would not accept its possibility because the Lord's Supper does not appear in Q, which is supposed to have been complete by or at the charge of the twelve apostles. Although Jesus is called "Lord" in Q (Q^3 6:46; 7:6–7), it is not clear whether he was the person who instituted the Lord's Supper. In any case, it is to be admitted that, having mentioned the tradition of Lord's Supper or Table, Paul argued for its transmission from the Lord.

It seems that Paul inherited a couple of traditions in Jerusalem: Q and the Lord's Supper. Paul was good at handling them as a well-trained Pharisee. The most prominent matter was to associate the Son of God revealed to him with Jesus, whose disciples he had persecuted. Having done this successfully, Paul could have identified Jesus as the Lord Christ Son of God. This made Paul armed with many lessons in connection with the Lord Jesus Christ Son of God.

The First Missionary Trip

Paul left Jerusalem for a missionary trip to the Gentiles. Contrary to the description generally known to us, Paul spent at least eleven years all the way down to Corinth of Achaia. It seems that the first missionary trip was initiated by Barnabas. At any rate, Paul and Barnabas finished it with a great achievement among the Gentiles.

The first missionary trip was made immediately after Paul's first visit to Jerusalem. It seems that Syria and Cilicia were the first destinations (Gal 1:21). However, the reason that he headed there has not been known.

---

30. Cf. Conzelmann, *I Corinthians*, 196.

From the fact that Barnabas was active in Antioch of Syria (2:11–14), it is very likely that he took Paul there. Thus, it is reasonable to think that Paul met Barnabas in Jerusalem at least and followed him to Antioch (2:1–2).[31] There is, however, no clue as to whether Paul met Barnabas before the first visit to Jerusalem. Cilicia could be the next stop because it was next to Syria and is supposed to be the hometown of Paul, if the Lucan description is correct (Acts 22:3). However, I do not want to draw a hasty conclusion on this.

Without doubt, Paul visited Galatia after he had left Syria and Cilicia. This can be inferred from the description that Paul informed the Galatians of his second visit to Jerusalem with Barnabas (Gal 2:1).[32] If they had not been to Galatia before the visit to Jerusalem for the apostolic meeting, Paul could not have mentioned him in Galatians.[33] This means that Paul and Barnabas visited Galatia during the first missionary trip. In addition, Titus was also known to the Galatians before the apostolic meeting (Gal 2:2–3). This informs us that Paul and Barnabas visited Galatia on their way back to Jerusalem from the place where they had met Titus during the first missionary trip. This may have been the second visit to Galatia that was made after the first visit to proclaim the gospel and establish a church in Galatia. If they had not established a church there, they could not have visited a second time. It is then definite that Paul had visited Galatia with Barnabas at least twice before the apostolic meeting.

It is likely that Paul and Barnabas went up to Corinth of Achaia via Asia and Macedonia after they had left Galatia. Although there is no concrete evidence, this can be known from the fact that Barnabas was mentioned in the letter that Paul sent to the Corinthians later (1 Cor

---

31. It is described in the book of Acts that Barnabas took Paul to Antioch after he had introduced him to the apostles of Jerusalem and then sent to Tarsus (Acts 9:23–30; 11:25–26). However, in his epistles, Paul did not describe Barnabas taking him to the apostles of Jerusalem from Damascus.

32. Lüdemann definitely argues for Paul's first visit to Galatia before the apostolic meeting (*Paul*, loc. 519 of 3299). On the other hand, it is mentioned in the book of Acts that Paul visited Jerusalem with Barnabas after the first missionary trip to Syria and Cicilia without the visit to Galatia (Acts 13:1—15:5).

33. According to the book of Acts, Paul visited Galatia for the first time after the apostolic meeting (Acts 16:6). It is, however, to be noted that if Paul had already separated from Barnabas just before the second missionary trip (15:35–41), he could not have been known to the Galatians and Paul could not have mentioned him in Galatians (Gal 2:1–2). It seems that Paul's description of the first missionary trip is different from what is described in the book of Acts.

9:6).³⁴ If Barnabas had not been there, Paul could not have mentioned him in the letter. Without doubt, they had visited Corinth before they broke up with each other later in Antioch (Gal 2:11–14). This informs us that the first missionary trip continued even to Corinth via Philippi, Thessalonica, and Athens.³⁵ It is also supported by the fact that Paul and Barnabas took Titus, born of a Greek, to the apostolic meeting held in Jerusalem around 49 CE (2:1–3). This means that Paul and Barnabas visited the region of the Greeks and met him there.³⁶ However, where they met him has not been described in detail. Nevertheless, from the fact that Macedonia and Achaia belonged to the Greek region, it can be said that Paul and Barnabas met Titus either in Macedonia or Achaia. It seems that Paul and Barnabas went to Corinth with Silvanus [Silas] and Timothy (2 Cor 1:19).³⁷ They delivered lessons and established churches there during the first missionary trip.

What Paul taught the Gentiles has not been known. It is, however, definite that Paul and Barnabas did not force them to be circumcised as reflected in the case of Titus (Gal 2:3). He accompanied Paul and Barnabas as a trophy of spiritual war achieved among the Gentiles. It seems

---

34. Knox argues that Paul already visited Corinth before the apostolic meeting in Jerusalem ("Chapters," 346–47). Later, having been acquainted with his view, Lüdemann argues for Paul's first visit to Corinth around 41 CE, before the apostolic meeting (*Paul*, locs. 184, 401, 495, 625 of 3299). To my judgment, it is not realistic that, having left Jerusalem in 38 CE and established churches in various places, Paul arrived in Corinth in 41 CE. Rather, it is likely that Paul was in Corinth two to three years before returning to Jerusalem in 49 CE.

35. It is written in the book of Acts that Paul visited Corinth during the second trip after the apostolic meeting in Jerusalem (Acts 18:1–2). If this were correct, Paul could not mention Barnabas in First Corinthians because Paul was already separated from Barnabas before the first visit to Corinth, according to the book of Acts (Acts 15:35–41). Then, Barnabas could not have been known to the Corinthians at all.

36. Titus Justus is mentioned in Acts 18:7. It is, however, unclear whether he was the man whom Paul and Barnabas took to Jerusalem on account of various reasons (Gal 2:1–3). Above all, he is not described as the one who accompanied Paul during the second missionary trip in the book of Acts. I wish, however, to believe that Titus was from Corinth because Paul had sent him there as his representative later (2 Cor 7:6–7).

37. It is described in the book of Acts that Paul took Silas [Silvanus] again at the very beginning of the second missionary trip to the Gentiles and met Timothy in the middle of it (Acts 15:40; 16:1). On the other hand, Paul himself did not talk about the time of taking Silvanus and Timothy in his letters. Paul eliminated the name of Barnabas because he was not with him any longer at the time of writing Second Corinthians.

that, having followed the case of the God-fearer at the synagogue of Jews in Diaspora, Paul allowed the Gentiles to remain uncircumcised. In addition, it seems that Paul delivered instructions on Jesus Christ based on the Jerusalem and Damascus traditions. At any rate, their proclamation seems to have resulted in an explosive response from the Gentiles. It seems that they made the first missionary trip for eleven years from 38 to 49 CE.

The Apostolic Meeting

Paul finally joined the apostolic meeting in Jerusalem around 49 CE. It was an important event for the mission to the Gentiles because of the exemption of Gentiles from circumcision. In addition, Paul had a chance to learn more about Jesus and his instruction from the apostles of Jerusalem.

Paul went up to Jerusalem with Barnabas. They reported what they had achieved among the Gentiles during the first missionary trip (Gal 2:1–2). The reputed apostles—that is, James the Lord's brother, Cephas, and John—accepted their achievement and recognized them as workers for the Gentiles (2:8–9). It is definite that they were pleased with their recognition. There were, however, a couple of problems to be noted. First, Paul and Barnabas privately reported what they had achieved only to several apostles (2:2); in other words, their report was not officially approved by the congregation of the Jerusalem church. Second, the majority of the Jewish congregation would not allow the Gentile Titus to be exempted from circumcision (2:3–6). They kept asking the Gentiles to be circumcised. This implies that the circumcision of Gentiles was not completely approved by the Jews of the Jerusalem church. Third, Paul and Barnabas were not commissioned as apostles of Gentiles. This is known from the fact that, while Cephas was described as the apostle of the circumcised, the title "apostle" was not applied to Paul and Barnabas (2:7). It seems that Paul and Barnabas were merely recognized as workers for the uncircumcised Gentiles at the apostolic meeting. This makes readers anticipate a serious argument over the authority of Paul in future. At any rate, the above descriptions imply that Paul was subordinate to the apostles at his second visit to Jerusalem.

It seems that Paul learned more about Jesus on the basis of the fourth redaction of Q. It is believed to have been complete during the resistance to the Roman emperor Gaius Caligula, who attempted to erect his statue in the temple around 40–41 CE.[38] The Jews dared to run the risk of death to keep the temple holy according to the Law. It seems that the members of the Q community—that is, the Jerusalem church composed of those who followed Jesus—were ready to devote themselves to observe the Law because they were also Jews. This tendency is reflected in the fourth redaction of Q.

The texts of the fourth redaction of Q seem to be as follows.[39]

1. The Texts Added to the First Redactional Layer

> Q^4 3:8bc (Luke 3:8bc / Matt 3:9bc)
> Q^4 4:1–13 (Luke 4:1–13 / Matt 4:1–11)
> Q^4 6:12–16 (Luke 6:12–16 / Matt 5:1a; 10:2–4)
> Q^4 6:20a (Luke 6:20a / Matt 5:1b)
> Q^4 6:23c (Luke 6:23c / Matt 5:12c)
> Q^4 7:28 (Luke 7:28 / Matt 11:11)
> Q^4 16:16 (Luke 16:16 / Matt 11:12–13)
> Q^4 16:17–18 (Luke 16:17–18 / Matt 5:18, 32)
> Q^4 7:35 (Luke 7:35 / Matt 11:19c)

2. The Texts Added to the Second Redactional Layer

> Q^4 9:59–60a (Luke 9:59–60a / Matt 8:21–22)
> Q^4 10:3 (Luke 10:3 / Matt 10:16a)
> Q^4 11:24–26 (Luke 11:24–26 / Matt 12:43–45)
> Q^4 11:47–51 (Luke 11:47–51 / Matt 23:29–31, 34–36)
> Q^4 12:4–5 (Luke 12:4–5 / Matt 10:28)
> Q^4 12:10 (Luke 12:10 / Matt 12:32)
> Q^4 12:11–12 (Luke 12:11–12 / Matt 10:18–19)
> Q^4 16:13 (Luke 16:13 / Matt 6:24)
> Q^4 14:26–27 (Luke 14:26–27 / Matt 10:37–38)
> Q^4 17:33 (Luke 17:33 / Matt 10:39)

---

38. This is the conclusion that I have drawn from the argument of Theissen, who understood the temptation of Jesus in light of the event of the Roman emperor Gaius Caligula (*Gospels*, 205–9). I believe that the temptation story seems to originate in the fourth redactional layer of Q (Ra, Q, 183–94).

39. Ra, Q, 179–239.

3. The Texts Added to the Third Redactional Layer

Q^4 12:49, 51–56 (Luke 12:49, 51–56 / Matt 10:34–36; 16:2–3)
Q^4 12:58–59 (Luke 12:58–59 / Matt 5:25–26)
Q^4 13:28–30 (Luke 13:28–30 / Matt 8:11–12; 20:16)
Q^4 13:34–35 (Luke 13:34–35 / Matt 23:37–39)
Q^4 14:5 (Luke 14:5 / Matt 12:11–12)
Q^4 14:11 (Luke 14:11 / Matt 23:12)
Q^4 14:16–24 (Luke 14:16–24 / Matt 22:1–10)
Q^4 14:34–35 (Luke 14:34–35 / Matt 5:13)
Q^4 15:4–7 (Luke 15:4–7 / Matt 18:12–14)
Q^4 17:1–2 (Luke 17:1–2 / Matt 18:6–7)
Q^4 17:6 (Luke 17:6 / Matt 17:20)
Q^4 17:37c (Luke 17:37c / Matt 24:28)
Q^4 19:12–26 (Luke 19:12–26 / Matt 25:14–30)
Q^4 22:30 (Luke 22:30 / Matt 19:28)

The texts listed above show the features inserted into the texts of previous redactions. The most prominent feature is the emphasis on the observance of the Law.

It is necessary to look at peculiar points that appear in the fourth redaction of Q. First, the disciples were advised to observe the Law even to death (Q^4 4:1–13; 6:23c; 11:47–51; 14:26–27; 16:16–18). Second, the twelve apostles had a self-understanding that God substituted them for the twelve patriarchs (6:13–16; 22:30). Then, the members of Q community had a strong unity with a self-consciousness as being the true people of God (3:8bc; 13:28–29). Third, the personified spirit is described as an entity superior to Jesus (4:1–2; 12:10). Fourth, the door to the Gentiles was open from an eschatological point of view (13:29). Rather, an eschatological reversal of position has been described between Jews and Gentiles (13:30; 14:24). These lessons would have made Paul widen his theological understanding of Jesus.

It seems that Paul accepted the instruction embedded in the fourth redaction of Q. As a former Pharisee, Paul was zealous for the Law at that time even after receiving the revelation and finishing the first missionary trip. Thus, Paul was able to recognize the authority of James, the Lord's brother, who had a conservative position on the Law (Gal 2:9). In addition, Paul had a theological foundation to be more zealous for the ministry of making the Gentiles the people of God. Moreover, Paul himself was determined to fulfill this mission even to death. Finally, Paul and Barnabas returned to Antioch.

The Theological Controversy in Antioch

There was a theological controversy between Paul and Cephas over the Gentile table in Antioch. It seems to be a turning point that Cephas turned the back on Paul. In addition, having stood on the side of Cephas, Barnabas also left Paul. As a result, the apostles of Jerusalem decided to send representatives to the Gentile churches to check Paul and the gospel he had proclaimed.

Cephas visited the Antiochene church. It seems that Barnabas invited some members of the Jerusalem church around 50 CE in gratitude of their warm welcoming at his previous visit to Jerusalem (Gal 2:11–14). However, a theological controversy occurred between Paul and Cephas over the Gentile table. It started with the news that the people of James, the Lord's brother, had just arrived in Antioch. Then, having heard of news, Cephas as well as Barnabas withdrew from the table fellowship in front of Paul. It seems that they were afraid of James, who held the leadership of the Jerusalem church and emphasized observance of the Law. Having seen the withdrawal from the Gentile table, Paul rebuked Cephas for the ignorance of Gentiles by saying, "You are a Jew, yet you live like a Gentile and not like a Jew. How is it, then, that you force Gentiles to follow Jewish customs?" In fact, Paul was not authoritative enough to rebuke Cephas at that time. However, Paul could not help but say so because he had to protect the Gentiles from Judaization and wanted to keep them exempted from circumcision. In this respect, Paul did not want the gospel of Christ to be in jeopardy and in vain among the Gentiles.

The controversy over the Gentile table resulted in a loss of supporters. First of all, having been rebuked, Cephas turned the back on Paul. It seems that Cephas thought Paul was not in a position to rebuke him. Thus, it was scandalous to him. Second, having stood on the side of Cephas, Barnabas left Paul and stopped helping him. Third, having followed Barnabas, the members of the Antiochene church quit supporting Paul. With regard to this, Lüdemann says that they should not be regarded as the founders of Christianity because "in a moment of crisis their solution was to incorporate Gentiles into a new form of that old dispensation."[40]

40. Lüdemann, *Paul*, loc. 2523 of 3299.

In any case, fourth, those sent by James, the Lord's brother, acknowledged that Paul had been more in the favor of Gentiles than of Jews. In consequence, it was a big loss for Paul that the members of the Jerusalem church and Antiochene church stayed away from him.[41] Finally, since there was no one other than the Gentiles on his side, Paul had no choice but to leave for the Gentile churches he had established during the first missionary trip.[42]

Since then, the situation seems to have gotten even worse for Paul. Having returned to Jerusalem, Cephas reported to the leaders of the Jerusalem church what had happened in Antioch; and then he probably criticized Paul against his ungratefulness and arrogance. Cephas seems to say, "It is not right to allow the Gentiles exempted from circumcision." Then, the apostles of Jerusalem agreed with him and decided to inform the Gentiles of Paul's insufficiency. They tried to let them know that Paul had not been commissioned as an apostle of Gentiles and that the gospel of Christ had not been entrusted to him. It was not thorough enough to make them the people of God.[43] In addition, the apostles of Jerusalem asked the Gentiles to observe the Law, to be circumcised, and to keep the special days. The Gentiles were also asked to follow the instruction of Jesus embedded in Q. It seems that some of Gentile members of churches agreed with the apostles of Jerusalem because they were the disciples of Jesus, more authoritative than Paul.

Only a small amount of information was given about the representatives sent to the Gentile churches. For instance, Cephas visited Corinth and baptized some of the Corinthians (1 Cor 1:12). However, those sent to other churches have not been specifically known. Later, Paul described them as "tempters" (1 Thess 3:5), "dogs" and "evildoers" (Phil 3:2), and "agitators" (Gal 5:12). These expressions were made to criticize those sent

41. Lietzmann, *Beginning*, 108–10. Cf. Beker, *Paul*, 64, 130; Betz, *Galatians*, 103–4; and Patte, *Paul's Faith*, 37, 366.

42. As for the importance of the theological controversy in Antioch with regard to Paul's later struggle with the opponents in the Corinthian and Galatian churches, see Bauer, *Paul*, 1:245–65. In a similar manner, Lüdemann argues that the event of Antioch resulted in the vision and self-assuredness to insist on its truth and that they "were the spark and the fuel which powered the immense missionary effort that made Paul the founder of Christianity" (*Paul*, loc. 2424–27 of 3299).

43. Barrett believes that the opponents were those who followed Judaism but not the apostles of Jerusalem (*Second Epistle*, 30, 286–87). On the contrary, Cho insists on the affinity of Paul's opponent with those sent by the apostles of Jerusalem ("Paul's Opponent," 444, 465, 471).

by the apostles of Jerusalem to the Gentile churches. Paul's mentioning of "super apostles" indicates the severe critique against the apostles of Jerusalem (2 Cor 11:5, 13). These expressions reflect the fact that the distrust of the apostles of Jerusalem toward Paul was enormous. In any case, it is important that they sent representatives to the Gentile churches to keep Paul in check.

B. THE SECOND MISSIONARY TRIP

There was an aftereffect of theological controversy over the Gentile table taken place in Antioch. Paul seems to have maintained a Jewish perspective in the early days of the second missionary trip.[44] Having been challenged by some Gentiles in the middle of it, Paul made a theological transformation of decoupling from the apostles of Jerusalem. Finally, Christianity was born with a focus on the cross of Christ for the salvation of people.

The Beginning of the Second Missionary Trip

Without knowing that the apostles of Jerusalem had decided to send representatives to the Gentile churches, Paul went on the second missionary trip. Even if Paul was aware of their decision, there was nothing that Paul could do. He simply tried to make the Gentiles remain in the gospel he had preached.

Having left Antioch of Syria, Paul headed for Cilicia, Galatia, and Asia. However, nothing has been said about what he did there. Since he did not write any letters to the churches there, no information has been left. Paul probably taught by adding what he learned from the fourth redaction of Q to what he had delivered during the first missionary trip. Among them, the most distinctive one was the instruction on the observance of the Law without circumcision. In other words, it seems that he delivered an instruction that was not much different from what he had taught during the first missionary trip. It seems that the theological controversy in Antioch did not bring about a major change in his proclamation.

It is necessary to describe the life of Paul in connection with his letters sent to the Gentile churches. It seems that after leaving Asia he

44. Lüdemann, *Paul*, locs. 1095, 1108–30 of 3299.

kept going to Macedonia and Achaia in the opposite direction from Jerusalem. It is highly possible that Titus accompanied Paul to his hometown, possibly Corinth. This is supported by the fact that he worked for Paul afterwards. In this respect, Paul must have walked once again on the path he had done during the first missionary trip.

Thess(A)

Paul seems to have sent a letter to the Thessalonians during his stay in Philippi, which was a gateway to the region of Macedonia in Europe. It was written to inform them of his upcoming visit (1 Thess 2:2). It seems that Paul did not know that the apostles of Jerusalem had decided to send representatives to the Gentile churches.

The first letter can be isolated from 1 Thessalonians and named Thess(A). Its texts can be listed as follows:

1. Beginning Part of Letter (1:1)
2. Reason to Thank the Thessalonians (1:2–10)
3. Paul's View on the Thessalonians (2:1–12)
4. Relationship between Paul and the Thessalonians (2:13–16)
5. Paul's Encouragement (4:1–8)
6. Ending Part of Letter (5:26–27)

The texts presented above show the contents to be sufficient enough to make up a personal letter. Paul expressed his opinion in a strong tone in Thess(A).

Paul wrote Thess(A) with the apostolic authority in various ways. Above all, Paul expressed his desire to define himself as an apostle (1 Thess 2:7). Then, the relationship between parents and children was applied so as to heighten his spiritual authority over the Thessalonians (2:11–12). In addition, Paul insisted that the command he had given to them was delivered under the authority of the Lord Jesus (4:2). Thus, Paul was able to encourage the Thessalonians to keep up with what he had taught before. This implies that Thess(A) was written before the challenge of those sent by the apostles of Jerusalem arose in Thessalonian church.

Little information has been left about the composition of Thess(A). It seems to have been written in Philippi during the summer of 51 CE, not far from the time of theological controversy in Antioch around 50.

However, who delivered it has not been known. Since Silas and Timothy were co-senders, neither of them were its deliverer (1 Thess 1:1). It is then possible that Titus delivered Thess(A) on his way to Corinth ahead of Paul and his companions.

Cor(A)

After the visit to Thessalonica, Paul headed for Corinth. Before the departure from Thessalonica to Athens of Achaia, a letter was sent to the Corinthians to inform of his upcoming visit. This is the first letter sent to the Corinthians. Thus, it can be called Cor(A).

The texts of Cor(A) can be identified on the basis of 1 Cor 5:9–13, in which phrases such as "I have written you in my letter" and "But now I am writing you" are found. They inform that 1 Cor 5:9–13 was a part of the second letter at least. Then, the content of Cor(A) can be abstracted on the basis of it. Paul taught the Corinthians to avoid fornication as he had mentioned it in Thess(A) (1 Cor 5:9, 11; 1 Thess 4:3–5). In addition, the issue of idolatry seems to be treated in Cor(A) as it was mentioned in Thess(A) (1 Cor 5:10–11; 1 Thess 1:9–10). At any rate, Cor(A) seems to include instruction on the sexually immoral, the greedy and swindlers, and the idolaters in addition to his plan to visit Corinth a second time.

The texts of Cor(A) can be isolated from 1 and 2 Corinthians as follows:[45]

1. Greetings (removed at the time of compilation)
2. Reasons to Thanks God (1 Cor 1:4–9)
3. Instruction on the Relationship (2 Cor 6:14—7:1)[46]
4. The Saints as the Temple of God (1 Cor 3:16–17)
5. Instruction on the Greedy and the Sexually Immoral (6:9–20)
6. Instruction on Idolatry and Sexual Immorality (10:1–22)
7. Instruction on Woman (11:2–16; 14:33b–36)
8. Instruction on the Better Way (12:31b—14:1a, 14:20–22)
9. Authoritative Statement (14:37–38)

---

45. Ra, *Corinthians*, 67–100.

46. Some critical scholars believe that 2 Cor 6:14—7:1 is a non-Pauline text interpolated into its present place. See Fitzmyer, "Qumran," 271–80.

10. Plan to Visit (16:5–6)

11. Plea for Timothy (16:10–11)

12. Greetings (16:13–14)

The texts listed above show a series of contents long enough to make up a letter to a community. As the case of Thess(A), Paul seems to have unfolded Cor(A) with authority.

Paul wrote basic lessons in Cor(A) with regard to how the Corinthians could be holy and blameless. Above all, a strict standard for relations with unbelievers was put forth from a Jewish perspective (2 Cor 6:14—7:1). Then, having reflected the Jewish tradition, Paul showed the preference to the holy temple and the positive stance on the Law (1 Cor 3:16–17; 6:19; 14:21, 34). The Corinthians were advised to be righteous to inherit the kingdom of God (6:9–11). Love is strongly emphasized with a large amount of text (13:1–13). Paul exhorted them with authority as the founder of the Corinthian church. For this, the phrase "Lord's command" was used to make the Corinthians to observe what he had taught before (14:37). It reminds readers of the previous expression "instruction by the authority of the Lord Jesus," written in Thess(A) (1 Thess 4:2). Finally, Paul asked the Corinthians to send a certain number of people with Timothy returning from Corinth after the delivery of Cor(A) (1 Cor 16:10–11).

There are some comments on the situation when Cor(A) was being written. It is noteworthy that the relationship with the apostles of Jerusalem is not reflected yet in Cor(A) as it was not in Thess(A). This tells readers that Cor(A) was written not too far from the time of writing Thess(A). It seems that Cor(A) was written in Thessalonica in the early fall of 51 CE, before the coming of winter (1 Cor 16:6). Without doubt, it was delivered by Timothy to the Corinthians (16:10).

Cor(B)

It is necessary to describe what happened on his way to Corinth, possibly in Athens of Achaia. Paul met the household of Chloe accompanied with Timothy returning from Corinth after the delivery of Cor(A) (1 Cor 1:11). They were those sent by the Corinthians in response to Paul's request as written in Cor(A) (16:11). It is reasonable to surmise that they reported to Paul what had happened among the Corinthians and delivered the questions raised by the Corinthians after reading Cor(A). Then, Paul had to answer the questions and give instructions in regard to the matters that he had heard from the people of Chloe.

The answers and new instructions were written down in the second letter, which can be called Cor(B). Its texts might be as follows:[47]

1. Greetings (removed at the time of compilation)
2. Regarding the Division Caused by Baptism (1 Cor 1:10–17)
3. Regarding the Sexual Immorality (5:1–5, 9–13)
4. Regarding the Lawsuits (6:1–8)
5. Regarding the Relationship between Husband and Wife (7:1–17)
6. Regarding the Virgins (7:25–40)
7. Regarding the Food Sacrificed to Idols (8:1–13; 10:23—11:1)
8. Regarding the Division Caused by Supper (11:17–29, 33–34)
9. Regarding the Spiritual Gifts (12:1, 4–12, 14–31a; 14:1b–19, 23–33a, 39–40)
10. Regarding the Resurrection (15:12–28)
11. Regarding the Collection (16:1–4)
12. Regarding Apollos (16:12)
13. Greetings (16:15–18)

The texts listed above are logical enough to show that they consist of answers to the Corinthians. Probably, there is no letter that has an external form as systematic as Cor(B).

The contents of Cor(B) can be divided into two parts. One is the part where Paul offered a solution after he had heard of news about the problematic matters happened among the Corinthians, and the other is the part where he answered the questions raised by them. The latter is known by the phrase περὶ δὲ. To the former belong the division caused by baptism (1 Cor 1:10–17), the fornication among the family members (5:1–5), the lawsuits among the members of church (6:1–8), the conflict at supper (11:17–29, 33–34), and the doubt of resurrection (15:12–28). To the latter belong the relationship between husband and wife (7:1–17), the issue of "virgins" (7:25–40), the food offered to idols (8:1–13; 10:23—11:1), the spiritual gifts (chapters 12, 14), the issue of

---

47. Ra, *Corinthians*, 101–60.

collection (16:1—4), and the invitation of Apollos (16:12). It is characterized in Cor(B) that Paul offered solutions to problematic matters that the Corinthians had faced.

In particular, the visit of Cephas to Corinth should not be overlooked. It seems that the apostles of Jerusalem sent him as a representative and that he baptized some Corinthians (1 Cor 1:12).[48] In addition, he seems to have taught them to follow the Jewish precepts; in other words, they were asked to observe the Law and to be circumcised. While Paul comparatively took a long time to arrive at Corinth by traveling on foot, Cephas probably took a shortcut across the Mediterranean by ship. Having heard of Cephas's activity in Corinth, Paul did not seem to take it seriously. This can be drawn from the fact that Paul did not say anything about him at all in Cor(B). It seems that Paul did not recognize the side effects of division caused by baptism and the Jewish instruction.

A little information about the composition of Cor(B) can be detected. It seems to have been written in Athens of Achaia on his way to Corinth from Thessalonica. This can be deduced from the fact that Paul mentioned the house of Stephanas as the first fruit of Achaia (1 Cor 16:15). In addition to Stephanas, Fortunatus and Achaicus were introduced as those living in Athens (16:17). Without doubt, it was delivered by the people of Chloe returning to Corinth. Finally, it can be said that Cor(B) was possibly written in the mid-fall of 51 CE.

Thess(B)

Another letter was written in Athens. Having heard of news from Timothy about the Thessalonians shaken by those come from the Jerusalem church, Paul sent a second letter to the Thessalonians. Thus, it can be called Thess(B).

The texts of Thess(B) can be isolated from 1 Thessalonians by excluding those of Thess(A) as follows:

1. Beginning Part (removed at the time of compilation)
2. Paul's Willingness to Visit (1 Thess 2:17–20)
3. Reason to Send Timothy (3:1–5)
4. Report of Timothy (3:6–7)

---

48. Vielhauer, "Paul," 129–42.

5. Paul's Joy over the Thessalonians (3:8–10)
6. Paul's Wish to Revisit Thessalonica (3:11–13)
7. Answer to the Question about Brotherhood (4:9–12)
8. Answer to the Question about the Dead (4:13–18)
9. Answer to the Question about the End of World (5:1–11).
10. Paul's Encouragement (5:12–25, 28)
11. Ending Part (removed at the time of compilation)

The texts listed above show a well-composed aspect of a letter in spite of worry about the Thessalonians. It seems that Paul wrote Thess(B) with relief.

The contents of Thess(B) can be divided into two parts. The first one is about Paul's reassurance of the Thessalonians, and the other is about his answer to their questions. The Thessalonians were shaken by the "tempter" as he had expected (1 Thess 3:4–5); however, Paul was relieved because they had decided to stay in the gospel (3:6–7). The tempters are supposed to be those sent by the apostles of Jerusalem. The word "tempter" reflects the fall of Thessalonians into a more difficult situation than the division among the Corinthians resulted from the baptism by Cephas as written in Cor(B). Paul's answer to the questions of the Thessalonians appears with an expression of περὶ δὲ in Thess(B) (4:9, 13; 5:1). This is in common with that found in Cor(B) (1 Cor 7:1, 25; 8:1; 12:1; 16:1, 12). Although Paul's use of it shows the contemporaneity of Cor(B) and Thess(B), the latter seems to have been written a little later than the former. This is because a more serious conflict with those outside the church is found in Thess(B) than in Cor(B).

The mission of Paul to the Gentiles can be divided into two parts. They are before and after writing of Thess(B). Prior to writing it, Paul knew nothing about those who had made the Gentiles challenge against him, except Cephas, who had visited Corinth. However, at the time of writing Thess(B), Paul's tone became aggressive as he was aware of the adversary. In this respect, a watershed is found in terms of his attitude toward the apostles of Jerusalem. Thus, it can be concluded that Christianity was conceived among the Gentiles at the time of writing Thess(B) in opposition to the Jewish community led by the apostles of Jerusalem.[49]

---

49. I do not agree with Lüdemann, who defines the members of the Jerusalem church as Jewish Christians (*Paul*, loc. 394 of 3299). No Christian instruction is found

Paul left some information about the composition of Thess(B). It was definitely written in Athens (1 Thess 3:1). In addition, it seems to have been written in the late fall of 51 CE just after sending Cor(B). Moreover, Paul asked Timothy to deliver Thess(B) because he had come to him with good news that the Thessalonians had decided to stay in the gospel (3:2–3, 6). This implies that between Paul's writing of Thess(A) and Thess(B) Timothy was sent to the Thessalonians or had remained in Thessalonica. Either way, it does not change the situation that there was a vivid communication between Paul and the Thessalonians.

Phil(A)

A situation similar to that of the Thessalonians happened to the Philippians. Having left Athens, Paul heard of news that the Philippians had been shaken a little by those come from Jerusalem but that they remained in the gospel. So, Paul sent a letter to the Philippians with relief.

The first letter sent to the Philippians can be called Phil(A). Its texts can be isolated from Philippians as follows:

1. Greetings (removed at the time of compilation)
2. Paul's Status and Attitude (Phil 3:1b–16)
3. Paul's Encouragement (3:17—4:1)
4. Paul's Recommendation (4:2–3)
5. Ending Part of Letter (4:8–9)

The texts listed above shows a well-composed aspect of a letter sent to a community of people. Paul showed an aggressive attitude toward the adversaries in it.

Paul presented a couple of new instructions in Phil(A). The faith of Christ is introduced anew for the righteousness of God (Phil 3:9). On the other hand, Paul expressed dissent against those who had made the Philippians confused in the life of faith by using words such as "dogs," "those men who do evil," "those mutilators of the flesh," and "the enemy of Christ's cross" (3:2, 18). They are stronger expressions than "tempter" as used in Thess(B) (1 Thess 3:5). Especially, the self-interactive saying "we who are the circumcision" implies that circumcision was an important issue to the Philippians. Then, it can be surmised that those sent by

---

in the Jerusalem tradition represented by Q.

the apostles of Jerusalem asked the Philippians to be circumcised. At any rate, the Philippians refused the Jewish instruction; rather, they stayed in the gospel Paul had preached (Phil 4:1). In the meantime, Christianity was born to the Gentiles.

Little information has been left for the composition of Phil(A). It seems to have been written a little bit later than Thess(B) in that Paul used more aggressive words in Phil(A). Thus, it can be said that it was written in the early winter of 51 CE on his way to Corinth from Athens or in Corinth. However, no information has been given about its deliverer. Nevertheless, Paul left traces in that he wanted to send Timothy back, but he could not, as written later in Phil(B) (Phil 2:19–24). This implies that Timothy had once visited Philippi before Phil(B) was delivered. If so, it is likely that he delivered Phil(A) to the Philippians.

Cor(C)

Paul left a lot of information about the Corinthians. Having finally arrived at Corinth again, Paul faced the challenge of some Corinthians sponsored by the apostles of Jerusalem. Paul was under great duress over the situation. Having retreated to Ephesus, Paul sent a letter with tears of grief, which was the third letter.

Paul faced the reality of the Corinthians at the second visit to Corinth. A certain number of Corinthians seriously challenged him against the gospel and his authority. This made Paul defend himself; however, he was weak, full of fear, and trembled while staying in Corinth (1 Cor 2:3). After all, having failed to persuade them to stay in the gospel, Paul left Corinth with a promise to come back after spending some time in Macedonia (2 Cor 1:16–17). However, he was not able to keep the promise on account of an unknown reason; rather, he went to Ephesus (1 Cor 16:7–9; 2 Cor 1:8). There a letter was written with tears of grief and sent to the Corinthians (2 Cor 2:4). This is Cor(C), the "Letter of Tears."[50] It has been argued that the text of 1 Cor 9:15 is the best candidate that Paul wrote with tears.[51] At the time of writing Cor(C), he was with Aquila and Priscilla, who had stayed Ephesus of Asia (1 Cor 16:19).

50. Furnish, *II Corinthians*, 397–98, 414. Paul once shed tears of delight when he wrote Phil(A) on the way to Corinth (Phil 3:18); on the contrary, having been challenged seriously by some Corinthians, Paul was forced to retreat to Ephesus and could not help but write a letter with tears of grief.

51. Barrett, *First Epistle*, 208; and Conzelmann, *I Corinthians*, 157.

The texts of Cor(C) can be separated from 1 Corinthians by eliminating those belonging to Cor(A) and Cor(B).[52] They can be listed as follows:

1. Greetings (1 Cor 1:1–3)
2. The Cross of Christ (1:18—3:15; 3:18–23)
3. Apostle as the Model (4:1–21)
4. Attitude that the Corinthians Should Take (5:6–8; 7:18–24)
5. Paul's Defense of Apostleship (9:1–27; 11:30–32)
6. Paul's Confidence in the Gospel and Apostleship (12:2–3, 13; 15:1–11)
7. The Resurrected Life (15:29–58)
8. Plan to Visit Corinth (16:7–9)
9. Greetings (16:19–24)

The texts listed above show Paul's strong tone for the defense of the gospel and his apostolate. Paul showed an increasingly aggressive attitude in the order of Thess(B), Phil(A), and Cor(C).

Paul put an emphasis on the apostolate as well as the gospel of Christ in Cor(C). Above all, salvation was presented in association with the cross of Christ for the first time (1 Cor 1:18—3:15; 3:18–23).[53] The crucifixion of Christ was the decisive weapon for Paul to keep the Corinthians and to break through the challenge initiated by the apostles of Jerusalem. With this, Paul began to develop Christian teaching. It seems that Paul was not challenged by the followers of Apollos because he was in good relationship with him (1:12; 16:12). Rather, those baptized by Cephas seemed to challenge Paul against the gospel and his authority (1:10–12). In response, Paul strongly defended himself for his apostleship (1:1; 9:1–15). At that time, Paul was concerned about the Corinthians and revealed his willingness to never give them up. In addition, the issue of redemption was introduced as the core of the gospel for the first

---

52. Ra, *Corinthians*, 161–222.

53. Critical scholars have argued that 1 Cor 1:17—4:21 is an integral unit from a literary perspective. See Welborn, "Discourse," 101–7; Wilkens, *Weisheit*, 68; and Conzelmann, *I Corinthians*, 37. It is, however, to be noted that, as I mentioned before, 1 Cor 1:17 and 3:16–17 reveal different characteristics from the rest of texts.

time (15:3). In this respect, Cor(C) occupies an important place in the process of the development of Christian theology.

It is necessary to take a look at Aquila and Priscilla. Paul was with them for a certain period of time in Ephesus, where they had stayed long enough to form a church at their house (1 Cor 16:8, 19). From the fact that Paul conveyed their regards to the Corinthians, it can be inferred that they had been known to the Corinthians. It seems that Aquila and Priscilla moved to Ephesus via Corinth after they had been expelled from Rome by the edict of the Roman emperor Claudius.[54] It is, however, unclear where and when Paul met them. It is most likely that Paul met them in Corinth. Although it is not clear whether their meeting was on Paul's first or second visit to Corinth, the former is preferred to the latter for three reasons,[55] First, their migration time from Rome and Paul's first visit to Corinth can match from a chronological perspective. Second, if they had met him at his second visit to Corinth, they would not have been with him on account of the challenge of some Corinthians against him. Third, if Paul had met Aquila and Priscilla in Ephesus, he would not have had an obligation to convey their regards to the Corinthians. It is legitimate to conclude that Aquila and Priscilla belonged to the first group of people converted by Paul during his first visit to Corinth, and then they migrated to Ephesus at an appropriate time after he had left. At any rate, Paul met Aquila and Priscilla again in Ephesus, and they got to know his negative view on the Law as reflected in Cor(C) (15:56). Afterwards, they returned to Rome after the edict of Claudius had been withdrawn; however, the exact time has not been known.

Paul left a little information about the composition of Cor(C). It was delivered by Timothy (1 Cor 4:17; cf. 2 Cor 2:12-13; 7:5-6).[56] He was employed so far to deliver most of Paul's letters. Cor(C) seems to have been written in Ephesus in the early spring of 52 CE because Paul revealed the intention to stay there until the coming Pentecost (16:8).[57]

54. Lüdemann claims that Paul met Aquila and Priscilla at Corinth in 41 CE (*Paul*, locs. 616, 625 of 3299). However, there must have been a certain period of time between the edict and their arrival in Corinth.

55. According to Acts, Paul met Aquila and Priscilla at Corinth during the second missionary trip (Acts 18:1-2). It is, however, to be noted that the author of Acts rearranged the historical facts according to his intention.

56. Barrett believes that the "Letter of Tears" was delivered to the Corinthians by Titus (*Second Epistle*, 94).

57. Lüdemann believes that First Corinthians was written in spring after spending at least one winter as reflected in 1 Cor 5:7; 16:8 (*Paul*, locs. 469, 478 of 3299).

If so, he would have gone through Athens, Thessalonica, Philippi, and Troas on his retreat to Ephesus.

Galatians

Having faced the severest challenge of the Galatians, Paul wrote a letter to them. Although he was quite upset by their challenge, he systematically revealed what he was trying to convey. Having emphasized the faith of hearing the gospel, Paul suggested the way to be the true people of God.

The challenge of the Galatians is inferred in three ways. The first material is found in Paul's urgency toward the Galatians from the beginning of Galatians (Gal 1:1). This shows that he faced severe challenges in connection with the apostolate. The second one is seen in the description that while he was staying in Ephesus a vast gate was open; however, there were a lot of enemies (1 Cor 16:8–9). This suggests a situation in which Paul heard news of the challenge against him in Ephesus from various surrounding areas, including Galatia. Third, he experienced severe sufferings beyond his ability in Asia (2 Cor 1:8–9). This reflects the fact that he was uncomfortable with the circumstances around him. The texts listed above imply that, having already been hurt by some Corinthians, Paul had a harsher time in Ephesus. This includes the news about the Judaization of the Galatians that made him terrified. Since Paul would have felt a crushing fall, he had no choice but to write a letter with a strong tone for the Galatians.

Galatians seems to be integral from a theological perspective. Its texts can be categorized as follows:[58]

1. Prologue (Gal 1:1–5)

2. Instruction Based on the Experience with the Apostles of Jerusalem (1:6—2:14)

    a. Rebuke against the Galatians (1:6–10)

    b. The Revelation of God Paul Received (1:11–24)

    c. Discussion on Getting into the People of God (2:1–10)

    d. Discussion on Staying in the People of God (2:11–14)

3. Intermediate Conclusion (2:15–21)

---

58. Ra, *Galatians*, 41–462.

4. Instruction Based on the Experience with the Galatians (3:1—6:10)

    a. Rebuke against the Galatians (3:1)

    b. The Spirit That the Galatians Experienced (3:2–5)

    c. Discussion on Getting into the People of God (3:6—5:12)

    d. Discussion on Staying in the People of God (5:13—6:10)

5. Epilogue (6:11-18)

Galatians is a well-composed letter with a structure of parallelism. Having sent a systematically formed letter even in urgent circumstances, Paul revealed his earnestness for the Galatians.

Paul systematically preached in Galatians. Having based on his experience of revelation, Paul described how the Gentiles became the people of God (Gal 2:1-10) and how they maintained this status (2:11-14). Then, based on the spiritual experience of the Galatians, Paul treated the issue of becoming the people of God (3:6—5:12) and maintaining this status (5:13—6:10). This implies that Paul acknowledged a crisis for the identity of the Galatians. They were taught not to be Jewish; rather, they had to walk on the path of becoming the people of God as Gentiles.

Paul strongly defended the gospel and his apostolate by criticizing those who had challenged him.[59] When he said that he had not been an apostle by or through people, he was speaking with the apostles of Jerusalem in mind, who had the authority to appoint him as an apostle or not (Gal 1:1). Then, there was a certain number of people sent to the Galatians by the apostles of Jerusalem, described in various ways: those of alienating the Galatians (4:17), those of being compared to leaven (5:9), the agitators to be emasculated (5:12), and those of boasting of flesh (6:13). They asked the Galatians to observe the Law and follow the instruction of Jesus, probably represented by Q, so that they could be the people of God. Having followed the instruction of the apostles of Jerusalem, the Galatians refused the gospel and the authority of Paul. Their challenge against him reflects the fact that he was in a crisis in relation to the Galatians. Thus, Paul could not help but write a letter with an

---

59. Beker identifies Paul's opponent with the itenerant Jewish-Christian missionaries who were in connection with the Jerusalem church (*Paul*, 42, 45–46). However, I am not sure whether they could be regarded as Christian missionaries. Rather, they belonged to those of the Jesus movement.

extremely negative view on the Law (3:19). At that time, Paul's Christian teaching also seems to have reached its climax.

Paul left little information about the composition of Galatians. It seems to have been written in Ephesus of Asia at the beginning of the summer of 52 CE after he had sent Cor(C) to the Corinthians. This is supported by the fact that Paul further developed his theological interpretation in Galatians than in Cor(C). However, it has not been known who delivered Galatians since no clue is found in this regard.

Cor(D)

Paul sent a fourth letter to the Corinthians. Having heard an optimistic report from Titus, Paul was full of hope to restore his relationship with them. Accordingly, Paul tried to write Cor(D) as carefully as he could.

There was a period of hope for Paul. Having sent Cor(C) and Galatians in Ephesus, Paul went to Troas to meet Titus, returning from Corinth (2 Cor 2:12–13). It seems that after Timothy had delivered Cor(C) and returned, Paul sent Titus to Corinth and promised to meet in Troas. However, things went wrong, and Paul had to leave for Macedonia without any notice to him. Nevertheless, fortunately Paul met Titus there and heard of optimistic news about the Corinthians. Perhaps Titus thought that they had regretted and repented to some extent after reading Cor(C). Having heard the report of Titus, Paul was so pleased that he might think of their return to the gospel and restoration of relationship. Therefore, he wrote Cor(D) with a tender tone.

The texts of Cor(D) can be isolated from 2 Corinthians from a redactional perspective as follows:[60]

1. Greetings (2 Cor 1:1–2)
2. Introduction: Comfort (1:3–7)
3. Apology for the Past (1:8—2:4)
4. Comfort from Worry about Titus (2:5–13; 7:5–16)
5. Plea for Collection (8:1–24)[61]

---

60. Ra, *Corinthians*, 223–56.

61. It has been generally agreed that chapter 9 originated in a different letter from that to which chapter 8 belonged. See Betz, *2 Corinthians*, 3–4. It is also kept in mind that chapter 8 has been generally written earlier than chapter 9. Cf. Bornkamm, "History," 258–63.

6. Greetings (13:11–13)

The texts listed above are logical enough to appeal for the restoration of relationship. Paul wrote the letter with care, so that they might not miss the opportunity to return to the gospel of Christ.

Paul focused on two topics in Cor(D). One is the apology for not keeping the promise to revisit without any notice, and the other is the forgiveness of those who had challenged him and the provision of comfort to those who had been depressed on account of conflict. It was written as carefully as possible in order that Paul would not miss the opportunity to recover the relationship. In the meantime, Paul asked them to participate in the collection he had requested a year ago. This shows that Paul was full of hope and expectation at the time of writing Cor(D).

There is a little information about the composition and delivery of Cor(D). It seems that Paul wrote it in the mid-summer of 52 CE, a year after he had mentioned the collection for the first time in Cor(B) (1 Cor 16:1; 2 Cor 8:10). Cor(D) seems to have been written in Philippi of Macedonia, where Paul fortunately met Titus returning from Corinth with an optimistic report (2 Cor 2:13; 7:5–7). It seems that Titus and his companion delivered Cor(D) to the Corinthians (8:16–18, 23). It is, however, to be remembered that not everything is going as expected.

Cor(E)

It seems that the Corinthians were sober toward Paul. Having received Cor(D), they did not respond to him as much as he had expected. They did not give a firm answer to the request for collection. Paul once again carefully wrote a letter on reconciliation.

The fifth letter can be called Cor(E), whose texts would be as follows:[62]

1. Greetings (removed at the time of compilation)
2. Introduction: the Apostolate (2 Cor 2:14–17)
3. The Minister of the Spirit (3:1—4:6)
4. The Minister of Resurrection (4:7—5:10)
5. The Minister of Reconciliation (5:11—6:13; 7:2–4)

62. Ra, *Corinthians*, 257–94.

6. Collection (9:1–15)

7. Greetings (removed at the time of compilation)

The texts listed above are abundant enough to constitute a letter to a community. It shows consistency in regard to the ministry of Paul.

Paul still expressed hope for reconciliation with the Corinthians in Cor(E). This is found in the description of his identity as the servant of God in various ways: a worker of a new covenant, a servant of life, and a reaper of peace. Then, he expected the Corinthians to donate some money in response to his ministry for the poor saints in Jerusalem. On the other hand, Paul criticized those who had challenged him; according to him, they were those who had made a mess of God's word for their own profit (2 Cor 2:17). They were more likely to be sent by the apostles of Jerusalem (3:1; 4:2).[63] However, Paul expected the Corinthians to defeat them and return to the gospel he had preached.

There is a little information about the composition and delivery of Cor(E). From the description that Paul boasted to the Macedonians of the offering gifts promised by the Achaians from a year ago, it can be known that Cor(E) was also written a year later than Cor(B) (2 Cor 9:2; cf. 8:2). Then, it seems to have been written in the late summer of 52 CE in Thessalonica, not far from the time of sending Cor(D). Cor(E) seems to have been delivered by a couple of people sent to carry the expected collection (9:3, 5). However, later in Cor(F), Paul revealed that they were Titus and his companion (12:18). It is, however, to be remembered that not everything is going as expected.

Cor(F)

Paul wrote the sixth letter, Cor(F), to the Corinthians with a strong tone. This is because they would not accept the gospel to the end. However, Paul did not give up his passion to make the Corinthians remain in the gospel of Christ.

Having sent Cor(E), Paul kept traveling the region of Macedonia. It seems that he finally arrived at Illyricum, located at the western end of Macedonia (Rom 15:19). There he heard of news that the Corinthians had not accepted his request in the end. Therefore, he turned to a tough stance against them. Still, the Corinthians rejected the gospel of Christ,

---

63. Barrett, *Second Epistle*, 128.

denied his authority, and refused to donate money. Paul was so hard-pressed that he could not find any hope from the Corinthians. Thus, he sent forth Cor(F) with a bold tone.

The texts of Cor(F) can be isolated from 2 Corinthians by eliminating those belonging to Cor(A), Cor(D), and Cor(E) as follows:[64]

1. Greetings (removed at the time of compilation)
2. Instruction: the Authority (2 Cor 10:1-11)
3. Paul's Boast in the Lord (10:12—12:13)
4. Warning (12:14—13:10)
5. Greetings (removed at the time of compilation)

The texts listed above show a consistent flow of content to criticize those who would not accept the gospel of Christ. Cor(F) seems to have been written with an emphasis on the authority of the Lord Jesus Christ.

Having revealed a tough atmosphere, Paul would not leave the Corinthians alone. So he warned them to be ready for his third visit (2 Cor 12:14; 13:1). This made them anticipate that Paul would punish them. Thus, he criticized those who regarded him as the one working according to "flesh" (10:2). In addition, he linked the super-apostles to Satan (11:5, 13-15). They were none other than the apostles of Jerusalem. This is the severest critique of Paul against them. On the other hand, Paul tried to touch the hearts of the Corinthians with spiritual parenting.

Paul did not leave any information about the place of writing Cor(F). It was probably written in Illyricum after traveling all the way up to the western end of Macedonia as reflected in Cor(D) (2 Cor 2:13) and Romans (Rom 15:19). More specifically, having left Ephesus, Paul crossed Macedonia and arrived at Illyricum. It is likely that Cor(F) was written at the end of 52 CE. However, it has not been known who delivered it to the Corinthians.

Paul finally visited Corinth a third time. As he foretold in Cor(F), he rushed to Corinth (2 Cor 12:14; 13:1). However, little has been known about what he did there on his third visit. It would not be easy for Paul to punish those who had challenged him because they would not be subordinate. Anyway, it seems that Paul headed for Jerusalem after he had left Corinth to deliver the collection before the visit to Rome (2 Cor 1:16; Rom 15:25-26, 30-32). Paul is likely to have gone to Jerusalem because

---

64. Ra, *Corinthians*, 295-332.

he already had the money collected among the Gentiles.⁶⁵ It has been, however, unknown at all whether or not the apostles of Jerusalem welcomed him. Paul wrote nothing about it.

C. THE THIRD MISSIONARY TRIP

Paul went on the third missionary trip from Jerusalem to Rome. However, on the way to Jerusalem, Paul started sending a letter to the Romans with an intention to get the financial support for the proclamation of the gospel even to Spain. However, it seems that his wish was not accepted on account of the conflict with the Romans, especially the Jewish members, over his negative view on the Law. On the other hand, he sent two letters while being imprisoned in Rome.

Rom(A)

Paul wrote the first letter, Rom(A), to Rome. Paul wrote it as carefully as he could because it was his first encounter with the Romans, whose church he had not established. However, he himself seems to have never predicted that his negative view on the Law would lead to things going the wrong way.

A mission to Spain was the final goal of Paul. For this, he tried to get financial aid from the Romans in exchange for preaching the gospel. Although he did not establish the church, Paul would have believed that he had coworkers, Aquila and Priscilla, with whom he spent a certain period of time in Ephesus. He tried to make the Roman church a forward base for the mission to Spain. Thus, Paul could not help but write Rom(A) as politely as possible to win the hearts of the Romans.

---

65. According to the book of Acts, having left Corinth of Achaia in Europe, Paul visited Ephesus and then went up to Jerusalem a third time (Acts 18:18–23). However, Paul did not report the third visit to Jerusalem in his letters. Then, it is said in the book of Acts that Paul went back to Ephesus (19:1), Macedonia, and finally Achaia (19:21–22; 20:1–2). If this description is historically correct, it refers to the second visit to Corinth. Having spent three months in Achaia, Paul visited Troas on his way to Jerusalem for the fourth visit (20:3–6, 13–16). If description written in the book of Acts is correct, this is contradictory to what Paul wrote in his letters. However, it is to be believed that Paul visited Jerusalem a third time to deliver the collected money as written in Rom 15:26.

The texts of Rom(A) would be as follows:[66]

1. Beginning Part (Rom 1:1–7)
2. Intention to Visit Rome (1:8–15)
3. Righteousness by Faith (1:16–17; 4:1–25)
4. The Love of God (5:1–11; 8:31–39)
5. The Ethics of Saints (12:3–13; 14:1–12)
6. Intention to Visit Rome (15:22–29)
7. Recommendation (16:1–2)
8. Greetings (16:3–16)
9. Benediction (16:21–27)

The texts presented above show that Paul constituted a letter with regard to the gospel for the Romans. It is likely that Rom(A) was a summary of the gospel that Paul wanted to preach to the Romans.

Rom(A) is conducted on two axes. They are the gospel and the mission grant. In other words, Paul wanted to preach the gospel to the Romans and in return expected their financial support for the mission to Spain. Here the righteousness of God by faith is presented, which was already claimed in Phil(A) (Phil 3:9) and Galatians (Gal 2:16). Paul emphasized the love of God, who had given his Son to save people from the status of sinner. By this, according to Paul, the mission God entrusted to him would be fulfilled. However, not everything seems to be done according to one's expectations.

A little information has been known in regard to the composition of Rom(A). It seems that Paul wrote Rom(A) in Corinth. This is known from the fact that Gaius is mentioned in Cor(B) and Rom(A) (1 Cor 1:14; Rom 16:23). This means that Gaius was with Paul in Corinth when he wrote Rom(A). It seems to have been written in the early days of 53 CE. Definitely, it was delivered by Phoebe, a deaconess of the Cenchrean church, located near to Corinth (Rom 16:1–2).

---

66. Ra, *Romans*, 31–100.

Rom(B)

Having sent Rom(A), Paul seems to have expected the Romans to accept his will. However, the Romans did not seem to be pleased with the gospel Paul had presented, especially his negative view on the Law, and asked him to clarify it. This was probably known to Paul from Phoebe returning from Rome. Accordingly, Paul sent another letter, Rom(B), to them.

There was a reason that Paul sent Rom(B). It is because some of the Romans would not agree with Paul that the Law brings wrath and transgression, as written in Rom(A) (Rom 4:15). Aquila and Priscilla seem to have had limitations for the interpretation of Paul's negative view on the Law because they had never heard of such an extreme teaching. They were aware of the negative view on the Law to the extent recorded in Cor(C) because it had been written while they were staying in Ephsesus with Paul (1 Cor 15:56). However, the negative view recorded in Galatians that the Law had been added because of transgression was not known to them (Gal 3:19). Aquila and Priscilla were not aware of it because Paul unfolded such an instruction after they had left for Rome. In addition, it seems that the Romans were not so enthusiastic about Paul's request for financial support. It seems that the Romans, especially the Jewish members, raised questions to make a clear statement about the Law in order to get the missionary fund. Thus, Paul had to explain his view on the Law more in detail in his following letter, Rom(B).

The texts of Rom(B) can be listed as follows:[67]

1. Beginning Part (removed at the time of compilation)
2. Wrath of God (Rom 1:18—2:11)
3. Limitation of the Law (2:12—3:18)
4. Righteousness of Faith than the Law (3:19-31)
5. Ethics of Saints (12:14—13:7; 14:13-23)
6. Encouragement and Benediction (15:30-33)
7. Ending Part (removed at the time of compilation)

The texts listed above are logical enough to constitute a letter with regard to the role of the Law. Paul was unintentionally compelled to explain the relationship of the Law to wrath and transgression.

---

67. Ra, *Romans*, 101–58.

Paul worked hard on explaining the relationship between the wrath of God and the Law. Having considered that the majority of the Roman congregation was supposed to be Jews, Paul treated the issue of wrath, the limitation of the Law, and the righteousness of God by faith. He did his best to make the Romans accept his gospel and support him financially. In particular, the circumstances at the time of writing Rom(A) should be taken into account. Since the Roman church was not established by Paul, the apostles of Jerusalem did not send a representative there. So he seems to have thought that the Romans would not challenge him against his view on the Law. However, it seems that the Jewish members of the Roman church were enthusiastic to raise critiques against it.

Little information about the time and place of composition has been known. It seems that Paul wrote Rom(B) on his way to Jerusalem from Corinth because he had still worried about not being welcomed by the apostles of Jerusalem (Rom 15:31). Rom(B) was probably sent to Rome in the middle of 53 CE by unknown person. This shows that Paul was able to communicate with the Roman church without any difficulty.

Rom(C)

Paul was forced to write another letter in response to the critique of the Romans against his negative view on the Law. They did not seem to be satisfied with his answer to their questions as written in Rom(B). Tensions between Paul and the Romans seem to have risen at the time of writing Rom(C).

Relations with the Roman congregation became increasingly difficult. It seems that, having read Rom(B), the Romans, especially the Jewish members, were not satisfied with his answer. Rather, they asked him to explain his view on the relationship between the Law and sin that was written in Rom(B) (Rom 3:20). This implies that they became unfriendly to Paul with a critique against his position. Thus, Paul could not help but write another letter to explain his view on the relationship between them.

The third letter, Rom(C), carries the texts listed as follows:[68]

1. Beginning Part (removed at the time of compilation)
2. The Law and Sin (Rom 5:12—6:23)
3. The Law and Faith (7:1–25)

68. Ra, *Romans*, 159–222.

4. Christ and the Spirit (8:1–30)
5. Ethical Instruction (13:8–10; 15:1–13)
6. Encouragement and Benediction (16:17–20)
7. Ending Part (removed at the time of compilation)

The texts listed above show Paul's consistency with regard to his negative view on the Law. However, they show that he tried to avoid the critique of the Romans while giving sin a negative role.

Paul described the relationship between the Law and sin in Rom(C). It has been claimed that sin abused the Law. Instead, Paul emphasized the way of being righteous by faith again. Paul did not give up the core of the gospel he was trying to preach. In this way, Paul tried to avoid the accusations of the Jewish members of the Roman church. Then, he delivered lessons centered on Christ and the spirit of God. Thus, Paul tried to persuade the Romans to accept the gospel and support him financially; however, it is not clear whether his attempt was successful.

Little is known about the information related to the writing of Rom(C). However, internal evidence tells that Rom(C) was written at the end of the 53 CE after arriving at Jerusalem or on his way to Rome.[69] However, no mention is made of the person who delivered it to the Roman church.

Rom(D)

It seems that the Romans were not friendly to Paul, yet. Since Paul dealt with the matter of sin from a pan-anthropological perspective in Rom(C), the Jewish members of the Roman church seem to have asked him to answer the question about the reason of proclaiming the gospel to the Gentiles. Thus, Paul unfolded his view on the salvation of people in his fourth letter, Rom(D).

Paul presented his view on the mission to the Gentiles. Rom(D) was probably composed of texts listed below:[70]

1. Beginning Part (removed at the time of compilation)

---

69. In the book of Acts, it is described that Paul was arrested in Jerusalem and taken to Rome (Acts 21:27—28:15). However, this is considered to be parallel with Jesus' arrest described in Luke's Gospel (Luke 22:47—23:49). Paul left no clue as to the fact that he was arrested and taken to Rome.

70. Ra, *Romans*, 223–72.

2. Paul's Passion for the Jews (Rom 9:1–5)
3. God's Selection (9:6–29)
4. God's Plan of Salvation (9:30—10:21)
5. Relationship between Jews and Gentiles (11:1–36)
6. The Ethics of Saints (12:1–2; 13:11–14)
7. Encouragement and Benediction (15:14–21)

The texts listed above are logical enough to constitute a letter regarding the reason to proclaim the gospel for the salvation of people. This seems to be Paul's response to the critique raised by the Romans for reading Rom(C).

Paul described the relationship between Gentiles and Jews in connection with God's plan of salvation. It was written to show the legitimacy of mission to the Gentiles. To this end, Paul wrote it with a strong tone from a standpoint that he received the mission from God. In addition, he also mentioned that God had not forsaken the Jews. By this, he once again revealed the enthusiasm to preach the gospel to the Romans. However, it has not been known whether such a plan had been implemented.

Little information about the writing of Rom(D) remains. It was not until the early 54 CE that Paul wrore Rom(D) on his way to Rome. However, no clue has been found about who delivered Rom(D). Paul was probably heading to Rome with a fear that the Romans might not welcome him.

Phil(B)

Paul finally went to Rome. It is, however, likely that the Romans did not welcome him and that he was imprisoned there on account of unknown reasons. He wrote a letter to the Philippians in gratitude of their financial support. This is the second letter to them, Phil(B).

Paul was diligent in preaching the gospel even in prison. Anyway, he sent a letter of thanks to the Philippians, who had financially helped him. This can be called Phil(B), whose texts can be isolated from Philippians by eliminating those of Phil(A) as follows:

1. Beginning Part (Phil 1:1–2)
2. Thanks and Benediction (1:3–11)

3. Paul's Situation (1:12–26)
4. Encouragement (1:27—2:18)
5. Recommendation (2:19–30)
6. Paul's Final Encouragement (3:1a; 4:4–7, 10–19)
7. Benediction (4:20–23)

The texts listed above show the contents are logical enough to constitute a personal letter of gratitude to the Philippians. It was full of joy.

Gratitude seems to have been the foremost theme in Phil(B). The financial support of the Philippians made Paul glad and show a friendly attitude toward them. He was zealous enough to preach the gospel to the family members of Caesar or his relatives while being in custody (Phil 1:12–17). He also emphasized that the Philippians should be delighted because he had been so happy. Although he referred to enemies, it seems to mean those who would not accept the gospel (1:28).

Little is also known about the writing of Phil(B). It seems that Phil(B) was written in the prison of Rome at the end of 55 CE.[71] It is definite that Epaphroditus delivered it on his way back to Philippi after he had delivered money to Paul (Phil 2:25; 4:18). There was no reason for Paul to send it by anyone. No further information about the composition of Phil(B) remains.

Philemon

Paul was able to preach the gospel to Onesimus in prison; probably, it was in Rome. Onesimus was a slave who had stolen money and ran away from his master. According to the contemporary custom, he was unforgivable. Accordingly, it seems that Paul wrote Philemon for his pardon.

Paul wrote a letter to Philemon to ask for the forgiveness of Onesimus. This is Philemon, whose texts are as follows:

A Greetings and Benediction (Phlm 1–3)

---

71. It is difficult to decide when Phil(B) was written. The imprisonment is an important factor to decide it (Phil 1:13). Paul's imprisonment in Rome is mentioned in both the book of Acts and Paul's epistles. Especially, it is said in the book of Acts that Paul was under house arrest as soon as he arrived in Rome (Acts 28:16, 23) and spent two years there (28:30). However, Paul said of nothing about the period in the prison of Rome. No other clue is found in Phil(B) that shows when it was written except the imprisonment. It was definitely written in the prison of Rome later than Rom(D).

B Reaction to the Act of Philemon (4–7)

  C Plea for Onesimus to Philemon (8–10)

    D Request for Onesimus (11–13)

      E Request for Philemon's Voluntary Decision (14)

    D' Request for Onesimus (15–16)

  C' Plea for Onesimus to Philemon (17–19)

B' Plea for Philemon to Do (20–22)

A' Greetings and Benediction (23–25)

The texts shown above definitely reveal a chiastic structure from a literary perspective. Philemon seems to be a logical letter to present its typical form as a personal letter.

Philemon is composed of a chiastic structure from a literary perspective. This shows that the most important theme lies in the middle. Paul asked Philemon for the emancipation of Onesimus. However, few theological topics were covered except it. In addition, Paul also revealed the typical picture of a house church in this letter. Moreover, Paul expressed his sincere heart for Philemon. Therefore, Paul could not help but write a letter in a humble manner.

Paul left little information on the work of Philemon. It seems to have been written in the prison of Rome after Phil(B) was written.[72] Thus, it can be said that Philemon was written in the early 56 CE. In addition, it is logical to say that it was delivered by Onesimus on returning to his master to be forgiven his sins. However, it seems that more research is needed on this.

D. CONCLUSION

The reconstructed life of Paul provides a stepping stone for tracing the process of how he developed his theological interpretation on various topics. This can be seen on the basis of examining his letters sent to the Gentile churches. After Paul had received the revelation about the Son of God, he inherited the tradition about Christ from the religious predecessors in

---

72. Lüdemann claims that Paul sent a letter to Philemon in the prison of Ephesus near to Colosse on the basis of 2 Cor 1:8 and Col 4:9 (*Paul*, loc. 701 of 3299). According to him, Colosse was supposed to be a hometown of Onesimus. It is, however, to be noted that there is no concrete evidence for this.

Damascus, learned about Jesus from Cephas in Jerusalem, went out the first missionary trip, set up churches, and continued having fellowship with them. In the meantime, Paul sent letters to the Gentile churches. Having examined them in chronological order, the process of formation and development of each theological topic will be revealed. Although many scholars have tried to trace how Paul formed his theology on various topics, they have failed to provide satisfactory interpretations. This is because they have been based on the hypothesis that each epistle of Paul in the present form is integral. Therefore, I have analyzed each epistle by subdividing them into short letters and concluded that sixteen letters had been sent to the Gentile churches. They can be listed as follows: Thess(A), Cor(A), Cor(B), Thess(B), Phil(A), Cor(C), Galatians, Cor(D), Cor(E), Cor(F), Rom(A), Rom(B), Rom(C), Rom(D), Phil(B), and Philemon, in the chronological order according to the degree of tension in the relationship with the apostles of Jerusalem. For their interpretation, it is important to observe that Paul was checked by them after the theological controversy over the Gentile table in Antioch. He was challenged by some Gentiles under their sponsorship. In response, Paul suggested a theological alternative centered on the crucifixion of Christ and tried to make the Gentiles stay within the gospel he had preached. This will be evident while tracing the process of how Paul described Christology, the death of Christ, his role for the redemption and salvation of people, the view on the Law, the end of world, the spirit of God, and the church of God. Then, it will be shown that when Paul was checked by the apostles of Jerusalem and challenged by some Gentiles, he made a major change in theology. In the middle of theological conflict between Paul and the apostles of Jerusalem, Christianity was born among the Gentiles.

2

The Lord Jesus Christ Son of God

THE VIEW PAUL HAD about Jesus Christ should be addressed first. His christological understanding has been closely related to topics such as the death of Christ on the cross, the salvation of people, the Law, the end of world, the spirit of God, and the church of God. Paul enhanced his christological understanding on the basis of traditions handed down to him.[1] However, the challenge of some Gentiles against him was a factor that formed a watershed in his christological interpretation. Having faced the challenge sponsored by the apostles of Jerusalem after the theological controversy over the Gentile table in Antioch, Paul began to advance in the direction of centering on Christ. Paul founded Christianity by defining Christ as the savior in the middle of the second missionary trip.

A. THE FIRST MISSIONARY TRIP

Paul provided a certain amount of information about what had happened after receiving the revelation about the Son of God. It seems that Paul identified the Son of God with Christ, inherited from the religious predecessors in Damascus, and then linked him with Jesus, learned from Cephas on the basis of Q in Jerusalem. It seems that his interpretation of the Lord Jesus Christ Son of God was not much different from that of Jews about the servant of God in Judaism.

---

1. Lüdemann says, "Christology, instead of the kingdom of God, stands at the center of Paul's system" (*Paul*, loc. 2387–88 of 3299).

The Event of Revelation

It has been alleged that God revealed his Son to Paul. He was confused as to whom he had to discuss with regard to the Son of God revealed to him. It was not easy to identify the Son of God immediately after he had received the revelation.

God revealed his Son to Paul in Damascus. According to Paul, God revealed his Son to him so that he might preach the Son of God to the Gentiles (Gal 1:16). Hereby, the Son of God emerged as an important figure; however, Paul did not say anything more about him. What mattered to Paul was who the Son of God is. It is not clear whether Paul knew of the Son of God as Jesus Christ from the moment of receiving the revelation. Therefore, the process in which the concept of the Son of God was formed must be studied. However, this is not necessarily the case in the current context of Paul's description about it.

It seems that Paul had heard about Jesus before he received the revelation. This is known from the fact that he persecuted the church of God, composed of the disciples of Jesus (1 Cor 15:9; Gal 1:23; Phil 3:6). Without some knowledge of him, Paul could not have persecuted his disciples. It seems, however, that Paul did not meet the historical Jesus who had worked in Galilee. In addition, it is unclear when Paul heard about him for the first time and what his first impression was. Perhaps Paul learned about him on the basis of teachings that his disciples had addressed to people in public. Otherwise, Paul could not have found a way to know about Jesus. Anyway, it is likely that Paul had had a little knowledge of Jesus before he received the revelation about the Son of God.

The revelation of God should be understood against the backdrop of prophetic tradition. According to Paul, God had chosen him in his mother's womb by grace before he received the revelation (Gal 1:15–16). Having reminded readers of Jeremiah, Paul described his birth to be understood from a prophetic viewpoint (Jer 1:5). It is, however, unclear when Paul had a prophetic self-understanding. Was it at the very moment of receiving the revelation, after the successful mission to the Gentiles, or at the time of writing Galatians? In addition, it is necessary to identify who the Son of God revealed to Paul was because various groups of people were described as the Son of God in the Scriptures. For instance, angels, kings, servants of God, and Israelites have belonged to the category.[2] However, Paul did not talk about the Son of God in relation

---

2. Dunn, *Christology*, 12–22.

to the messianic figure listed above. It is, then, necessary to define the identity of the Son of God revealed to Paul more in detail.

Paul left a clue to the identity of the Son of God revealed to him. First, it is said that he had not discussed with his "flesh and blood" (Gal 1:16). This literally means that Paul did not ask any Pharisaic teachers or Jewish colleagues to identify the Son of God. It is likely that the Son of God revealed to him was different from the messianic figure about whom he had learned or known before in Judaism. This seems to have been shocking to him. Then, having stated that he did not consult with "flesh and blood," Paul wanted to show his independence from the Jewish tradition with regard to the revelation about the Son of God. However, this did not mean a complete break with his past. Rather, it seemed to reflect the complete separation from the Pharisaic Judaism with regard to the interpretation of the Son of God. At any rate, Paul wanted to put an emphasis on a new perspective on the Son of God.

Second, the apostles of Jerusalem are mentioned in association with the identification of the Son of God. Paul did not consult them right after he had received the revelation (Gal 1:17a). Whereas this may make readers perceive that the apostles of Jerusalem had nothing to do with the Son of God, this could rather mean that the Son of God revealed to Paul had some connection with Jesus whom they had followed. I prefer the latter to the former. If the Son of God revealed to Paul had nothing to do with Jesus, he would not have implicated them in this context. Perhaps Paul was embarrassed when he received the revelation about the Son of God while persecuting the disciples of Jesus. Thus, having mentioned the apostles of Jerusalem, Paul wanted to imply that the Son of God had something to do with Jesus to some extent. Otherwise, there is no reason to say that Paul did not want to meet the apostles right after receiving the revelation. At any rate, the disciples of Jesus had already advanced to Jerusalem when God revealed his Son to Paul around 35 CE. It seems that Paul needed a certain amount of time to consider how Jesus was related to the Son of God without the help of apostles. In consequence, it can be said that Paul took in mind the connection of the Son of God with Jesus from the very moment of receiving the revelation.

Third, Paul stated that he had gone to Arabia (Gal 1:17). This literally means that Paul went to Arabia after the event of revelation. Some scholars have argued that this refers to the Nabataean kingdom.[3] However,

---

3. See Lüdemann, *Paul*, loc. 277 of 3299.

there is a lack of consensus with regard to the location of Arabia. This is probably because they approached it from a geographical point of view. Unlike this, I would point to the description that Paul mentioned Arabia in connection with Hagar and Mount Sinai in Galatians (4:25). Even if there is no direct connection between Arabia and Hagar, it seems that a certain relationship is detected with Mount Sinai, where the Law was given. If so, Arabia should be interpreted as a place associated with the Law. Probably, Paul tried to say that as Moses received the Law from God in a lonely place, so he went to a certainly isolated place to ask God for help to identify the Son of God revealed to him. However, his attempt seems to have been unsuccessful. He failed to identify him in light of the Law. This is supported by the fact that Paul said of nothing about what happened in Arabia.

Paul talked about how he had progressively defined the Son of God revealed to him with the three narratives. It seems that for a while Paul did not find any legitimate answer to the question of who the Son of God revealed to him was. Although Paul had not excluded the possibility that the Son of God had referred to Jesus, he hesitated to admit it because he had persecuted the church of God, which consisted of the disciples of Jesus. Paul walked in a way that made it possible to interpret the Son of God against the backdrop of the Law in Arabia, but he failed.

The Damascus Tradition

Paul met a group of people in Damascus. It seems that they transmitted to Paul the tradition about Christ which had been closely related with prophecies written in the Scriptures. Probably, Paul understood the Son of God revealed to him in light of Christ as learned from the religious predecessors in Damascus.

Damascus was a meaningful place to Paul. This is supported by the description that, having received the revelation about the Son of God and then gone to Arabia in vain, Paul finally returned to Damascus (Gal 1:16–17). This means that he visited Damascus twice in a short period. If the revisit had not been related with the revelation about the Son of God, Paul should not have mentioned his return to Damascus. However, Paul did not say anything about what happened there. The only thing we can tell is that some people helped him to escape there (2 Cor 11:32–33; cf. Acts 9:23–25). They would have been friendly to Paul.

It is necessary to investigate what happened in Damascus. Paul probably received the tradition about Christ as the gospel there. Otherwise, no clue is found in his letters about where Paul received the gospel of Christ (1 Cor 15:1–3). As I mentioned in chapter 1, it seems that the people who helped Paul to escape Damascus had given him the gospel. It consists of four elements: death, burial, resurrection, and epiphany of Christ. The religious predecessors handed the gospel of Christ over to Paul; however, they did not mention who the Christ was in a definite way at all. Christ could refer to anyone who meets the conditions, even someone other than Jesus. Nevertheless, it seems that, having received the gospel of Christ, Paul identified the Son of God with Christ. Despite that the gospel of Christ did not actually fit in the Jewish concept of messiah on account of his death, Paul dared to equate the Son of God revealed to him with Christ. The reason that Paul accepted the Damascus tradition has not been known. It seems that after Paul had failed to define the Son of God in Arabia, he was delighted with the gospel of Christ that made him able to define who the Son of God was. This is supported by the fact that Paul often used the title "Christ" in connection with "Son of God" in his letters (Rom 1:4; 1 Cor 1:9; Gal 2:20).

Paul identified the Son of God with the Christ handed down from the religious predecessors in Damascus. Damascus was an important place to Paul in that he received the Damascus tradition represented by the gospel of Christ for the identification of the Son of God revealed to him. This is to be accepted because Paul developed various interpretations on the basis of the Damascus tradition, as we shall see.

The Jerusalem Tradition

Paul went up to Jerusalem three years after he had received the revelation. There he met Cephas and learned more about Jesus. The reason that Paul visited him is because the Son of God revealed to him could be identified with Jesus.

The encounter between Paul and Cephas in Jerusalem is important. It was around 38 CE, three years after Paul had received the revelation (Gal 1:18–19). At that time, the first three redactions of Q had been complete in Galilee. Jesus was defined as the "Son of God" in two places. First, the heavenly voice announced Jesus as "My Son!" after he had been baptized (Q^3 3:21–22). This means that God designated Jesus as his Son through a mysterious phenomenon. Thus, Paul seems to have regarded it as the theological foundation upon which he could identify the baptized Jesus with the Son of God revealed to him. Second, Jesus revealed his status to the disciples by calling himself the "Son of God" and said that only a person who received the revelation according to his wish could know God the Heavenly Father (Q^3 10:22). While the nature of revelation was not specifically explained, it is presumed to be a mysterious way to know God. It is, however, important that the "Son of God" and "revelation" appear in both texts. In this regard, Paul was able to more closely reconcile the revelation about the Son of God to Jesus because he was portrayed as the Son of God known through revelation in Q.

It is likely that Cephas taught Paul another identity of Jesus. He is the "Lord" (Q^3 6:46–47; 7:6–7). In fact, the title "LORD" was applied to God according to the Jewish tradition as reflected in the first redaction of Q (Q^1 3:4; Isa 40:3). The third redactor, however, applied it to Jesus the Son of God. Nevertheless, it does not mean that Jesus was to be regarded as God. Thus, Paul was able to define the "Son of God" revealed to him as the "Lord Jesus Son of God" described in Q. It was possible for Paul to interpret it that way because he was a well-trained Pharisee for the reinterpretation of previous traditions. Paul began to use the title "Lord Jesus Son of God" on the basis of Q, with which he had been acquainted in Jerusalem.

Paul also learned that Jesus had been portrayed as the "Son of Man." It deserves our attention in that the third redactor of Q applied it to Jesus (Q^3 17:24, 26). He is the Son of Man who will appear in a supernatural way at the end of world. It has been generally agreed that the title "Son of Man" has been used against the backdrop of Daniel 7:13 in terms of a transcendental and eschatological figure. However, Paul did not use the title "Son of Man" in his letters because the Jewish title was not understandable to the Gentiles. He used the title "Son of God" rather than the "Son of Man" because the former was familiar to the Gentiles. It is important that Paul recognized the Son of God as the Lord Jesus Son of Man coming from heaven to the earth at the end of world. This seems to be what Paul learned from Cephas on the basis of Q, which represents the Jerusalem tradition.

It was not easy for Paul to recognize Jesus as the messianic Son of God revealed to him in Damascus. This is because he persecuted the disciples of Jesus. However, Paul identified the "Son of God" with the Lord

Jesus learned from Cephas on the basis of Q in Jerusalem. In this way, Paul developed his christological interpretation step by step.

The First Missionary Trip and Thereafter

Having been equipped with the concept of the Lord Jesus Christ Son of God, Paul set out the first missionary trip around 38 CE. What he taught the Gentiles about Jesus Christ is unclear because no record has been left. Having returned to Jerusalem after the first missionary trip, Paul had another chance to learn more about Jesus from the apostles of Jerusalem on the basis of the fourth redaction of Q.

It seems that during the first missionary trip Paul delivered an instruction on the Lord Jesus Christ Son of God based on the traditions that he had received. To them belong the revelation about the Son of God, the Damascus tradition about Christ, and the Jerusalem tradition about the Lord Jesus. Paul would have preached what he had learned, so that the Gentiles could accept the Lord Jesus Christ as the Son of God revealed to him. The resurrection of Christ was possibly proclaimed as handed down from the Damascus tradition; in addition, the transcendental coming of the Son of God at the end of world would be included in his teachings as inherited from the Jerusalem tradition. However, what he proclaimed in detail has not been known because there are no records of it. It seems that there was no external influence that led him to a new interpretation. The first missionary trip ended up with a tremendous achievement among the Gentiles, and Paul returned to Jerusalem for the apostolic meeting after eleven years of traveling.

Having returned to Jerusalem around 49 CE, Paul had another chance to learn more about Jesus. Paul was acquainted with the fourth redaction of Q, which had been complete around 41 CE. Jesus was more specifically described as the Son of God as found in the story of temptation and a proverbial saying (Q^4 4:1–13; 12:10). However, Jesus the Son of God was portrayed as an entity inferior to the spirit of God. This seems to make Paul associate the Son of God revealed to him more closely with Jesus. It is also noteworthy that Jesus was described as the one representing the twelve tribes of Israel (3:8bc; 4:1–13; 6:13–16; 22:30). Thus, Paul was able to proclaim that the Gentiles should also become the people of God by observing the instruction of Jesus. Then, Jesus was defined as "Wisdom," which seems to be personified being (Q^4 7:35; 11:49) He reminds readers of "wisdom" described as a tool for the creation of world (Prov 8:22–31). In addition, the personified aspect of wisdom seems to be described against the backdrop of Jewish tradition in that wisdom returned to the heavenly house located among the angels (1 *En.* 42:1). Although Jesus was not definitely described against the backdrop of "wisdom" in Q, this seems to have given Paul a foothold to regard Jesus as a divine agent of God. These are what Paul learned about Jesus during the second visit to Jerusalem.

Later, Paul had a theological controversy with Cephas in Antioch around 50 CE (Gal 2:11–14). It was a huge loss for them that they turned their back on each other. However, it seems that there was no effect on Paul's christological interpretation. This is verified by the fact that Paul continuously used the title "Lord Jesus Christ Son of God" in his letters written later. This means that although Paul turned his back on Cephas, he did not abandon the instruction of Jesus he had learned from the apostles of Jerusalem. If so, it means that Paul had the historical Jesus in mind from the time he had received the revelation of God about his Son.

Summary

As we have seen above, Paul seems to have added the understanding of the Son of God revealed to him over time. First, Paul associated the Son of God with Christ inherited from the religious predecessors in Damascus. Then, Christ the Son of God was understood in connection with the Lord Jesus learned from Cephas and then the apostles of Jerusalem on the basis of Q in Jerusalem. It seems that Paul was able to build up his own interpretation of the Lord Jesus Christ Son of God step by step because he was a former Pharisee well trained for the reinterpretation of tradition transmitted from ancestors. In this respect, Paul made a significant contribution to christological interpretation. However, it is to be admitted that Paul did not specifically address the process of interpretation made up to the end of the first missionary trip.

B. THE SECOND MISSIONARY TRIP

Paul set on his second missionary trip after the theological controversy over the Gentile table in Antioch around 50 CE. It seems that, having received the report from Cephas, the apostles of Jerusalem got annoyed with Paul and in return decided to send representatives to the Gentile churches that he had established during the first missionary trip. However, Paul did not know what would happen to the Gentile churches at that time. As time passed, Paul faced the challenge of some Gentiles sponsored by the apostles of Jerusalem. The more seriously he had been challenged, the more emphasis was put on the role of Christ as the redeemer and savior. In the meantime, Christianity was born.

Thess(A)

Paul sent Thess(A) ahead of his second visit to Thessalonica. The christological titles appear in it such as "Son of God," "Lord," and "Christ" for Jesus. It seems that, having relied mainly on the Jerusalem tradition, Paul delivered lessons on the Lord Jesus Christ from a Jewish standpoint.

Thess(A) begins with a reference to the Lord Jesus Christ. Paul mentioned the Thessalonian church in God the Father and the Lord Jesus Christ (1 Thess 1:1). The Lord Jesus Christ appears in parallel with God the Father; however, this does not mean that Jesus Christ is equal to God. At any way, the "Lord Jesus" is combined with "Christ." While the former originated in the Jerusalem tradition, the latter came from the Damascus tradition. This makes readers assume that the title "Lord Jesus Christ" was also used during the first missionary trip before Paul wrote Thess(A). At any rate, it attracts the attention that the Lord Jesus Christ was mentioned as the foundation of the church in parallel with God the Father in the first letter sent to the Gentiles.

Paul used the title "Lord Jesus Christ" again. It appears in connection with "the work produced by faith, the labor prompted by love, and the endurance inspired by hope" (1 Thess 1:3). The Lord Jesus Christ is presented as a source of faith, love, and hope. It seems that Paul presented the combination of faith, love, and hope against the backdrop of Jewish tradition, as Lüdemann says that "passages like Wisd. of Sol. 3:9; 7:25 or 4 Macc. 17:2–4 shed further light on the traditional character of the triad in 1 Cor. 13."[4] If his interpretation is acceptable, it can be said that Paul creatively connected the Lord Jesus Christ with the matter of faith, love, and hope from a Jewish perspective. It was possible for him because he was a well-trained Pharisee to interpret the tradition in a certain way. In

---

4. Lüdemann, *Paul*, loc. 1177 of 3299.

this respect, Paul used the christological title for the purpose of something he had wanted to deliver in Thess(A).

The phrase "words of the Lord" is mentioned for the first time. According to Paul, the "words of the Lord" came out of the Thessalonians and spread in all directions (1 Thess 1:8). It is clear that "the Lord" here refers to Jesus. If Paul used the phrase "words of the Lord" against the backdrop of that used in Q, this would be understandable (Q^3 6:46–47; 7:6–7). It is then likely that Paul taught the Gentiles lessons on the Lord based on Q even in the second missionary trip. This implies that the theological debate in Antioch had no effect on Paul's christological interpretation. Paul continued to rely upon the Jerusalem tradition represented by Q even in the early days of the second missionary trip.

Paul then described Jesus the Son of God as a transcendental figure. This is implied in the description that Jesus the Son of God rose again from the dead, would come from heaven, and would deliver people from the coming wrath (1 Thess 1:10). Paul listed at least three elements to be considered. First, the resurrection of the Son of God catches our attention because the combination of two traditions is found: the revelation about the Son of God and the Damascus tradition about the resurrection of Christ. It is, however, noteworthy that Paul did not use the title "Christ" in association with the issue of resurrection here. This indicates that, having put forth the historicity of resurrection of Jesus, Paul showed the intention to combine the Jerusalem tradition and Damascus tradition from a christological perspective. Second, Paul defined the Son of God as a transcendental figure coming from heaven. However, no verb is used for "coming" in the Greek version; nevertheless, from the context, scholars have interpreted that he would come in a certain future. This reminds readers of the "Son of Man" appearing supernaturally in the sky as written in Q (Q^3 17:24, 26). Having substituted the title "Son of God" for "Son of Man," Paul tried to make the Gentiles understand the eschatological coming of a messianic figure from heaven. This means that Paul heavily relied upon the Jerusalem tradition learned from Cephas. Third, Jesus is designated as a figure who will deliver people from the coming wrath. The coming wrath is reminiscent of Q describing John as the preacher of it. The Greek word ὀργή is commonly used in both texts (Q^1 3:7; 1 Thess 1:10). Having substituted Jesus for John with regard to deliverance from the coming wrath, Paul attributed the salvific role to Jesus. This implies his dependence upon the Jerusalem tradition at the time of writing Thess(A).

The title "Christ" appears in connection with "apostle." This is found in the wish that Paul would be regarded as an apostle (1 Thess 2:7). The title "apostle" was used for the twelve disciples of Jesus in Q (Q^4 6:13–16). Paul certainly wanted to enjoy the authority that they had enjoyed. However, the title "apostle" is associated with "Christ" rather than "Jesus" in Thess(A). Since Thess(A) was written first after the theological controversy in Antioch, Paul did not conceal his wish to set himself apart from the twelve apostles of Jerusalem. As for his identity, it seems that Paul preferred "Christ" over "Jesus." In this way, Paul used a mixture of the Jerusalem and Damascus traditions.

In Thess(A), Paul used all the christological titles that he had inherited. To them belong "Lord," "Jesus," "Christ," and "Son of God." It is, however, important that Paul tended to rely more upon the Jerusalem tradition than the Damascus tradition from a christological perspective. This means that the Jewish perspective dominated his christological understanding even in the early days of the second missionary trip.

Cor(A)

Paul enhanced his christological view in Cor(A) further than in Thess(A). It is revealed in the fact that new roles were imposed upon the Lord Jesus Christ. In particular, Paul attempted a creative interpretation of Christ from a Jewish perspective on the basis of the Jerusalem tradition represented by Q.

At the beginning of Cor(A), Paul used the title "Lord Jesus Christ" three times in a row from an eschatological context (1 Cor 1:7–9). First, the title is used in connection with the word "manifestation [ἀποκάλυψις]" (1:7). This reminds readers of its infinitive form, "to reveal [ἀποκαλύψαι]," used for the Son of God revealed to Paul (Gal 1:16). It seems that Paul attempted to relate the manifestation of the "Lord Jesus Christ" with the Son of God revealed to him in Damascus. It is, however, noteworthy that the tile "Lord Jesus Christ" was used instead of the "Son of God." This shows Paul's effort to understand the revelation in connection with the tradition that he had inherited from the religious predecessor and the apostles of Jerusalem. Second, the "Lord Jesus Christ" is defined as an eschatological figure that will solidify the Corinthians with blamelessness until the day of judgment (1 Cor 1:8). This is reminiscent of an instruction that those who have waited for Jesus the Son of God coming from heaven will be delivered from wrath as written in Thesss(A) (1 Thess 1:10). The role of the Lord Jesus Christ in Cor(A) is fortified in comparison with that of the Son of God in Thess(A) because the Lord Jesus Christ will keep the Gentiles blameless up to the time of eschatological judgment. The difference between them shows that Paul developed the christological interpretation with regard to the role of Jesus Christ. Third, the "Son of God Jesus Christ our Lord" is mentioned for the fellowship of the Corinthians (1 Cor 1:9). God is described as the one who initiates the fellowship between the Son of God and the Corinthians. It seems that this was a way of solidifying them not to be reproached on the day of eschatological judgment. Whereas the title "Son of God" was already used for the transcendental and eschatological coming from heaven in Thess(A), it is presented as the corresponding part for the fellowship of the Corinthians in Cor(A). In this way, Paul attributed a new role to the Son of God, so that the Corinthians could be closer to the Lord Jesus Christ. In consequence, it can be said that Paul made a significant contribution to christological interpretation in Cor(A).

The title "Lord Jesus Christ" appears in connection with the spirit of God. According to Paul, the Corinthians should be cleansed, sanctified, and righteous "in the name of the Lord Jesus Christ and in the spirit of God" (1 Cor 6:11). Having set the "name of the Lord Jesus Christ" in parallel with the "spirit of God," Paul gave them equal authority. This is somewhat different from Q, where Jesus is described as an entity inferior to the spirit of God (Q^4 4:1–2; 12:10). In any case, having put the Lord Jesus Christ in parallel with the spirit of God, Paul tried to show that a spiritual power was imposed upon the Lord Jesus Christ to ensure his authority. In addition, having put the Lord Jesus Christ just after the issue of inheriting the kingdom of God, Paul strengthened the salvific role of Jesus Christ. In this respect, Paul made a contribution to christological interpretation as time passed.

Paul portrayed Christ from a typological perspective. Having mentioned the forefathers walking under the cloud and passing through the sea, Paul interpreted it as the baptism into Moses. Then, Christ is portrayed as the rock out of which spiritual drink comes (1 Cor 10:1–4). Without doubt, the baptism into Moses and the rock of Christ are described against the backdrop of Exodus (Exod 13:21; 14:21–30; 17:6). It is then necessary to take a look at the baptism and temptation of Jesus described in Q (Q^3 3:21–22; Q^4 4:1–13). While the baptism of Jesus reminds readers of the Israelites crossing the Red Sea, his temptation makes people think of temptation that they did against God in the wilderness. In both texts of Q, Jesus was identified as the "Son of God" (Q 3:22; 4:3, 9). Having compared the typological description of Paul and the stories in Q, it comes to the fore that Paul applied the instruction of Q to his reinterpretation of Exodus in Cor(A). While Jesus the Son of God was focused in Q, Christ was the main figure to be considered in Paul's reinterpretation of Exodus. In this way, Paul enhanced christological interpretation on the basis of the Jerusalem tradition from a Jewish perspective.

Christ is mentioned in connection with the Lord's Table. The cup is linked with the blood of Christ and the bread with his body (1 Cor 10:16). Paul put forth the participation of the Corinthians in the table of Christ that was contrasted with that of demon (10:21). The issue of eating and drinking was already dealt with in Q (Q^2 12:29; Q^3 7:33-34; 17:27). While this is related to the practical life in Q, it was applied to the ritual service related to Christ in Cor(A). The Corinthians were advised to be united with Christ by taking part in the Lord's Table. In this respect, Christ was presented as the center to which the Corinthians should be united from a spiritual point of view. This indicates that Paul developed the role of Christ in relation to ritual service.

Paul tried to theologize the Lord Jesus Christ Son of God in Cor(A). Having attributed new roles to him, Paul described him as the one who had made the religious life of people possible. To this end, Paul enhanced christological interpretation on the base of the Jerusalem tradition represented by Q. Paul, as the founder of the Corinthian church, seems to have been so authoritative that no one could raise objections to his christological interpretation at the time of writing Cor(A).

Cor(B)

Paul communicated Jesus Christ as the center of the religious life of people in Cor(B). The christological interpretation was given to solve the practical matters that they had faced in their religious life. For this, Paul creatively used his christological interpretation.

Paul used the title "Lord Jesus Christ" to encourage the Corinthians. This appears in Paul's exhortation in the "name of the Lord Jesus Christ" (1 Cor 1:10). Paul made Christ a platform to encourage the Corinthians. The phrase "name of the Lord Jesus Christ" was used to refer to his authority as already mentioned in Cor(A) (6:11). Thus, Paul was able to use it in connection with his counsel in Cor(B). Paul thought that the Corinthians should be subordinate to the authority of the Lord Jesus Christ whom he had preached. In this respect, Paul developed his christological interpretation little by little as time went by.

The intensive description of Christ appears once again. Having used the title "Christ," Paul connected it with baptism and the cross in Cor(B) (1 Cor 1:12–13, 17). Christ is portrayed as the basis of authority to resolve the division among the Corinthians resulted from their alliance with the baptizer: Paul, Apollos, and Cephas (1:12). Paul presented the cross of Christ as a solution, so that the Corinthians might be united around him. In addition, Paul defined himself as the one sent by Christ (1:17). This reminds readers of Jesus sending his disciples for the proclamation of the kingdom of God and the healing ministry (Q^3 10:2; Q^2 10:4–11; Q^3 10:16). However, Paul could not help but replace "Jesus" with "Christ" as the sender of ministers for two reasons. First, since he had never met the historical Jesus, Paul could not claim to be an apostle sent by him; and second, Paul was a little uncomfortable with Cephas, who had supposed to claim to be an apostle commissioned by Jesus. Having turned back on Paul in Antioch, Cephas came to Corinth, baptized some of the Corinthians, preached the Jewish lessons, and resulted in the division among them. Having heard of these side effects, Paul moved away from the Jerusalem tradition to the Damascus tradition a little. In this way, Paul made christological interpretations taking into account the situation of the Corinthians at the time of writing Cor(B).

Paul portrayed the Lord Jesus Christ as a means of creation. This is revealed in the description that all things and human beings originated in God through the Lord Jesus Christ (1 Cor 8:6). Paul described the role of the Lord Jesus Christ with a reference to the creation of world. It seems that Paul understood the Lord Jesus Christ in light of "wisdom" personified as a tool for the creation of world (Prov 8:22–31). In other words, the role of wisdom was applied to Christ against the backdrop of creation. This is quite abrupt, but a meaningful description for the role of Christ. The term "wisdom" is mentioned for Jesus in Q (Q^4 7:35). "Wisdom" was used to explain the relationship with her children; however, she does not appear as a medium of creation in Q. Therefore, it seems that in Cor(B) Paul tried to describe the theme of creation and the relationship with the Corinthians on the basis of previous descriptions. This means that Paul shared the wisdom tradition for christological interpretation in Cor(B).

In this way, Paul creatively developed his christological interpretation to define the Lord Jesus Christ as the wisdom of God.

The Lord Jesus is dealt with from an eschatological point of view. According to Paul, one's participation in eating the bread and drinking the cup means to make a promise to proclaim the death of the Lord until he comes (1 Cor 11:24–26). The tradition of supper handed down from the Lord Jesus was interpreted in association with his death and eschatological coming. As shown before, the coming of Jesus the Son of Man was mentioned in Q (Q^3 17:24–26), and then it continued in the description of Jesus the Son of God coming from heaven in Thess(A) (1 Thess 1:10). In this vein, Paul mentioned the coming of the Lord Jesus in Cor(B). In addition, the issue of eating and drinking appears again that was already mentioned in connection with Jesus the Son of Man in Q (Q^2 12:29; Q^3 7:33–34; 17:27) and in association with the Lord Christ in Cor(A) (1 Cor 10:3–4, 16–22). However, Paul treated it against the backdrop of proclaiming the death of the Lord until he comes in Cor(B). This shows that Paul creatively developed the role of Jesus Christ the Son of God over time. In this respect, he made a significant contribution to christological interpretation.

Paul described Christ as the center to which the congregation should be united. It is said, "The body is a unit, though it is made up of many parts; and though all its parts are many, they form one body. So it is with Christ" (1 Cor 12:12). Paul attributed a new role to Christ from religious and sociological perspectives. The issue of unity was already dealt with when the cross of Christ was suggested as a remedy of division among the Corinthians (1:13, 17). This means that Paul tried to settle the dispute among the Corinthians with christological instructions. This becomes evident that the unity with Christ was seen from ethical and ritual perspectives when compared to the account in Cor(A) (6:15; 10:16–17). On the other hand, Paul asked the Corinthians to constitute one body of Christ with regard to the spiritual gifts in Cor(B) (12:12, 14–27). In this way, Paul gave Christ the role of uniting the divided Corinthians. This made a step of progress in christological interpretation.

Christ is portrayed as a new ancestor from a spiritual viewpoint. Having emphasized Christ as the first fruits, Paul referred to the resurrection of those who belonged to him (1 Cor 15:20–23). Then, Christ is presented in contrast with Adam from a typological view.[5] This is a more

---

5. Beker, *Paul*, 100.

advanced description than what Paul said about the resurrection of the Lord and saints in Cor(A) (6:14). This means that Paul defined Christ as the one who brought new life to people with a reference to the new ancestor of mankind in Cor(B) (15:22). This shows Paul's use of Adamic Christology in order to include the Gentile Corinthians into the people of God. It can be then said that, having a basis in the resurrection of Christ originated in the Damascus tradition, Paul developed the idea that Christ became the new ancestor of mankind from a spiritual standpoint. In consequence, Paul was the first person who creatively applied the Adamic typology to Christ.

Paul tried to present his christological interpretation from various perspectives in Cor(B). Having received traditions, he used them in combination in any direction he wanted. He was creative while trying to show new interpretations. In response to Cephas's visit to Corinth and his baptism of some Gentiles with an instruction on the observance of the Law, Paul delivered a christological interpretation that shows the tendency to be away from the Jerusalem tradition represented by Q. The christological interpretations were given to solve the practical matters that the Corinthians actually had faced in their life of faith.

Thess(B)

Paul presented christological lessons in connection with salvation in Thess(B). This resulted from Paul's active response to the changed circumstances of the Thessalonians caused by those come from the Jerusalem church. In the meantime, Paul attributed a salvific role to Christ.

The coming of the Lord Jesus Christ is mentioned several times. Paul used the Greek word παρουσία in connection with the "Lord Jesus" three times (1 Thess 2:19; 3:13; 4:14–16) and with the "Lord Jesus Christ" once (5:23). The "Son of God" was defined as the transcendental figure coming from heaven with a reference to Jesus in Thess(A) (1 Thess 1:10), and the coming [παρουσία] of Christ was mentioned for the first time in Cor(B) (15:23). Without doubt, his coming was described against the backdrop of the transcendental coming of Jesus the Son of Man from heaven as mentioned in Q (Q^3 17:24). However, having heard of news about the Thessalonians being agitated by the tempters (1 Thess 3:5), Paul mentioned the transcendental advent of the Lord Jesus "Christ" in Thess(B). As the tempter sent by the apostles of Jerusalem had asked the

Gentiles to accept the Jewish teachings and challenge Paul, he showed a tendency to rely upon the Damascus tradition by using the title "Christ" in connection with the issue of transcendental coming.

Paul presented the Lord Jesus Christ in connection with salvation for the first time. According to him, God erected people to be saved by the Lord Jesus Christ, who died for them (1 Thess 5:9–10). The word "salvation" appears in connection with his death for the first time. Whereas Paul treated the deliverance of people from wrath by Jesus the Son of God coming from heaven in Thess(A) (1 Thess 1:10), the death of Jesus Christ was introduced for their salvation in Thess(B). This kind of christological interpretation was made at the time of being challenged by the apostles of Jerusalem. This means that Paul developed the salvific role of Jesus Christ, which did not appear in the Jerusalem tradition represented by Q. In consequence, it can be said that Paul enhanced christological interpretation in connection with the salvation of people in the rapidly changed circumstances of the Thessalonians.

Paul described the Lord Jesus Christ as a transcendental figure for the salvation of people in Thess(B). This was one of Paul's responses to the challenge of those sent by the apostles of Jerusalem, who tried to make the Thessalonians follow the instruction of Jesus and the Law. In this context, Paul suggested christological teachings for the salvation of people. In the meantime, Christianity was conceived among the Gentiles.

Phil(A)

Paul made a turning point in terms of christological interpretation in Phil(A). This appears in the fact that the Lord Jesus Christ is defined as the savior from heaven. Paul provided a christological declaration in response to the challenge against him.

The term "faith" is connected with Christ. According to Paul, everyone can be righteous by the "faith of Christ" (Phil 3:9). Paul understood Christ in association with faith for the first time here. The "faith of Christ" is to be understood as a subjective genitive from a grammatical point of view. This means the faith that Christ had in God and showed to people. In this respect, Christ, not Jesus, was presented as an example for those who would have faith in God. Paul taught that the Philippians should believe just as Christ had believed in God. This reflects the fact that Paul was inclined toward the Damascus tradition centered on Christ.

Jesus Christ is portrayed as a savior who would come from heaven. According to Paul, the Philippians had to wait for a "savior" Lord Jesus Christ, who would come "from there" (Phil 3:20). The word "savior" is used for the first time so far among the Pauline letters. Then, the phrase "from there" refers to "from heaven" in this context. The "coming from heaven" was already treated in association with the "Son of God" in Thess(A) (1 Thess 1:10), with "Christ" in Cor(B) (1 Cor 15:23), and with the "Lord Jesus" three times and with the "Lord Jesus Christ" once in Thess(B) (1 Thess 2:19; 3:13; 4:14–16; 5:23). As discussed before, the coming from heaven was described against the backdrop of the Son of Man appearing in the sky as mentioned in Q (Q^3 17:24). Then, Paul was able to mention the coming of the Lord Jesus Christ from heaven with a reference to the savior in Phil(A). This indicates that Paul to some extent relied upon the Jerusalem tradition represented by Q even at the time of writing Phil(A). It is, however, noteworthy that whereas the phrase "coming from heaven" and the word "salvation" were separately used in Thess(B) (1 Thess 2:19; 5:9), the "coming from there" and "savior" appear at a place in Phil(A). Hereby Paul stressed that the Lord Jesus Christ was an eschatological and transcendental savior. This shows that Paul made a contribution to christological interpretation at the beginning of the challenge against him.

Paul developed his christological interpretation while the challenge against him was getting stronger. As discussed in chapter 1, the expressions "dogs," "evildoers," and "mutilators of flesh" refer to those sent by the apostles of Jerusalem to make the Philippians observe the Law and challenge Paul against the gospel and his authority (Phil 3:2). The expression of challenge against him was getting stronger as time went by: Cephas in Cor(B) (1 Cor 1:12), the "tempter" in Thess(B) (1 Thess 3:5), and "dogs," "evildoers," and "mutilators of flesh" in Phil(A), listed according to the chronological order of composition. This implies that the stronger challenge Paul had faced, the further he developed his christological interpretation in connection with the salvific role of Jesus Christ.

Paul made Christianity be born among the Gentiles by portraying the Lord Jesus Christ as a transcendental savior. The salvation by the savior Christ refers to the experience of "a new birth in Christ."[6] Although Paul was not yet completely independent from the Jerusalem tradition,

---

6. Lüdemann, *Paul*, loc. 2412 of 3299. He further says, "The notion of God who had sent his Son into this world in order to save people was a core element of the Christianity that Paul founded" (loc. 2458).

his dependence on it has been significantly reduced. This is verified by the fact that no christological interpretation was made except for the transcendental advent from heaven. In consequence, Paul made a turning point in terms of christological interpretation in Phil(A).

Cor(C)

Paul wrote various accounts of Christ in Cor(C). Among them, the crucified savior comes to the fore. In addition, Paul used the typological approach to describe the salvific role of Christ. Paul developed a christological interpretation that enriched the view on Jesus Christ the Son of God in response to the direct challenge of some Corinthians.

Christological titles are used at the beginning of Cor(C). The "Lord Jesus Christ" is used two times, and "Christ Jesus" appears twice (1 Cor 1:1–3). Since they were already used in the letters written earlier, it is not foreign to use them again here. It is noteworthy that "Christ Jesus" appears as the one who called Paul to be an apostle and the Corinthians to be the saints. This kind of statement appears for the first time so far. On the other hand, the "Lord Jesus Christ" is presented as the object whose name the Corinthians were calling to be endowed with grace and peace. In this way, Paul elevated the Lord Jesus Christ to the level of choosing God's people.

Christ is introduced as the crucified savior. Paul defined the crucified Christ as the power and wisdom of God for the salvation of those who had been called by God (1 Cor 1:23–24). The crucifixion of Christ appears for the first time in connection with the salvation of people. The death of "our Lord Jesus Christ" was once connected to salvation in Thess(B) (1 Thess 5:9–10); however, how his death affects the salvation of people was not clearly described there. Accordingly, Paul focused the death of Christ on cross in terms of salvation in Cor(C). As the "Lord Jesus Christ" was described as the savior coming from heaven in Phil(A) (Phil 3:18–20), Paul portrayed the crucified Christ as the way of salvation in Cor(C). Thus, the salvific role of Christ was more embodied in Cor(C) than in Thess(B) and Phil(A). It seems that Paul developed the christological instruction anew on the basis of the Damascus tradition, which deals with the death of Christ according to the Scriptures. When the challenges of some Corinthians sponsored by the Jerusalem apostles were intensifying, Paul had no reason to rely on the Jerusalem tradition.

Paul identified Christ Jesus against the backdrop of wisdom tradition. This appears in the saying that Christ Jesus had become the wisdom of God—that is, righteousness, holiness, and redemption [ἀπολύτρωσις]" (1 Cor 1:30). Paul once stated that everyone could be washed, sanctified, and righteous "in the name of Jesus Christ" in Cor(A) (6:11) and insisted that one can obtain the righteousness of God by the faith of Christ in Phil(A) (Phil 3:9). However, in Cor(C), Paul defined Christ Jesus as the wisdom of God that was in contrast with the human "wisdom" for which Greeks looked (1 Cor 1:22). In addition, Paul already wrote an instruction on Christ against the backdrop of wisdom tradition in Cor(B) (1 Cor 8:6; Prov 8:22–31). Paul's use of wisdom shows a great difference from what is described in Q as the one to send prophets (Q^4 7:35; 13:34). Thus, in Cor(C), Paul was able to define Christ as the wisdom of God independent from what is described in Q. This was another way to portray him as the savior of people. In consequence, Paul creatively developed his christological interpretation with regard to the salvific role of Christ to be independent from the Jerusalem tradition.

Christ is metaphorically presented as the foundation upon which a man builds a house. According to Paul, no one can lay any foundation other than Christ, which he had already laid (1 Cor 3:10–11). Paul presented Christ in comparison to the foundation upon which people build their spiritual houses. This means that the Corinthians should not rely on teachings other than Christ preached by Paul. This may have something to do with the teachings written in Q because the metaphor reminds readers of the parable of two builders (Q^3 6:48–49). Whereas the main topic was whether to live according to the words of the Lord Jesus or not in Q, Paul changed it into the issue of whether the Corinthians accepted Christ or not in Cor(C). This indicates that Paul used the Jerusalem tradition in the direction of emphasizing the salvific role of Christ at the time of being challenged by some Corinthians.

Paul also attributed the role of mediator to Christ. This is revealed in the expression that the Corinthians were of Christ and that Christ was of God (1 Cor 3:23; cf. 1:30). Paul heightened the relationship of Christ between God and the Corinthians with a form of possessive genitive. This makes readers think of Q, in which the relationship among God, Jesus, and his disciples is described (Q^3 10:16). Although there are a couple of elements that show differences between the instructions of Paul and Q, it should be admitted that the relationships among God, Jesus/Christ, and disciples/Corinthians is found in common. It seems that Paul had adopted the mediatory role of Jesus found in Q and adapted it to the description of Christ with a modification. This shows that, having described the role of Christ, Paul gradually shifted the center of weight from the Jerusalem tradition to the Damascus tradition.

Christ is described as the lamb of Passover. This refers to Paul's account of Christ as the sacrifice of Passover (1 Cor 5:7). Christ was once described against the backdrop of Exodus in connection with baptism and temptation in Cor(A) (1 Cor 10:4; Q 3:21–22; 4:1–13). Then, Paul chose the metaphor of the lamb of Passover for the designation of Christ as the sacrificed savior from a typological perspective in Cor(C). As the lamb of Passover was a symbol of sacrifice for the deliverance of Israelites from the bondage of Egypt, so Christ is defined as the sacrificed savior for the salvation of Gentiles from their sins. This is a way of describing the crucified Christ as the sacrificed lamb of Passover to save people. This shows how Paul strengthened the salvific role of Christ from a typological viewpoint.

Paul portrayed Christ as the core of gospel. It is written that if one holds firmly to the gospel consisted of the death, burial, resurrection, and epiphany of Christ, he or she would be saved (1 Cor 15:1–5). The redemptive death of Christ attracts the most attention; however, it will be dealt with more in detail in chapter 4. Having mentioned the death and resurrection of Christ as the events according to the Scriptures, Paul presented him as the savior who has fulfilled the prophecies. In this way, Paul tried to understand Christ in light of the Hebrew Scriptures. This was a way to strengthen the redemptive and salvific role of Christ. As discussed in chapter 1, the gospel of Christ Paul had preached was developed from the Damascus tradition. In consequence, Paul developed his christological understanding in response to the challenge of some Corinthians sponsored by the apostles of Jerusalem.

Christ is once again described from a typological perspective. For this, a series of description appears. Having distinguished the spiritual body [σῶμα πνευματικόν] from the natural body [σῶμα ψυχικόν] (1 Cor 15:44), Paul insisted that Christ, the last Adam, became a life-giving spirit [πνεῦμα ζῳοποιοῦν], while the first Adam had become a living being [ψυχὴ ζῶσα] (15:45). Finally, Paul stated that the natural body [τὸ ψυχικόν] had come first, and then the spiritual body [τὸ πνευματικόν] came (15:46). The contrast between ψυχή and πνεῦμα appears three times. This means that Christ as the last Adam was to be understood as a new ancestor of those who have the spiritual body that represents the saved people of God. In this respect, Paul described Christ from a perspective of Adamic typology in a more advanced form in Cor(C) than in Cor(B) (1 Cor 15:21–22). Having been challenged directly by some Corinthians, Paul fortified his typological interpretation of Christ with the contrast between ψυχή and πνεῦμα.

Paul developed his christological understanding by attributing the redemptive and salvific role to the crucified Christ in Cor(C) This is a more advanced interpretation than the previous one to solve the practical matters in Cor(B). The stronger the challenge Paul experienced, the more he inclined to fortify his christological interpretation with a description of the redemptive and salvific role of Christ. He seems to be dependent upon the Damascus tradition more than the Jerusalem tradition. This means that he was getting independent from the apostles of Jerusalem. Meanwhile, Christianity was growing.

Galatians

Paul introduced Christ as a redeemer as well as a savior in Galatians. For this, the concepts of "descendant of Abraham" and "posterity of a woman" were added. Paul developed his christological interpretation further when the challenge against him reached its peak. Thereby his view on Christ seems to be completely independent from the teachings of the apostles of Jerusalem.

Christ is presented as a redeemer as well as a savior at the beginning of Galatians. According to Paul, Christ gave himself for the sins of people to rescue them from the present evil age according to the will of God (Gal 1:4). There are several elements to be compared with those embedded in the core of the gospel (1 Cor 15:3–5). First, having substituted "the Lord Jesus Christ gave himself" for "Christ died," Paul stressed the spontaneous death of Christ. Second, the phrase "for our sins" is used in Galatians as well as in Cor(C). This implies Paul's confidence in the redemptive role of Christ. Third, the expression of "according to the will of God" appears in Galatians instead of "according to the Scriptures" used in Cor(C). It seems that Paul tried to show the direct relationship of Christ with God. Finally, the phrase "to rescue us from the present evil age" attributes the salvific role to Christ in comparison with the summarized form of the gospel described in Cor(C). These changes were made when the Galatians harshly challenged Paul under the sponsorship of the apostles of

Jerusalem. In the meantime, Paul developed his christological interpretation on the basis of the Damascus tradition as an answer to the challenge of the Galatians against the gospel and his authority.

Christ is portrayed as the one who gave himself. According to Paul, Christ the Son of God was crucified for his sake (Gal 2:20). The Son of God showed his love by giving up his life for people. Paul mentioned the voluntary death of Christ for people in a couple of places such as Cor(B) (1 Cor 8:11) and Thess(B) (1 Thess 5:10). It is, however, only in Galatians that Paul connected the spontaneous death of Christ with the love of the Son of God. Christ the Son of God was portrayed as the one who showed his love by sacrificing himself for people. This is meaningful in the fact that it was told to the Galatians when their challenge reached its peak. In consequence, it can be said that Paul presented his own christological interpretation while coping with the changed relationship with the Gentiles.

Paul described Christ as a redeemer. This is found in the description that Christ has been cursed for people and thus redeems them from the curse of the Law (Gal 3:13). Paul changed the personal confession that Christ the Son of God died for him to a statement that Christ died to redeem people from the curse of the Law. This is a more advanced statement than the previous one that Christ died "for our sins" as written in Cor(C) (1 Cor 15:3) and Galatians (Gal 1:4). In this way, Paul enhanced his christological interpretation in connection with the redemptive role in terms of how to redeem people from sin and curse at the time of the most severe challenge by the Galatians.

Christ was defined as the descendant of Abraham. Having pointed out that it was used in the singular form, Paul identified Christ as the descendant of Abraham (Gal 3:16). Without doubt, the descendant of Abraham has something to do with the people of God. It is reminiscent of John's proclamation written in Q that God could make stones the descendants of Abraham (Q^4 3:8bc). However, it seems that the instruction of John about the descendant of Abraham had been ignored by Paul. Rather, he applied the issue of being the descendant of Abraham to Christ in Galatians. In other words, Christ was portrayed as the only one who could make the Gentiles the people of God by faith. Thus, it can be said that Paul presented Christ as a new ancestor of the people of God in terms of faith. This is the christological interpretation that Paul presented against the apostles of Jerusalem, who had attempted the Judaization of Gentiles.

Paul used the concept of "posterity of a woman" for the Son of God. This is revealed in the saying, "When the time had fully come, God sent his Son, born of a woman, born under the Law, to redeem those under the Law, that we might receive the full rights of sons" (Gal 4:4–5). There are three elements to be taken into account. First, the description that the time had fully come means that God had set a time. In the Hebrew Scriptures, there are many prophecies about the servant of God coming to the world. Therefore, it is necessary to deal with two more elements to decide which prophecy Paul referred to in this context. Second, the Son of God born of a woman implies a descendant who came to the world through a designated woman. Then, the prophecy told in the garden of Eden is the best candidate for the prophecy that deals with both time and woman at the same time (Gen 3:15). It seems that Paul regarded the Son of God revealed to him as the "posterity of a woman." Third, Paul saw the purpose of the coming of Jesus Christ to the world in terms of redemption. He claimed that the Son of God came under the Law to redeem those under the Law. This should be taken as a follow-up declaration to the previous statement regarding the remission of sins written in Cor(C) (1 Cor 15:3) and Galatians (Gal 1:4; 3:13). This indicates that Paul enhanced his christological interpretation in terms of the redemptive role of Christ.

Paul added christological accounts in Galatians. Among them, the role of a redeemer seems to have been emphasized most. The ideas of "descendant of Abraham" and "posterity of a woman" were added to heighten the role of Christ, who could make the Galatians the people of God. Paul created christological teachings in response to the most serious challenge of the Galatians sponsored by the apostles of Jerusalem. As the challenge against him grew, Paul was getting more independent from the Jerusalem tradition. In the meantime, the amount of Christian instruction increased.

Cor(D)

Paul presented a new understanding of Christ in Cor(D). His role of comforting the Corinthians reflects the expectation that he wanted to restore his relationship with them. For this, Paul did not rely upon the tradition that he had inherited.

Two different roles of Christ are presented. First, Paul portrayed Christ as a "comforter" in the context of his effort to console the

Corinthians (2 Cor 1:5). The issue of comfort is mentioned to restore the deteriorated relationship with them. Second, Paul presented Christ as the one who had been rich but became poor for the Corinthians (8:9). It is, however, noteworthy that this appears in the context of effort to collect more money for the poor saints of the Jerusalem church. Paul did not portray Christ as the transcendental figure coming from heaven, nor as the redeemer crucified for the remission of sins. Christ is regarded as the model for the consolation of the Corinthians and the sacrifice for them. It can be then said that Paul interpreted the role of Christ anew.

There is a reason that Paul assigned a new role to Christ. Having received the optimistic report of Titus about the Corinthians, Paul was confident in the restoration of relationship with them. It was then necessary for Paul to put an emphasis on the ability of Christ to console them. Paul seems to believe that there was no more challenge against him; in addition, the apostles of Jerusalem were out of his sight. There was no reason for Paul to portray Christ as the redeemer and savior that made the Corinthians allergic to the gospel he had preached. This may have been the christological lesson Paul could offer to restore his relationship with them in a changed circumstances.

Paul was independent from the previous traditions with regard to his christological interpretation while writing Cor(D). No clue is found that he reflected the influence from the Damascus and Jerusalem traditions. There is no text that mentions the death of Christ or the transcendental coming of Jesus from heaven. It seems that Paul simply focused on the restoration of relationship when he presented a new interpretation with regard to the role of Christ. In Cor(D), Paul seems to have made the least christological interpretations.

Cor(E)

Paul described Christ from a typological perspective in Cor(E). Christ was compared to the first human being created at the beginning of world, far beyond Moses. Having thought that the challenge against him seemed to have disappeared, Paul creatively developed his own christological interpretation with a hope to be reconciled to the Corinthians.

Christ is portrayed in connection with the creation of God. Having mentioned the fading glory of Moses covered with a towel (2 Cor 3:13–14), Paul introduced the glory and image of God embedded in Christ

(4:4). With this comparison, the superiority of Christ to Moses is communicated to the Corinthians. This shows a typological approach applied to Christ against the backdrop of the first human being created in the image of God (Gen 1:27). It seems that Paul used a rabbinic interpretation to describe Christ as a better man than Moses.[7] Perhaps the reason Paul took a typological approach to the beginning was to bring the Gentiles into the people of God beyond the Judaization of them.

Paul presented Christ as a person who makes man a new creature. This appears in the saying that everyone in Christ becomes a new creature (2 Cor 5:17). The new creature should be understood against the backdrop of God's creation. This probably means that Christ restores the nature of man that God originally created. For this, Christ was the model who had been created in the image of God. In other words, according to Paul, everyone should recover it in Christ. In this way, Paul applied the typology of creation to Christ in order to include the Gentile Corinthians into the people of God. This shows how Paul treated the Corinthians when they had inclined to follow the Jewish instruction initiated by Cephas as a representative of the apostles of Jerusalem.

The christological interpretation was enhanced from a typological perspective in Cor(E). Paul once presented Christ as the image of God in Cor(A) (1 Cor 11:3, 7), as the agent of creation in Cor(B) (8:6), and as the last Adam in Cor(C) (15:45–47). In this vein, Paul portrayed Christ as the one who makes people new creatures in Cor(E). This shows that the typological approach to the beginning of world for the description of Christ was continuously used for the Corinthians. It seems that Paul was independent from the traditions handed down to him with regard to his typological interpretation of Christ. In consequence, it can be said that Paul developed his own christological interpretation in his letters sent to the Corinthians in sequence.

Cor(F)

Paul applied Adamic typology to Christ in Cor(F). Having defined Christ as a husband, Paul compared the Corinthians to Eve seduced by the serpent. This means that Christ was to be interpreted in light of Adam. This is how Paul presented a christological interpretation in response to the challenge of some Corinthians.

7. Furnish, *II Corinthians*, 226.

Christ is defined as a husband from a symbolic perspective. This is found in the description that Paul introduced the Corinthians as a pure virgin to Christ the husband (2 Cor 11:2). Whereas they were compared to Eve seduced by the serpent in the garden of Eden, Christ was indirectly identified as Adam her husband (Gen 3:1–6; 2 Cor 11:3). Paul applied Adamic typology to the relation between Christ and the Corinthians in terms of spiritual marriage. This means that the Corinthians should be united to Christ. The analogy of marriage was used for the first time to carry the christological interpretation that expresses the desperate heart of Paul toward the Corinthians.

Paul developed a christological interpretation in association with Eve in Cor(F). This seems to have been possible because he had previously established a connection to it. In Galatians, Paul described Jesus Christ the Son of God as the posterity of a woman whom God had promised to Eve and the serpent in the garden of Eden (Gal 4:4–5; Gen 3:15). Thus, Paul was able to portray Christ in light of Adam, the husband of Eve, representing the Corinthians in Cor(F). However, the role of Christ has been severely restricted. This seems to reflect the fact that Paul knew that his christological instructions were ineffective for the Corinthians.

It seems that Paul made his own christological interpretation in response to the challenge against him. As shown before, the "serpent" makes readers think of those who seduced the Corinthians to challenge Paul against the gospel and his authority. They were none other than those sent by the apostles of Jerusalem. Then, the deceit of serpent refers to their teachings that made the Corinthians leave the gospel of Christ preached by Paul (2 Cor 11:3). This means that the Corinthians did not stop challenging Paul. Then, the optimistic report of Titus about their situation was proved wrong and made Paul misunderstood them (7:6–7). Having realized the opposite, Paul presented his own christological interpretation to defeat their challenge in Cor(F). This indicates that Paul continuously developed his christological interpretation to meet the challenge of the Corinthians.

Summary

Paul experienced a drastic situation during the second missionary trip. This is well reflected in the christological teachings delivered to the Gentiles. It seems that Paul did not have any information that the apostles of

Jerusalem had decided to send representatives to the Gentile churches at the time of writing Thess(A) and Cor(A). The challenge was getting stronger among the Gentiles as reflected in Cor(B), Thess(B), Phil(A), Cor(C), Galatians, and Cor(F). In the first half of the second missionary trip, Paul relied upon the Jerusalem tradition represented by Q with a reference to the transcendental coming of Jesus Christ for the eschatological judgment. On the other hand, the stronger the challenge he faced, the less transcendental aspect was attributed to Christ. Rather, Paul presented the crucified Christ as the redeemer and savior based on the Damascus tradition. In addition, various interpretations about the role of Christ were added to make the Gentiles stay in the gospel that he had preached. For this, a typological approach was applied to Adam, Abraham, Moses, and the posterity of a woman in order to describe the role of Christ. This indicates that Paul developed his christological interpretation in response to the challenge of some Gentiles sponsored by the apostles of Jerusalem. Meanwhile, Christianity was born and grew among the Gentiles.

C. THE THIRD MISSIONARY TRIP

Paul continued creating his christological interpretation during the third missionary trip to or in Rome. Having faced no interference of the apostles of Jerusalem, Paul delivered his christological instruction in connection with the birth, death, resurrection, and exaltation of Christ in his first letter. On the other hand, having responded to the critique raised by the Romans regarding his negative view on the Law, Paul had to respond on the basis of a christological interpretation for the salvation of people. This will show Paul's ability to meet the changing circumstances.

Rom(A)

Paul wrote a wide range of christological accounts of Jesus Christ in Rom(A). The birth, death, resurrection, and exaltation of Christ come to the fore. In this respect, he contributed to christological interpretation in his own way.

The Davidic lineage of the Lord Jesus Christ is mentioned for the first time. According to Paul, the Son of God was a descendant of David as to his human nature (Rom 1:3). This is the first case that deals with the lineage of Jesus Christ among Paul's letters. This reminds readers of

Q in which Jesus was called "God's Son" (Q^3 3:22). As most scholars have agreed, it originated in Psalm 2:7, which is supposed to have been written by David. Having acknowledged common elements between the two texts, Paul was able to portray the Lord Jesus Christ Son of God as the descendant of David. Without doubt, the descendant of David had been regarded as a messianic figure according to the Jewish concept (2 Sam 7:11–14; Ps 2:7; 4QFlor. 1.10f; 4QpsDan A). It seems that Paul treated the issue of Davidic lineage because the Roman church had been established by Aquila and Priscilla, who were Jews once expelled from Rome; later, they stayed with Paul in Ephesus and then finally returned to Rome (1 Cor 16:19; Rom 16:3). This indicates that Paul treated the Davidic lineage of Christ in consideration of Jewish members of the Roman church.

Paul introduced the Lord Jesus Christ as the Son of God from a spiritual viewpoint. It is said that through the spirit of holiness the Lord Jesus Christ was declared with power to be the Son of God by his resurrection from the dead (Rom 1:4). This is a messianic concept that contemporary Jews would not accept. This is because, according to the Pharisaic conviction, one who suffered death could not be the Messiah. However, Paul connected resurrection from the dead to the messianic "Son of God" revealed to him. It is important that Paul was able to connect the spirit of holiness with the messianic "Son of God" at the time of writing Rom(A). This implies that Paul tried to understand the messianic feature of the Lord Jesus Christ Son of God in connection with resurrection from the dead. It seems that, having relied upon the Damascus tradition, the christological view of Paul went through a process of development in consideration of the Jewish members of the Roman church.

The Lord Jesus Christ is defined as the savior. According to Paul, Christ died for the ungodly, and people are justified by his blood and saved from wrath through him (Rom 5:6, 9). Here Paul dealt with the love of God shown through the death of Christ, the righteousness of people by his blood, and the salvation from wrath all together. The love of Christ the Son of God for Paul was once mentioned in regard to his death in Galatians (Gal 2:20), the deliverance from wrath was already treated in Thess(A) (1 Thess 1:10), and the salvation of people resulted from the death of Christ was dealt with in Thess(B) (1 Thess 5:9–10), Phil(A) (Phil 3:18–20), Cor(C) (1 Cor 1:18–25), and Galatians (Gal 1:1–4). Thus, Paul was able to comprehensively describe the role of Christ in Rom(A). In consequence, it can be said that Paul progressively developed his christological interpretation that the Lord Jesus Christ is the savior of all in consideration of the circumstances of the Romans.

Paul described the exalted Jesus Christ as a mediator in heaven. He wrote, "Christ Jesus, who died—more than that, who was raised to life—is at the right hand of God and is also interceding for us" (Rom 8:34). This is a christological issue that appears only in Rom(A). The death, resurrection, and exaltation of Jesus Christ make readers think about his ascension ahead of eschatological advent referred to in Thess(A) (1 Thess 1:10), Cor(B) (1 Cor 15:23), Thess(B) (1 Thess 4:16), and Phil(A) (Phil 3:20). Paul wanted to describe the exalted feature in order to fill up the gap between the resurrection and advent of Christ in Rom(A). This is probably the most advanced among the christological narratives so far. It seems that Paul described the exaltation of Christ against the backdrop of Psalm 110:1, which is supposed to have been written by David. The reason Paul gave the Davidic character to Christ is because the majority of those in the Roman church were supposedly Jews. It is, however, noteworthy that Paul's mention of the birth and exaltation of Christ seems to be new to Aquila and Priscilla because no mention of them had been made Cor(C), which is supposed to have been written in the Ephesus of Asia. In this respect, Paul made christological lessons, taking into account the circumstances of the Romans.

In Rom(A), Paul made a theological account of birth, death, resurrection, and exaltation of Christ. In addition, Christ is introduced as the descendant of David for the first time. It seems that Paul enhanced his christological interpretation taking into account the circumstances of the Roman church, which is supposed to have been composed of mostly Jews. These christological interpretations enriched the teaching of Christianity.

Rom(B)

Paul gave Jesus Christ a role for the redemption of people in Rom(B). This reaches the peak in the expression of "a sacrifice of atonement." Perhaps Paul presented his christological interpretation in answering the question raised by the Romans, whose majority was supposedly Jews.

Jesus Christ was portrayed as an example for the Romans in their life of faith. According to Paul, the righteousness of God comes through the faith of Jesus Christ to all who believe in God (Rom 3:22). Here, Jesus Christ is connected to faith in the form of the subjective genitive as already used in Galatians (Gal 2:16). In addition, whereas Paul portrayed Abraham as the model for the righteousness of God by faith in Galatians (Gal 3:6–15) and then repeated it in Rom(A) (Rom 4:1–15), he admonished the Romans to have the faith of Jesus Christ for the righteousness of God in Rom(B). In this respect, Jesus Christ was presented as an example for the Romans in their life of faith. This is the most basic christological instruction of Paul in relation to the righteousness of God that refers to the status of salvation.

Paul mentioned redemption [ἀπολύτρωσις] in Jesus Christ. This is shown in the description that the Romans could be righteous by the redemption in Christ Jesus (Rom 3:24). Paul argued that the Romans should be released from sin through Christ Jesus to be righteous before God. The concept of salvation is closely connected with redemption in this context. Since Paul already mentioned redemption in connection with Christ in Cor(C) (1 Cor 1:30), he was able to present the concept of "redemption in Christ Jesus" in Rom(B). This means that the Romans could be set free from sin when they had the faith in God that Jesus Christ had shown. In this respect, Paul developed his christological interpretation in association with the concept of redemption.

Jesus Christ was defined as the "sacrifice of atonement [ἱλαστήριον]." According to Paul, God made Jesus shed blood and become the sacrifice of atonement (Rom 3:25). Whereas the term "blood" was already used in Rom(A) (5:9), the word "sacrifice of atonement" is used for the first time in Rom(B). This is reminiscent of the sin or guilt offering that the Jews dedicated in the tabernacle or temple (Lev 4:1—5:19). It seems to be also related to the role of the suffering servant of YHWH (Isa 53:10). In this vein, Paul described in Cor(C) that Christ died for the sins of human beings (1 Cor 15:3). However, the concept of redemption was developed in connection with the "sacrifice of atonement" in Rom(B). Paul seems to have attributed the redemptive role to Jesus Christ from a Jewish standpoint, taking into account the Romans, whose majority was supposedly Jews. In this way, Paul contributed to christological interpretation by giving Christ Jesus a redemptive role.

Paul presented his christological interpretation in connection with the concept of redemption and salvation in Rom(B). Above all, Paul seems to have put in mind that the majority of the Romans were supposedly Jews. This is supported by the words "his blood" and "sacrifice of atonement," reminiscent of the sin or guilt offering given to God at temple. Paul gave them an answer that only the "sacrifice of atonement" through the blood of Christ would lead them to the righteousness of God. This is another way to express Christ as the redeemer who leads people to the righteousness of God, which is the status of being saved. In this way, Paul made a significant contribution to christological understanding.

Rom(C)

Paul portrayed Jesus Christ as a deliverer of people from sin and death to life in Rom(C). This is a christological interpretation given in response to the critique that the Romans had raised after reading Rom(B). As a result, Paul enhanced his christological interpretation in consideration of the circumstances of the Romans.

Jesus Christ is described as a deliverer of people from sin and death in two ways. First, having introduced Adam as the type of the "one to come," Paul presented Christ from a perspective of Adamic typology;[8] and second, he described Christ as the one who let grace overflow to people for their life, contrasted with the sin and death that came into the world through Adam (Rom 5:12–21). This shows Paul's attempt to define Jesus Christ as the redeemer and savior of people from a perspective of Adamic typology. It seems to result from a progressive interpretation of Christ having died for the remission of sins as written in Cor(C) (1 Cor 15:3) and Galatians (Gal 1:4). In this vein, Paul was able to portray Jesus Christ as the redeemer who delivers people from sin and death in Rom(C). In addition, while the contrast between life and death appears in terms of "one man" in Cor(B) (1 Cor 15:21–22), the contrast between "a living being" and "a life-giving spirit" is found in terms of "man" in Cor(C) (1 Cor 15:45). Thus, Paul was able to set "sin and death" through the Law in contrast with "life" given through Christ in Rom(C). Paul described the salvific role of Jesus Christ against the backdrop of Adam, who had committed sin in the garden of Eden.

Paul tried to explain the role of Christ Jesus in relation to the Law. The law of the spirit of life in Christ Jesus set people free from the law of sin and death, and God sent his own Son in the likeness of sinful man (Rom 8:2–3). Paul believed that God had sent his Son Jesus Christ to free people from sin and death. In this respect, Jesus Christ is portrayed as the redeemer and savior of people from sin and death to life. Paul made a comment on God having sent his Son to the world on the basis

---

8. Scroggs, *Adam*, 92; and Wright, "Adam," 371.

of previous statements written in Galatians (Gal 4:4) and Rom(A) (Rom 5:8–10). In addition, the concept of "the Law of the spirit of life in Christ" reminds readers of "the Law of Christ" written in Galatians (Gal 6:2). It is then definite that Paul presented the understanding of the role of Christ in connection with the Law in more advanced level in Rom(C) than that found in Galatians.

Paul developed his christological interpretation in consideration of circumstances that the Romans faced. In response to their critique against his previous statement in Rom(B) that the Law makes people realize sin (Rom 3:20), Paul tried to explain the role of Christ in connection with the Law in Rom(C). Jesus Christ was portrayed as the redeemer and savior delivering people into life from sin and death resulting from observance of the Law. This means that Paul provided his christological interpretation taking into account the circumstances of the Romans, who had sincerely observed the Law.

Rom(D)

Paul described Jesus Christ from a soteriological point of view in Rom(D). This is supported by the words "righteous" and "save" used for the description of the role of Jesus Christ. Paul seems to have given a basic lesson from a christological perspective because of the consistent critiques of the Romans.

Christological interpretation is presented in a couple of places. First, it is said, "Christ is the end of the Law, so that there may be righteousness for everyone who believes" (Rom 10:4). Paul presented how to be righteous by saying that everyone can become the righteous people of God not by the Law but by faith in God. Hereby Paul described the role of Christ in demonstrating the fulfillment of the Law. His description of Christ as the end of the Law reminds readers of fulfilling the Law of Christ as written in Galatians (Gal 6:2). Paul replaced the phrase "fulfill the Law of Christ" with "Christ as the end of the Law" in Rom(D). This was made in the middle of continuous critiques of the Romans against Paul. It seems that Paul wanted to deliver an instruction on the salvation of people by the faith of Christ in God that supersedes the observance of the Law. In consequence, it can be said that Paul made a contribution to christological interpretation in connection with the salvation of people.

Second, Jesus was introduced as an object of religious confession. It is said that if one confesses with one's mouth "Jesus is Lord" and believes that God raised him from the dead, he or she will be saved (Rom 10:9–10). The Romans were advised to confess Jesus Christ as "Lord." Paul taught the Romans an instruction on salvation resulted from their confession. This reminds readers of what Paul said in Cor(C): no one can say "Jesus is Lord" except by the holy spirit of God (1 Cor 12:3), and everyone is saved by the belief in the gospel (15:1–2). However, Paul put the themes of confession and salvation together in Rom(D) and described them from a christological perspective. Hereby, Christ was presented as the object of confession. This shows that Paul developed his christological interpretation step by step in response to the changing circumstances of the recipients of his letters.

Paul emphasized the salvific role of Christ in Rom(D). As for this, faith, the lordship of Christ, and belief in God who raised him were suggested. Paul presented christological interpretations in response to the consistent critiques of the Romans, especially the Jewish members. In this way, Paul further strengthened the status of Jesus Christ in his letters sent to the Romans. As a result, christological interpretation became more and more abundant among the Christians in the region of Gentiles.

Phil(B)

Paul presented a christological hymn in Phil(B).[9] This is a well-composed hymn consisting of two parts: the stance of Christ and God's reward (Phil 2:5–11). At the end of his life in the prison of Rome, Paul showed his most advanced interpretation of Christ, far beyond what he had done before.[10]

In the first half of the christological hymn, three different stances of Jesus Christ are described in the direction of descent. First, the divine nature is mentioned. It is said that, having been in very nature [μορφή] of God, Jesus Christ did not consider equality with God something to be grasped (Phil 2:6). This is the only text that mentions the equality of

---

9. The question of an appropriate author and date of composition for the christological hymn constitutes one of the perennial conundrums of studies of Philippians. For the authorship of Paul, refer to Hofius, *Christushymnus*, 3–17; and Kim, *Origin*, 147–49. For the pre-Pauline authorship, see Beare, *Commentary*, 77.

10. Seeley lists the names of scholars of those pro or contra with regard to the matter of the pre-existence and incarnation of Jesus Christ ("Background," 49, n. 2).

Jesus Christ with God; in other words, no text delivers the divine nature of Jesus Christ among the Pauline epistles.[11] Although Paul once defined Christ as an agent through whom everything was created in Cor(B) (1 Cor 8:6), he never mentioned Jesus Christ in connection with the nature of God before. It is, however, described in Phil(B) that Jesus Christ voluntarily gave up equality with God. Paul showed himself beyond the traditions of Jerusalem and Damascus for the interpretation of the divine nature of Christ.

Second, the voluntary *kenosis* of Jesus Christ comes to the fore. According to Paul, having taken the very nature [μορφή] of a servant, having been made in human likeness, and having been found in appearance as a man, Jesus Christ made himself nothing (Phil 2:7).[12] The issue of the pre-existence and incarnation of Jesus Christ is out of discussion here; however, it is necessary to point out the extreme contrast between God and a servant in terms of "nature." The appearance of Jesus Christ in human likeness reminds readers of God who sent his Son born of a woman as written in Galatians (Gal 4:4) and being in the likeness of sinful man as written in Rom(C) (Rom 8:3). However, Paul added more theological meaning to the coming of Jesus Christ to the world of human beings with a reference to the nature of a servant and becoming nothing in Phil(B). It seems that Paul used this to create an interpretation to explain the nature of Jesus Christ.

Third, the death of Jesus Christ is mentioned. According to Paul, Jesus Christ "humbled himself and became obedient to death—even death on a cross" (Phil 2:8). Paul argued that Jesus Christ died on cross on account of humbleness and obedience. The death of Christ on cross was mentioned for the first time in Cor(C) (1 Cor 1:18; 2:2), and it reached its peak in Galatians (Gal 3:1, 13). It is, however, noteworthy that humbleness and obedience were more focused on in Phil(B). In this

---

11. There is an opinion that the christological hymn was described against the backdrop of the combination of Isaiah 45, stories of the Suffering Righteous, and Greco-Roman ruler worship. Seeley concludes that the hymn presents Jesus Christ as the strong and admirable leader "in a position of clear superiority vis-à-vis the emperor" and it "describes God as transferring to him the epithet 'LORD,' previously reserved for God alone." As for the question of whether the Greek word θεός refers to the God of the Bible or a god among those abundantly found in the Roman Empire, Seeley would like to interpret it against the backdrop of emperor worship ("Background," 49–72).

12. The term "likeness" seems to refer to similarity rather than homogeneity. As for its interpretation, see Brown, *Introduction*, 491–93.

way, the character of Jesus Christ was focused entirely, which seems to be what Paul was trying to emulate. The situation he was facing in the prison of Rome led him to describe the character of Jesus Christ in a different way from his previous description. Paul's christological view went through a process of change and development in response to his changing circumstances.

In the second half of the christological hymn, two different rewards of God are suggested in parallel. First, the exaltation of Jesus Christ is mentioned. According to Paul, "God exalted him to the highest place" (Phil 2:9). The Greek term for the highest exaltation is used only once here in the Christian Scriptures; however, Paul did not describe how God exalted Jesus Christ to the highest place in detail. For the plausible explanation, the intercessory role of Christ at the right hand of God deserves the highest place as written in Rom(A) (Rom 8:34). Otherwise, no text is detected for the expression of highest exaltation in other Pauline epistles. Then, it can be said that, having mentioned the intercessory role at the right hand of God in Rom(A), Paul was able to mention the highest exaltation to Jesus Christ in Phil(B). This shows that Paul creatively developed his christological interpretation step by step, having been independent from any traditions inherited by him.

Second, another reward given to Jesus Christ is presented in the christological hymn. According to Paul, God "gave him the name that is above every name" (Phil 2:9). This kind of reward is found only here; however, Paul did not explain its meaning in detail. Thus, it is necessary to see if there is any text that can explain the exaltation of the name of Jesus Christ. Although there are many texts that include the word "name" in connection with the Lord Jesus Christ (1 Cor 1:2; 5:4; 6:11; Rom 1:5; 10:13; 15:9, 20), no text refers to God bestowing the exalted status upon him. In this respect, it can be said that Paul created the idea that God gave Jesus Christ the name above every name. This kind of christological interpretation seems to reach a culmination with regard to the description of exaltation of Jesus Christ far beyond the traditions of Jerusalem and Damascus.

Then, two final clauses follow the main ones in the christological hymn. They are "at the name of Jesus every knee should bow in heaven and on earth and under the earth" and "every tongue confess that Jesus Christ is Lord" (Phil 2:10–11). According to Paul, God exalted him to the highest place and gave him the name that is above every name in order to make all the people bow at his name and everyone confess him as the

Lord. The description of bowing at his name appears only once in the christological hymn; on the other hand, everyone's confession of Jesus Christ as the Lord makes readers think of Paul's previous ones mentioned in Cor(C) (1 Cor 12:3) and in Rom(D) (Rom 10:9). Thus, in Phil(B) Paul was able to describe that God made all beings confess Jesus Christ as the Lord. In this respect, Paul enhanced his christological interpretation step by step depending upon the previous ones.

The christological hymn shows the most advanced form of confession of Jesus Christ. He is presented as the Lord of everything. This shows the most exalted aspect of the Lord Jesus Christ among Paul's letters. It is amazing that Paul wrote this kind of christological hymn in prison. This shows that as time passed Paul developed his christological view in response to the changing circumstances and resultantly strengthened the Christian instruction.

Summary

Paul continued developing his christological interpretation during the third missionary trip while heading for and staying in Rome. Jesus Christ was described as the savior in different way from the previous letters. Paul portrayed Jesus Christ as the redeemer and savior of people to be confessed as the "Lord." Finally, a description appears in the christological hymn that Jesus Christ humbled himself but God exalted him. Paul creatively worked on his christological interpretation over time. As a result, he gradually fortified Christian instruction with regard to the role and status of Jesus Christ far beyond the traditions of Jerusalem and Damascus.

D. CONCLUSION

I have traced how Paul developed his christological interpretation as time passed. It takes the central position in interpreting various topics addressed during the three missionary trips to the Gentiles. What Paul taught the Gentiles about the Lord Jesus Christ Son of God during the first missionary trip has not been known because there is no record on it. On the other hand, in the early period of the second missionary trip, Paul seems to have depended upon the Jerusalem tradition represented by Q more than the Damascus tradition for his christological interpretation.

This is found in the description of the transcendental Jesus Christ the Son of God coming from heaven at the end of world to deliver people from wrath. However, in the middle of the second missionary trip, there was a progressive change in his christological interpretation. Having faced the challenge of some Gentiles sponsored by the apostles of Jerusalem, Paul tended to deliver instruction centered on Christ more and more. Especially, Christ was introduced as the crucified redeemer and savior. In the midst of this, Christianity was born and raised in the area of the Gentiles. Later, Paul did not develop his christological interpretation much because there was no challenge during his third missionary trip to Rome. It is, however, noteworthy that Jesus Christ was described as the exalted intercessor at the right hand of God. This shows that Paul creatively developed his christological interpretation as time went by in response to the changing circumstances of the recipients of his letters. As we shall see, his christological understanding plays the role of a foundation upon which other theological topics rely, such as the death of Christ, redemption and salvation, the Law, the end of world, the spirit of God, and the church of God.

3

The Death of Jesus Christ

THE DEATH OF JESUS Christ is an important topic in Paul's theology. It has been interpreted in various ways according to his relationship with the recipients of his letters. It seems that Paul did not give much meaning to the death of Jesus Christ at the beginning of missionary trip to the Gentiles. Having followed the Damascus tradition, Paul simply mentioned the death of Christ. However, after the challenge of some Gentiles sponsored by the apostles of Jerusalem in the middle of the second missionary trip, Paul started imposing theological meanings upon the death of Christ. The theological account of his death was progressively developed. It reaches its peak at the description of his crucifixion as the means of salvation. Thus, it can be said that Christianity was born at the time of interpreting the death of Christ on the cross as a means of salvation. Later, in Romans, written during the third missionary trip, the blood of Jesus Christ was substituted for it on the premise that he had died for the redemption of people. This means that Paul changed his view on the death of Jesus Christ in response to the changing circumstances that he faced. In this meantime, Christian teaching on his death expanded.

A. THE FIRST MISSIONARY TRIP

Paul had definitely known of the death of Jesus before he received the revelation about the Son of God. Despite that he had inherited instruction on the death of Christ from the religious predecessors in Damascus and learned about the death of Jesus from Cephas in Jerusalem thereafter, he did not give a special meaning to it during his first missionary trip. Paul probably understood it in light of the martyrdom of prophets. However, no record on it has been left.

The Event of Revelation

It is a historical fact that Jesus died. However, the death of Jesus seems to have drawn little attention from his disciples from a theological perspective. Their proclamation of the executed Jesus may be one of reasons that made Paul persecute them. Paul did not give a particular meaning to the death of Jesus even after he had received the revelation about the Son of God.

Paul knew that Jesus died from a historical point of view. It seems that the Jews could not accept Jesus because of their religious belief that the slain one should not be a messiah sent by God. This would be one of reasons that made Paul persecute the disciples of Jesus who had proclaimed the instruction of the slain Jesus. If the disciples of Jesus had mentioned his death, they would have argued that he was martyred as a prophet. However, the disciples of Jesus did not make any comment on his death. At any rate, it is historically true that Paul persecuted the disciples of Jesus (Gal 1:22–23; Phil 3:6), but he did not mention whether the persecution was related to the death of Jesus or not.

It seems that the Son of God was irrelevant to the issue of death when Paul received the revelation. This is known from the fact that Paul did not say anything about the death of the Son of God in connection with the revelation (Gal 1:16).[1] If the revelation had been related to his death, Paul would have mentioned it with enthusiasm. As already discussed in chapter 2, having received the revelation, Paul acknowledged the possibility that the Son of God could be identified in connection with Jesus. However, it seems that he would want to clarify the relationship between them in more specific. Without doubt, Paul did not link the Son of God to the death of Jesus immediately after receiving the revelation. This is because he did not know exactly who the Son of God revealed to

---

1. It is described in the book of Acts that Jesus of Nazareth appeared to Paul in vision and said, "Why do you persecute me?" (Acts 9:5; 22:8; 26:15). The author did not mention the mission to the Gentiles given to Paul. Rather, it is Ananias who mentioned Paul's mission to the Gentiles (22:14). It is also to be noted that Paul never mentioned the heavenly saying of Jesus in his letters.

him was. Thus, it can be said that the Son of God had nothing to do with the death of a messianic figure at the time of receiving the revelation.

The Damascus tradition

Paul seems to have received the tradition about the death of Christ from the religious predecessors in Damascus. It is not until the time of receiving the gospel of Christ that Paul was able to connect the issue of death to the Son of God. However, no detailed description of the death of Christ had been made at that time.

After Paul had received the revelation about the Son of God, he inherited the tradition about the death of Christ. Without doubt, it is one of elements that consists of the gospel handed down to Paul (1 Cor 15:1–5). As discussed in chapter 1, those who transmitted the tradition about Christ are supposed to have been the religious predecessors of Paul in Damascus. However, it seems that they did not articulate the death of Christ further. They did not provide any clue about how Christ died, in addition to when, where, and why he died. The death of Christ was not associated with the cross, either. While no prophecy is definitely mentioned according to which Christ died, the statement "Christ died according to the Scriptures" could be understood against the backdrop of Isaiah 53:10. This means that even the religious predecessors did not talk much about the theological background of the death of Christ, either.

It is necessary to see whether Paul linked the death of Christ to the Son of God revealed to him. We do not know about it because Paul did not elaborate on it. Having heard about the death of Christ from the religious predecessors, Paul was probably embarrassed because of the Jewish tradition that the executed can never be a messiah. It is, however, important to observe that Paul used to mention the Son of God in connection with the issue of death in his letters written later, for instance, Thess(A) (1 Thess 1:10), Galatians (Gal 2:20), and Rom(A) (Rom 1:4). If Paul had not understood the Son of God in connection with the death of Christ, he could not have mentioned the death of the Son of God in his letters written later. Therefore, it is reasonable to conclude that Paul understood the death of Christ in association with the Son of God since he received the Damascus tradition. It must be, however, admitted that there is still much to be explained.

The Jerusalem tradition

The death of Jesus does not appear in the Jerusalem tradition represented by Q. It is not clear whether Paul linked the death of Christ to Jesus when he learned about him from Cephas in Jerusalem. It seems that no significant meaning was given to the death of Jesus at that time.

Little has been known historically about the death of Jesus. Paul went up to Jerusalem around 38 CE and learned from Cephas about the life and instruction of Jesus on the basis of Q. It seems, however, that Paul did not get any information about the death of Jesus because there was no text about it in the first three redactions of Q, which are supposed to have been completed in Galilee before the disciples of Jesus advanced to Jerusalem. This indicates that the disciples of Jesus did not impose any theological meaning upon his death. To my judgment, contrary to the general conviction that Jesus died for our sins, he in fact was killed because he had preached a teaching that the contemporary Jews could not accept; for instance, the commandment "Love your enemies" should be taken into consideration (Q^1 6:27; cf. 6:29–31). This is beyond the commandment to love one's neighbors as written in the Law (Lev 19:18). Then, the commandment to love one's enemy was therefore in direct opposition to the Law. This undermined the distinction between Jews and Gentiles because for the Jews loving their enemy could mean breaking their ethnic and religious boundaries. It could be understood as giving up their identity as the people of God. This kind of instruction was shocking to the Jews because they treated Gentiles as their enemy. Therefore, they had no choice but to regard Jesus as a very dangerous person and refused to accept his instruction to love their enemy. The Jews could not help but put him to death. If so, the disciples of Jesus would have understood his death as a prophetic martyrdom.

It is not clear whether Paul linked the death of Christ to Jesus. Paul went up to Jerusalem because he believed that the Son of God revealed to him had a connection with Jesus. Had it not been, Paul would not have had to meet Cephas in Jerusalem. However, it is another matter whether Jesus should be connected to the death of Christ. Since the death of Jesus was not mentioned in Q, Cephas had nothing to teach Paul with regard to it. This could be supported by Paul's allegation that the Jews killed Jesus as reflected in his first letter, Thess(A) (1 Thess 2:15). This means that even at the time of writing Thess(A) Paul did not attribute any theological meaning to the death of Jesus. This, in turn, implies that Paul hesitated to link the execution of Jesus by Jews to the death of Christ according to the Scriptures at the time of his first visit to Jerusalem to meet Cephas. Anyway, this seems to be a topic that needs to be studied further.

The First Missionary Trip and Thereafter

It seems that Paul did not impose any theological meaning upon the death of Jesus Christ during his first missionary trip. Since no text has been left, we are not sure what he preached with regard to it. It is not until his participation in the apostolic meeting around 49 CE that Paul was acquainted with the instruction on the cross. However, this does not mean that Paul gave a meaningful interpretation of the death of Jesus.

I wonder whether Paul delivered an instruction on the death of Jesus during the first missionary trip. Since Paul had received no theological significance from Cephas in connection with the death of Jesus, there was nothing to say about it. However, since Paul had a history of persecuting the disciples of Jesus for preaching the slain one, we can surmise that he mentioned the death of Jesus in a certain form of proclamation during the first missionary trip. If there was any rudimentary narrative, it would be that Jesus died. However, I would not believe that Paul proclaimed the death of Jesus in spite of no significant meaning. At least, Paul would have taught that the Jews killed Jesus without any theological meaning.

There is no doubt that Paul probably mentioned the death of Christ during his first missionary trip. This is because he learned about it from the religious predecessors in Damascus. We can surmise that the instruction on the death of Christ according to the Scriptures made Paul add something to it. Although no text has been left that reflects what he preached about it, we are sure of his effort to find out prophecies in the Scriptures to interpret the death of Christ. The best candidate is found in Isa 53:10. In consequence, it can be said that Paul dealt with the death of Christ from a theological perspective during the first missionary trip.

Paul had a chance to learn about the cross when he visited Jerusalem again around 49 CE. Having returned from the first missionary trip, he was exposed to the fourth redaction of Q, which is supposed to have been completed around 41 CE. There is an instruction that asks people to carry their cross to be the disciples of Jesus (Q^4 14:27).[2] As explained in

---

2. This kind of interpretation can be supported by the texts belonging to the fourth redactional layer of Q. For instance, several texts of it refer to the persecution

chapter 1, it was written during or immediately after the crisis initiated by the Roman emperor Gaius Caligula, who had tried to erect his statue in the temple of Jerusalem. The fourth redactor of Q made those who had followed the instruction of Jesus keep the temple holy according to the Law and run the risk of martyrdom.³ It seems that there were some killed to protect the temple from being polluted by the Roman soldiers (Q^4 13:34–35). It is, however, to be noted that this teaching does not refer to the crucifixion of Jesus.⁴ Although Paul did not experience the crisis while being on the first missionary trip to the Gentiles, he probably decided to run the risk of death for God after he had learned the instruction of Jesus on the basis of the fourth redaction of Q. Having gained support for the mission to the Gentiles, it seems that Paul returned to Antioch with Barnabas.

The theological controversy over the Gentile table occurred in Antioch around 50 CE. It seems to have had little to do with the death of Jesus Christ because the Gentile table was a matter totally different from it. Apart from the fact that Paul and Cephas had turned their back on each other, there was no chance to develop the instruction on the death of Jesus Christ. However, since Paul lost the support of those belonging to the Jerusalem church as well as the Antiochene church, he would have anticipated the sufferings to come. At that time, the only place he could lean on was the churches that he had established in the region of Gentiles during the first missionary trip.

---

and martyrdom of the disciples of Jesus. They had to face the suffering (Q^4 6:23c). Moreover, some of the disciples of Jesus were martyred in his name (11:47–51; 13:34–35). Having been understood against the backdrop of Deuternomic history, they were compared to the prophets who had been persecuted and martyred. In addition, the fourth redactor delivered the instruction that Jesus had come to the world to give the sword rather than peace in order to make the disciples fight against the attempt to erect the statue of the Roman emperor Gaius Caligula (12:49–53). This was how to imitate Jesus and keep the Law of God (4:1–13; 14:5; 16:16–18). As for the influence of Deuternomic history on Q, see Steck, *Israel*, 20–26, 257–60; and Kloppenborg, *Formation*, 173, 190.

3. Ra, Q, 218–20.

4. It is necessary to trace how the instruction on the cross was brought out. First, if Jesus had known about his crucifixion ahead of his execution and said the instruction about carrying the cross, he should have been considered a foreteller. Then, the death of Jesus on the cross should be understood as the martyrdom of a prophet. However, this kind of interpretation is not persuasive because Paul did not talk about it in his early letters. Second, if the disciples of Jesus created the instruction on carrying the cross after his death and attributed it to him, it is a prophecy told after the event (*vaticinium ex eventu*). The disciples of Jesus may have created such a teaching.

Summary

It seems that Paul did not pay much attention to the death of Jesus Christ at the beginning of his mission to the Gentiles. Although he learned about the death of Christ from the religious predecessors, he did not impose any theological meaning upon it. In addition, he did not get any instruction about the death of Jesus. Thus, no one knows what Paul had preached with regard to the death of Jesus Christ during his first missionary trip. Then, Paul was acquainted with the instruction about the cross that people should carry to be the disciples of Jesus. This became the foundation upon which Paul enhanced his theological interpretation of the death of Jesus Christ later. At any rate, Paul acquired more information as time went by, so that he might impose theological meaning upon the death of Jesus Christ.

B. THE SECOND MISSIONARY TRIP

Paul's interpretation of the death of Jesus Christ went through a drastic change during the second missionary trip. This happened in response to the challenge of some Gentiles sponsored by the apostles of Jerusalem. The more strongly they challenged Paul against the gospel and his authority, the more intensive instruction Paul delivered with a reference to the death of Jesus Christ on cross as the means of redemption and salvation. This informs readers of Paul's effort to enhance the theological interpretation of the death of Jesus Christ according to the relationship with the Gentiles. In this respect, Paul is to be regarded as the founder of Christianity.

Thess(A)

Paul referred to the death of the Lord Jesus Son of God from a historical point of view in Thess(A). However, Paul attributed no theological meaning to the death of Jesus yet. It seems that the Jerusalem tradition was preferred to the Damascus tradition with regard to the death of Jesus Christ.

The death of the "Son of God" is implied for the first time. According to Paul, God raised up his Son among the dead (1 Thess 1:10). This means that the Son of God died but God raised him. The "Son of God" is identified with Jesus coming from heaven in the immediate context. It is then noteworthy that death and resurrection are linked with Jesus the Son of God rather than Christ. As shown in chapter 1, the death and resurrection of Christ originated in the Damascus tradition. However, having connected them to Jesus the Son of God, Paul revealed his intention to put more weight on the Jerusalem tradition. This means that Paul converted the death and resurrection of Christ into those of Jesus the Son of God. In this respect, Paul combined the Damascus tradition with the Jerusalem tradition with regard to the death and resurrection of Jesus the Son of God in the early days of the second missionary trip. This indicates that Paul stayed at the level of regarding the issue of death as a preliminary step for resurrection.

Paul then mentioned the forced death of Jesus. This appears in the description that the Jews killed the Lord Jesus and the prophets (1 Thess 2:15). First, the name "Jesus" is mentioned rather than the title "Christ" here. This implies Paul's acknowledgement of the execution of Jesus from a historical standpoint. No theological meaning is given to the death of Christ here. However, nothing is said of how Jesus was killed. It is not clear even whether he was killed on a cross. Second, it is necessary to pay attention to the term "prophets" used immediately after "the Lord Jesus." They are none other than the disciples of Jesus because the term originated from Q, in which they were portrayed as prophets (Q^3 10:24; 11:32; Q^4 6:23c; 11:47; 13:34).[5] They were persecuted and even slain by their fellow Jews at that time (Q^4 11:47–51; 13:34–35). This shows that Paul applied to the death of Jesus and his disciples what he had learned from the apostles of Jerusalem on the basis of the fourth redaction of Q during his second visit to Jerusalem around 49 CE. If my argument is acceptable, it can be said that Paul tended to depend on the Jerusalem tradition with regard to the death of the Lord Jesus at the time of writing Thess(A). This means that he understood the death of Jesus and his disciples in light of the martyrdom of prophets, following the instruction of Q.

The death of Jesus the Son of God was focused without that of Christ in Thess(A). Although Paul had learned an instruction on the death of Christ from the religious predecessors in Damascus, he tended to connect it to Jesus as learned from Cephas even at the beginning of the second missionary trip. In addition, it seems that Paul regarded the death of Jesus the Son of God to be the martyrdom of a prophet.

---

5. Allison, *Jesus*, 58–60.

Cor(A)

Paul did not mention anything about the death of Jesus Christ in Cor(A). His death is simply implied in the description that God raised the Lord back to life. This probably plays the role of a turning point in terms of interpreting the death of Jesus Christ.

The death of Jesus Christ was not directly mentioned. Paul simply mentioned that God raised the Lord back to life (1 Cor 6:14). The death of the Lord is presupposed in the context. This is slightly different from what Paul expressed in Thess(A) that God raised his Son from the dead (1 Thess 1:10). Paul omitted the phrase "from the dead" in Cor(A). The fact that the Jews killed Jesus was not mentioned at all. These two elements suggest that Paul's view of the death of Jesus had changed. Perhaps Paul was preparing for a change from a historical approach to a theological one with regard to the interpretation of the death of Jesus Christ.

Paul used a different title for the description of the death of Jesus Christ. The title "Lord" is used instead of "Jesus Christ." This is slightly different from the description in Thess(A), which mentions the Son of God in connection with death and resurrection (1 Thess 1:10). Although "the Lord" refers to Jesus Christ in Cor(A) (1 Cor 1:7), it is necessary to examine the reason that Paul adopted the title "Lord" for the description of the implied death of Jesus Christ. To my judgment, as we shall see, Paul probably wanted to take a transitional step between the forced death of Jesus learned from the Jerusalem tradition and the spontaneous death of Christ inherited from the Damascus tradition.

The death of the Lord Jesus Christ attracted little attention in Cor(A). However, it seems that from the silence Paul tried to reveal a change in his theological position on the death of Jesus Christ. It can be said to be an intermediate point in changing Paul's view on the death of Jesus Christ from a forced one to a spontaneous and sacrificial one.

Cor(B)

Paul developed his theology of the death of Jesus Christ in Cor(B). His death was considered to be voluntary and sacrificial for the benefit of people. It seems that Paul attributed the sacrificial aspect of the death of Jesus Christ in response to the Jewish instruction delivered by Cephas as a representative of the apostles of Jerusalem that had resulted in the division among the Corinthians.

The cross of Christ is mentioned for the first time. The word "crucifixion" appears in the rhetorical question of Paul with an expected answer of "no" (1 Cor 1:13). Having mentioned his crucifixion with an unrealistic manner of speech, Paul hinted at the death of Christ on a cross. Then, the word "cross" is mentioned in his claim that he preached the gospel lest the cross of Christ be emptied of its power (1:17). This means that Christ died or was killed on a cross. Whereas Paul treated the death of Jesus by Jews without a reference to a cross in Thess(A) (1 Thess 2:15), he presented the death of Christ on a cross from a theological point of view in Cor(B). Two points must be considered here: one is the process in which the cross was mentioned as a means of death, and the other is the process in which it was linked to Christ, not Jesus. Since the cross was associated with the disciples of Jesus in Q (Q^4 14:27), Paul was able to adopt it in Cor(B). However, the question of why the cross was applied to Christ, not Jesus, is still unanswered. It seems that Paul had no choice but to interpret the phrase "Christ died according to the Scriptures," inherited from the Damascus tradition, in connection with the death on cross. As a result, the cross of Christ was suggested as a means of unity among the divided Corinthians in Cor(B). This marks a turning point with regard to Paul's interpretation of the death of Christ.

Paul presented the death of Christ with a reference to sacrifice for others. This is found in the saying of Christ's death for those who were weak in faith (1 Cor 8:11). Paul described the voluntary death of Christ for others for the first time here. In other words, the death of Christ was presented as a means of giving something beneficial to those who were weak in faith. This kind of description is possible because Paul already imposed a theological meaning upon the cross of Christ as a means of unity in the previous text (1:12–17). It is to be noted that the title "Christ" was used without the name "Jesus." In addition, the forced death of Jesus described in Thess(A) was changed to the spontaneous death of Christ in Cor(B). This marks a turning point in terms of interpreting the death of Jesus Christ. It seems that Paul tried to show his dependence upon the Damascus tradition with regard to the death of Christ as a sign of resistance to Cephas, who had visited Corinth, baptized some of the Corinthians, which resulted in the division among them, and produced those who were weak in faith. In this respect, the death of Christ on the cross was described to be voluntary and sacrificial for the benefit of others.

The death of the Lord Jesus is again presented as a means of giving something beneficial to others. This is found in the interpretation of the supper held at the night that the Lord Jesus was arrested (1 Cor 11: 23–26). According to Paul, the Lord Jesus mentioned the "bread for you" and the cup of a new covenant. Then, Paul added his interpretation that the Corinthians should proclaim the death of the Lord until he comes again. In this way, the forced death of Jesus turned into a spontaneous and sacrificial one. At this moment, it is noteworthy that the bread refers to the body of the Lord Jesus, who died for his disciples. This means that Paul introduced the death of the Lord Jesus as a means of giving something beneficial to them. In other words, the Lord Jesus is portrayed as the one who voluntarily gave himself for those following his instruction. As a result, the sacrificial death of the Lord Jesus seems to be used interchangeably with that of Christ on cross in Cor(B). This is a further developed interpretation of the death of Jesus Christ than that written in Thess(A).

Finally, the death of Christ is implied again. According to Paul, Christ was raised up among the dead (1 Cor 15:12). Of course, it is God who raised Christ from the dead. This reminds readers of the Son of God and the Lord whom God raised from death as written in Thess(A) (1 Thess 1:10) and Cor(A) (1 Cor 6:14). Thus, it was possible for him to mention the resurrection of Christ from death in Cor(B). It is important here that the death of the Son of God and of the Lord was replaced with that of Christ. In addition, whereas the focus is on God who raised the Lord or the Son of God in Thess(A) and Cor(A), it is on Christ who has been raised among the dead in Cor(B). This shows that as time passed Paul became inclined to Christ in connection with the matter of death. In this respect, Paul had a tendency to depend upon the Damascus tradition at the time of writing Cor(B).

Paul marked a turning point in connection with the death of the Lord Jesus Christ in Cor(B). This is revealed in the description that the forced death of Jesus by the Jews was changed to the voluntary death of Christ on the cross for the benefit of others. Then, the cross was mentioned in connection with Christ for the first time. This is probably the result of Paul's response to Cephas's visit to Corinth. In this respect, a significant advance was made in that Paul described Christ as the one who died for the Corinthians.

Thess(B)

Paul treated the death of Jesus Christ twice in Thess(B). It is characterized by spontaneous and sacrificial death. Perhaps Paul kept up with the interpretation of the voluntary death of Christ to make the Thessalonians resist the teachings of those sent by the apostles of Jerusalem.

First, the active role of Jesus is described in connection with death and resurrection. According to Paul, Jesus died and rose again (1 Thess 4:14). This differs from previous expressions in two ways. In Thess(A), the death of the Son of God was presumed with the phrase "raised among the dead" (1:10), and then the forced death of Jesus by Jews was mentioned (2:15). To the contrary, in Thess(B), Paul explicitly mentioned the voluntary death of Christ and his ability to rise with the active verbs of "die" and "rise." The voluntary death of Christ mentioned in Cor(B) (1 Cor 8:11) turned into that of Jesus in Thess(B); as a result, Paul changed the forced death of Jesus to a spontaneous one. With this, Paul began to attribute a theological meaning to the death of Jesus. This shows that Paul understood the death of Jesus in Thess(B) differently from that in Thess(A). This kind of change reflects that the situation of the Thessalonians changed between the times of writing Thess(A) and Thess(B). Thus, it can be said that Paul made a transition in the interpretation of the death of the Lord Jesus Christ Son of God in sequence of Thess(A), Cor(B), and Thess(B).

Second, the voluntary and sacrificial death of Jesus is mentioned in connection with salvation. According to Paul, the Lord Jesus Christ "died for us so that, whether we are awake or asleep, we may live together with him" (1 Thess 5:10). Living with the Lord Jesus Christ seems to refer to salvation mentioned in the previous verse (5:9). The phrase "for us" reminds readers of similar ones, such as "for the brothers who are weak in faith" and "for you" as written in Cor(B) (1 Cor 8:11; 11:24). Paul presented the voluntary and sacrificial death of the Lord Jesus Christ in connection with salvation for the first time in Thess(B). In this respect, Paul enhanced his interpretation of the death of the Lord Jesus Christ as time passed.

It seems that Paul dealt with the death of Jesus Christ to make the Thessalonians stay away from the instruction of those sponsored by the apostles of Jerusalem. As discussed in chapter 1, they were called the "tempter" (1 Thess 3:5). While Paul mentioned in Cor(B) that Cephas had visited Corinth and left only division among the Corinthians (1 Cor

1:11–12), he introduced the "tempter" who had tried to make the Thessalonians follow the Jewish instruction and stand up against Paul. It seems that, having mentioned the death of the Lord Jesus Christ as the means of salvation, Paul tried to keep the Thessalonians away from the instruction of the "tempter," who had no theological interpretation of the death of Jesus. This indicates that Paul relied upon the Damascus tradition in order to make the Thessalonians defeat the instruction delivered by those sent by the apostles of Jerusalem and rather stay firmly in the gospel he had preached. In this respect, Paul moved away from the Jerusalem tradition in his theological interpretation of the death of Jesus Christ as the challenge against him grew. In the meantime, Christianity was conceived among the Gentiles.

Phil(A)

Paul mentioned the "cross of Christ" in Phil(A). It appears there in association with salvation for the first time. This informs that Paul understood the cross of Christ from a soteriological point of view in response to the instruction delivered by those from the Jerusalem church.

The cross of Christ appears a second time among the Pauline letters. According to Paul, many were living as enemies of the cross of Christ (Phil 3:18). The cross of Christ was once mentioned as a means of unity among the divided Corinthians in Cor(B) (1 Cor 1:12–17). However, in Phil(A), the cross of Christ appears in connection with the "enemies" contrasted with those whose citizenship is in heaven and who eagerly await a savior from heaven, the Lord Jesus Christ (Phil 3:20). Paul indirectly attributed a soteriological meaning to the cross of Christ for the first time in that those who came near the cross of Christ had the heavenly citizenship while waiting for a savior from heaven. This shows how Paul laid the theological foundation for the birth of Christianity in connection with the soteriological role of the death of Christ on cross.

It seems that the cross of Christ was used to hold the Philippians firm in the gospel Paul had preached. He mentioned the "enemies of the cross of Christ," referring to those whose destiny was destruction, whose god was their stomach, and whose glory was in their shame (Phil 3:19). They were none other than those defined as "dogs," "those who do evil," and "those mutilators of the flesh" (3:2–3). Without doubt, they were those sent by the apostles of Jerusalem to make the Philippians keep the

Law and be circumcised. This was how to make the Philippians stand up against Paul. In response, having suggested the cross of Christ as the means of salvation, Paul tried to defeat their instruction. The cross of Christ was formed on the basis of the gospel of Christ, which thoroughly originated in the Damascus tradition. This shows that Paul kept moving away from the Jerusalem tradition in response to the challenge of the apostles of Jerusalem. The stronger the challenge Paul faced, the more theological meaning he attributed to the death of Christ on the cross.

Paul linked the cross of Christ to salvation for the first time in Phil(A). Having defined Christ as the savior, Paul presented the cross of Christ as a means of salvation. To this end, having relied on the Damascus tradition, which introduced the death of Christ, Paul tried to be independent from the apostles of Jerusalem. In this way, Paul sought to make the Philippians stay away from the instruction delivered by those from the Jerusalem church. In consequence, Paul started forming the Christianity among the Gentiles.

Cor(C)

Paul dealt with the death of Christ on the cross from a redemptive and soteriological perspective in Cor(C). This is an epoch-making interpretation in response to the serious challenge of some Corinthians against Paul. The more serious the challenge Paul faced, the more profound the interpretation he made with regard to the death of Christ on the cross.

The cross of Christ is introduced from a soteriological point of view. According to Paul, the message [λόγος] of the cross of Christ is the way of leading people to salvation (1 Cor 1:18). The crucified Christ is defined as the power and wisdom of God that brings righteousness, holiness, and redemption (1:23–24, 30). Therefore, Paul said that he knew nothing except Jesus Christ and his crucifixion (2:2). The message of the cross of Christ is known only to those led by the spirit of God (2:8–10). It is in Cor(C) that Paul treated the cross of Christ and his crucifixion most. Whereas the "cross of Christ" was mentioned once in Cor(B) (1 Cor 1:17) and once in Phil(A) (Phil 3:18), the "message of the cross of Christ" is introduced in Cor(C) (1 Cor 1:18). Paul developed the theological expression from the "cross of Christ" to the "message of the cross of Christ" as the challenge against him was getting stronger. And then, the crucifixion is mentioned for the first time in Cor(C) (1:23; 2:2, 8). Paul focused on the description of the "crucifixion of Christ" more than the "cross of Christ" in Cor(C). This shows Paul's creative attempt to interpret the death of Jesus Christ from a theological perspective.

It is necessary to take a look at why Paul put an emphasis on the crucifixion of Christ more than his cross in Cor(C). Paul seems to have wanted to reflect the painful situation resulting from the challenge of some Corinthians sponsored by the apostles of Jerusalem. As mentioned in chapter 1, Paul experienced a severe critique against the gospel and his authority at his second visit to Corinth. Having returned to Ephesus (1 Cor 16:8), he sent Cor(C), called the "Letter of Tears" (2 Cor 2:4). At that time, "crucifixion" was the most plausible word to express his painful situation. In other words, Paul made the Corinthians feel the same pain that he had felt, so that they might regret what they had done against him. Of course, he wanted them to accept the gospel he had preached and to refuse the instruction delivered by Cephas, who had visited Corinth as a representative of the apostles of Jerusalem. If my argument is acceptable, it can be said that Paul interpreted the death of Christ anew in response to the Jewish instruction delivered by Cephas.

The death of Christ gained weight from a theological point of view. This is found in the description that Christ died "for our sins" according to the Scriptures (1 Cor 15:3). The phrase of "for our sins" makes readers see the death of Christ from a redemptive perspective. As shown in chapter 1, the religious predecessors handed down the Damascus tradition, which included the statement that "Christ died according to the Scriptures." Having inherited this, Paul changed it into a sacrificial death for the brothers who were weak in faith in Cor(B) (1 Cor 8:11; cf. 11:24–26) and that "for us [ὑπὲρ ἡμῶν]" in Thess(B) (1 Thess 5:10). Finally, Paul changed it to death "for our sins [ὑπὲρ τῶν ἁμαρτιῶν ἡμῶν]" in Cor(C) (1 Cor 15:3). As a result, the sacrificial death of Christ was to be understood in light of redemption. This was a turning point for Paul in terms of interpreting the death of Christ.

It is necessary to take a look at why Paul understood the spontaneous and sacrificial death of Christ in association with redemption in Cor(C). It seems that Paul wanted the Corinthians to defeat the instruction delivered by Cephas, who was one of those in charge of formation of the Jerusalem tradition represented by Q. According to Q, John proclaimed to bear the fruit worthy of repentance to be forgiven one's sins (Q^1 3:8). In addition, Jesus taught the disciples to ask God for forgiveness of their sins because they already had forgiven everyone who had committed sins against them (Q^2 11:4). The disciples of Jesus were taught to forgive seven times a day (Q^2 17:4). It seems that Cephas delivered this kind of instruction about the remission of sins based on the works of repentance. In response to it, Paul could not help but suggest a totally different instruction on the forgiveness of sins. That is the redemption through the death of Christ according to the Scriptures on the basis of the Damascus tradition. In this respect, Paul imposed a redemptive role upon the death of Christ.

Paul presented a shocking interpretation of the death of Christ in Cor(C). The crucifixion was seen from redemptive and soteriological perspectives. This was given in response to the challenge of some Corinthians sponsored by the apostles of Jerusalem, including Cephas. With the instruction on the crucifixion of Christ, Paul tried to make the Corinthians stay away from the Jerusalem tradition represented by Q. In the meantime, the crucifixion of Christ Jesus began to establish itself as the core teaching of Christianity.

Galatians

Paul provided various descriptions with regard to the death of Jesus Christ in Galatians. They were made when Paul faced the severest challenge of the Galatians sponsored by the apostles of Jerusalem. Having been dependent upon the Damascus tradition, Paul attributed a theological meaning to the death of Jesus Christ.

Above all, the resurrection of Christ from the dead is written about at the beginning of Galatians. According to Paul, God raised Jesus Christ from the dead (Gal 1:1). This kind of description had already been mentioned in Thess(A) (1 Thess 1:10), Cor(B) (1 Cor 15:12), and Thess(B) (1 Thess 4:14). No more particular meaning was given to the death of Christ in Galatians in comparison with what had been expressed in the previous letters. However, having mentioned it at the beginning of Galatians, Paul tried to show that the death and resurrection of Christ would play a key role in Galatians. The conviction that God raised Christ from the dead was maintained on the basis of the Damascus tradition.

Paul maintained his redemptive and soteriological perspectives with regard to the death of Christ. This is seen in the description that Christ gave himself "for our sins" in order to rescue "us" from the present evil age (Gal 1:4). This is the interpretation of Paul about the reason that Christ died. The death of Christ "for our sins" should be understood from a redemptive point of view as it was in Cor(C) (1 Cor 15:3). Paul kept describing the death of Christ from a redemptive standpoint to defeat the instruction of those sponsored by the apostles of Jerusalem. This shows that Paul continued to give a theological meaning to the death of Christ on the basis of the Damascus tradition when the challenge of the Galatians against him reached its peak. In this respect, Paul stayed away from the Jerusalem tradition.

The motive of love is connected to the death of Christ the Son of God. Having mentioned the crucifixion with Christ, Paul talked about the love of the Son of God shown by giving himself (Gal 2:19–20). Two points will have to be addressed here. First, Paul used the word "crucified" again in connection with him since it had been used in Cor(B) (1 Cor 1:13). While Paul mentioned his crucifixion with an unrealistic manner of speech in Cor(B), he adopted it from a theological perspective in Galatians. As a result, the issue of crucifixion was developed from a theological point of view. Second, Paul put forth the issue that Christ gave himself for others. While Christ is mentioned as the one who gave himself for people in the previous text (Gal 1:4), the Son of God is portrayed as the one who gave himself for Paul here (2:20). The motive of love is added to the voluntary and sacrificial death of Christ the Son of God. This reminds readers of what Paul wrote in Cor(A): "If I . . . surrender my body to the flames, but have not love, I gain nothing" (1 Cor 13:3). It seems that the motives of surrendering one's body and loving others were applied in combination to the Son of God giving himself for loving Paul in Galatians. The internalization of the death of Christ the Son of God appears for the first time here. In this respect, Paul treated the death of Christ for him with love as soon as the challenge of some Galatians against Paul reached its peak. In consequence, it can be said that the voluntary and sacrificial death of Christ the Son of God on cross for loving people, including Paul, was given in response to the instruction of those sponsored by the apostles of Jerusalem.

Paul continued to present the death of Christ from a redemptive perspective. This is found in the saying, "Christ redeemed us from the curse of the law by becoming a curse for us, for it is written: 'Cursed is everyone who is hung on a tree'" (Gal 3:13). This means that Christ died on cross made of a tree as a curse to redeem [ἐξαγοράζω] people from the curse of the Law. Having set the death of Christ in parallel with the redemption from the curse of the Law, Paul assigned the redemptive role to the death of Christ. This is a more theological expression from a redemptive point of view than the previous ones that Christ died "for our sins" as written in Cor(C) (1 Cor 15:3) and in Galatians (Gal 1:4). In addition, the contrast between the death of Christ and the curse of the Law strengthens the fact that Paul had been challenged by those sponsored by the apostles of Jerusalem, who had asked the Galatians to observe the Law. This shows that the stronger the challenge Paul had faced, the more theological a meaning he imposed upon the death of Christ. Having stayed away from the Jerusalem tradition, Paul showed a tendency to rely upon the Damascus tradition with regard to the interpretation of the death of Jesus Christ.

The cross of Christ is presented in connection with the issue of becoming the people of God. This is seen in a contrast between the cross of Christ and circumcision (Gal 5:11; 6:12). Circumcision is a symbol for Jews of being the people of God. On the contrary, having set the cross of Christ in contrast with circumcision, Paul suggested it as the way of becoming the people of God. The issue of becoming the people of God was the top priority of the Gentiles in Paul's theology. In this respect, Paul progressively developed his interpretation of the death of Christ; for example, it was suggested as a way of unity among the divided Corinthians in Cor(B) (1 Cor 1:17), a criterion to distinguish the enemies from the heavenly citizen in Phil(A) (Phil 3:18), and the power of God for the salvation of people in Cor(C) (1 Cor 1:18). In this vein, in Galatians, the death of Christ is presented as a means for the Galatians to become the people of God. This indicates that Paul treated the cross of Christ as a theological tool to defeat the Jewish instruction of those sponsored by the apostles of Jerusalem.

Paul made a conclusion to his interpretation of Christ's death. It is revealed in the saying that Paul himself should never boast except in the cross of the Lord Jesus Christ (Gal 6:14). This reminds readers of the saying, "I resolved to know nothing while I was with you except Jesus Christ and him crucified" as written in Cor(C) (1 Cor 2:2). It is noteworthy that these two statements were said when Paul faced the challenge severely. It seems that the Galatians did not eventually accept the gospel Paul had preached. In this respect, the cross of Christ became the last bastion for Paul in a theological sense.

When the challenge against him was at its climax, Paul presented the cross of Christ as the core of the gospel that should not be abandoned. This is supported by the fact that the redemptive death of Christ on the cross does not appear anymore in the rest of Paul's letters. It is definite that the stronger the challenge Paul faced, the more he put an emphasis on the redemptive death of Christ depending on the Damascus tradition. In the meantime, the doctrine of Christianity had been formed more certainly.

Cor(D) and Cor(E)

Paul reduced his interest in the death of Christ in an effort to improve his relationship with the Corinthians. While the death of Christ is not mentioned in Cor(D), it is to a minimum in Cor(E). This shows that Paul adjusted his level of theological description according to the circumstances of the recipients of his letters.

The death of Jesus Christ is not treated in Cor(D). Although Paul defined God as the one who raises the dead, it is not related with Christ, but with Paul (2 Cor 1:9-10). There is no indication of the cross or crucifixion at all. It seems that Paul did not want to deal with the heavy topic of death in a situation where he was trying to improve relations by comforting the Corinthians. To my judgment, Paul should have emphasized the redemptive death of Christ in order to forgive the sins of the Corinthians committed against him. In any case, this shows that Paul dealt with the theological interpretation of the death of Christ in the direction he pursued according to the circumstances of the recipients of his letters.

Paul dealt with the death of Jesus Christ at a basic level in Cor(E). First, the death of Jesus is mentioned with a reference to burden (2 Cor 4:10). Having mentioned that he carried around in his body the death of Jesus, Paul tried to emphasize his own suffering. The death of Jesus was used as an analogy to explain Paul's suffering. In this case, the redemptive and soteriological role mentioned in Cor(C) was not assigned to the death of Jesus at all. There is no other theological significance in terms of interpreting the death of Jesus Christ.

Second, a customary phrase is found with regard to the role of God. According to Paul, God, who raised the Lord Jesus, will also raise people (2 Cor 4:14). Here, the death of the Lord Jesus was only premised. The same expression was only once used in Cor(A), which was written when Paul had been in good relations with the Corinthians (1 Cor 6:14). In this way, Paul showed in Cor(E) that he refrained from mentioning the death of Christ while trying to be reconciled to the Corinthians. This also shows that Paul adopted the description of the death of Jesus Christ according to the circumstances in which the recipients of his letters were placed.

Third, Paul linked the love of Christ with his spontaneous and sacrificial death. Paul said, "For Christ's love compels us, because we are convinced that one died for all, and therefore all died" (2 Cor 5:14). It is necessary for us to pay attention to two points. The first one is the issue of death associated with the love of Christ. Since Paul already linked the love of Christ the Son of God with the death for Paul and people in Galatians (Gal 1:4; 2:20), he could have presented this idea in Cor(E) as well. The second one is that Paul referred to the spontaneous and sacrificial death of Christ. This kind of interpretation was already found while the challenge against Paul was not as serious as reflected in Cor(B) (1 Cor 8:11) and Thess(B) (1 Thess 5:9). Similarly, Paul mentioned the spontaneous and sacrificial death of Christ in the context of seeking reconciliation with the Corinthians. It is, however, noteworthy that no redemptive role was attributed to the death of Christ in this context.

While trying to restore relations with the Corinthians, Paul kept the account of the death of Jesus Christ to a minimum as reflected in Cor(D) and Cor(E). No redemptive and soteriological meaning was given to it; rather, only spontaneous and sacrificial aspects were emphasized. Having relied on the Damascus tradition, Paul adjusted the level of theological narrative to suit the situation.

Cor(F)

Paul presented the crucifixion of Christ as a symbol of weakness in Cor(F). It is set in contrast with the power of God to raise Christ again. It seems that, having faced the consistent challenge of some Corinthians, Paul stopped attributing the redemptive and soteriological role to the death of Christ on cross.

The crucifixion of Christ is set in contrast with the power of God to raise him again. According to Paul, Christ was crucified because of weakness but was raised by the power of God (2 Cor 13:4). The resurrection of Christ from the dead by God was mentioned in Thess(A) (1 Thess 1:10), Cor(B) (1 Cor 15:12), Thess(B) (1 Thess 4:14), and Galatians (Gal 1:1). In addition, Paul once designated the crucified Christ as the power of God in Cor(C) (1 Cor 1:24). It is, however, noteworthy that the death of Christ and the power of God to raise him again are to some extent contrasted in

Cor(F). No redemptive and soteriological meaning was assigned to the death of Christ anymore. The crucifixion of Christ is simply presented as a symbol of weakness.

It is necessary to find out why Paul did not attribute a meaningful role to the crucifixion of Christ. To my judgment, the consistent challenge of some Corinthians made Paul abandon the confidence that the instruction on the death of Christ on cross could be influential enough to make the Corinthians return to the gospel. This shows that the theological interpretation of the death of Christ on cross was argued when Paul was confident in the possibility to persuade those who had challenged. However, Paul was quite upset when some Corinthians continued challenging him. This seems to be why Paul did not attribute a redemptive and soteriological role to the death of Christ on cross in Cor(F).

Summary

It seems that Paul's instruction on the death of Jesus Christ went through ups and downs during the second missionary trip. It depended on the circumstances that he had with the challengers against the gospel and his authority. The stronger the challenge of those sponsored by the apostles of Jerusalem became, the more emphasis Paul put on the redemptive and salvific death of Christ. The forced death of Jesus turned into the voluntary and sacrificial death of Christ as time went by. For this, Paul adopted words such as "cross" and "crucifixion." Paul came to the point of saying that he could not give up the cross of Christ. On the other hand, as the influence of the apostles of Jerusalem increased on the Gentiles, Paul abandoned the Jerusalem tradition represented by Q. Rather, Paul developed his interpretation of the death of Christ based on the Damascus tradition. This shows the process of establishing Christianity completely independent from the Jerusalem church.

C. THE THIRD MISSIONARY TRIP

Paul treated the death of Christ during the third missionary trip. Instead of the "cross" or "crucifixion," he used the word "blood" in order that the Romans might not be mistaken for traitors against the Roman Empire. While the critique against him was getting stronger, Paul consistently developed his theological interpretation of the death of Christ with a reference to redemption.

Rom(A)

Paul even described the death of Jesus Christ as a path to sublimation in Rom(A). Having introduced the blood of Christ as a means of redemption, Paul described the death of Jesus Christ in connection with love, salvation, and exaltation. Paul avoided using the terms "cross" and "crucifixion" so that the Romans might not be mistaken for traitors against the Roman Empire.

The death of Jesus Christ is indirectly handled in connection with resurrection. According to Paul, Jesus Christ the Son of God rose again among the dead by the spirit of sanctification (Rom 1:4). Here, the death of Jesus Christ itself is of little focus. It is, however, noteworthy that Paul used the term "dead" for the death of Jesus Christ, which was already used in Thess(A) (1 Thess 1:10), Cor(B) (1 Cor 15:12), and Galatians (Gal 1:1). Having compared with the expression that Christ died and "rose" from the dead in Thess(B) (1 Thess 4:14), Paul sought to convey the initiative of Christ in death and resurrection by using the word "rising" again in Rom(A). This means that Paul made it a customary form of expression for the death of Jesus Christ in connection with resurrection as time went by.

The redemptive death of Christ is presented with the motive of love. According to Paul, Christ died for the powerless, ungodly, and sinful people (Rom 5:6). The expression "he died for us" reminds readers of what was already used in Cor(B) (1 Cor 8:11), Thess(B) (1 Thess 5:9–10), Cor(C) (1 Cor 15:3), and Galatians (Gal 1:4). However, his voluntary, sacrificial, and redemptive death reaches its peak in Rom(A) with a saying that he died for sinners (Rom 5:8). In the meantime, the death of Christ is connected with the love of God for people. While the love of the Son of God is mentioned in connection with giving himself for Paul in Galatians (Gal 2:20), Paul put forth the love of God, who gave his Son to die for sinners in Rom(A). When compared between Galatians and Rom(A), the subject of giving love changed from the Son of God to God, and the scope of the object of being loved was extended from "Paul" to "all sinners." This indicates Paul's theological effort to widen the scope of redemption resulting from the death of Christ.

Paul adopted the term "blood" for the death of Christ. This appears in the saying that people have been righteous by his blood for the salvation from wrath and that they were reconciled to him through the death of God's Son (Rom 5:9–10). Parallels are found between "his blood" and "the death of the Son of God," and between "being righteous" and "being reconciled with God." They show that the death of Christ should be understood in light of righteousness and reconciliation. The term "blood" was adopted instead of "cross" or "crucifixion," which referred to the execution of traitors against the Roman Empire. In this way, Paul tried to keep the Romans away from being mistaken for traitors against the Roman Empire. Here is the narrative development of the death of Christ. As such, Paul enhanced his theological interpretation of the death of Christ on the basis of the Damascus tradition, taking into account the political situation of the Romans.

The death of Christ is presented as the first step in the process of exaltation. According to Paul, Christ died but was raised and then he has been alive at the right hand of God to pray for people (Rom 8:34). This is Paul's theological interpretation that the death of Christ paved the way to his exaltation as a mediator at the right hand of God. The exaltation of Christ is described against the backdrop of Psalm 110:1, in which the title "Lord" and the phrase "at the right hand" are used. This informs that the dead Jesus Christ became the Lord after God raised and exalted him. This is the theological interpretation that Paul presented in connection with the death of Christ for the first time. In this respect, a new interpretation of exaltation was created in regard to the death of Christ leading to his exalted status.

Paul mentioned the death of Christ from a christological point of view. It appears in the description that Christ died and rose again to become the Lord of both the dead and the living (Rom 14:9). The lordship of Christ refers to his exalted status after his death and resurrection. There would be no exaltation of Christ without his death. This reminds readers of Jesus Christ exalted for the intercessory role at the right hand of God after he was raised from death as written earlier (8:34). In this respect, Paul added the theological meaning of exaltation to the redemption resulting from the death and resurrection of Christ.

Having sent Rom(A) to the Roman church, which he did not establish, Paul imposed various meanings upon the death of Jesus Christ. It was described as a way to exaltation in addition to redemption and salvation. In addition, Paul used the word "blood" instead of "cross" or "crucifixion" in reference to Christ in order that the Romans might not be mistaken for traitors against the Roman Empire. The death of Christ Jesus was expressed as a way of God loving the sinner. It seems that Aquila and Priscilla were also exposed to this kind of instruction for the first time, although they had spent a certain period of time with Paul in Ephesus at the time of writing Cor(C) and returned to Rome later. In this respect, Paul continued to add theological meanings to the death of Christ Jesus. In the meantime, Paul was able to make the doctrine of Christianity more concrete.

Rom(B)

Paul mentioned the "sacrifice of atonement [ἱλαστήριον]" through faith in the blood of Christ in Rom(B). This brings us to Paul's view of the death of Christ with a new concept. However, he did not add anything to it.

The blood of Christ is mentioned again. The word "blood" is used in place of "death" on the cross (Rom 3:25). Paul avoided using the phrase "death of Christ on cross" or his crucifixion in Rom(B) as he did in Rom(A) in order that the Romans might be free from suspicion by the Roman authorities. Meanwhile, Paul tried to reveal the importance of the death of Christ to the Romans. It is noteworthy that the blood of Christ is associated with the "sacrifice of atonement," which was used for "the lid on the ark of the covenant, which was sprinkled with the blood of the sin-offering on the Day of Atonement" according to the *LXX* (Exod 25:17).[6] In this way, the redemptive role of the death of Christ is referred to in Rom(B). In this respect, Paul took the interpretation of the death of Christ to the next level from a Jewish perspective.

It seems that Paul was busy answering the question raised by the Romans while writing Rom(B). It was about wrath and transgression that the Law brings as written in Rom(A) (Rom 4:15). It seems that Paul did not pay much attention to the interpretation of the death of Christ in Rom(B). However, the death of Christ was interpreted in light of a "sacrifice of atonement" from a Jewish perspective in consideration of the fact that the majority of the Romans were supposedly Jews.

---

6. Bauer, *Lexicon*, 375.

Rom(C)

Paul attributed more theological meanings to the death of Christ in Rom(C). Having connected the death of Christ with baptism, Paul argued it for the way of leading the Romans to the eternal life connected with the resurrection of Christ. By this, Paul developed his theology of the death of Jesus Christ taking into account the continued critique of the Romans against him.

The death of Christ is presented in association with baptism. According to Paul, everyone who was baptized into Christ Jesus was baptized into his death (Rom 6:3). Baptism is presented as a way to share in the death of Christ. While Paul had criticized baptism for the dead in Cor(C) (1 Cor 15:29), he interpreted baptism as a way of sharing in the death of Christ in Rom(C). However, how baptism is a way to share in the death of Christ is not mentioned in detail. It is, however, noteworthy that whereas participation in the Lord's Supper was interpreted as a decision to preach the death of the Lord until he comes in Cor(B) (1 Cor 11:26), baptism was interpreted as a way of sharing in his death in Rom(C). This indicates that Paul developed his interpretation of the death of the Lord Jesus Christ in connection with the liturgical ritual as time went by. In this respect, Paul independently interpreted the death of Christ in connection with baptism.

Paul once again understood the death of Jesus Christ from a redemptive point of view. This is known by the saying that the old self was crucified with Christ "so that the body of sin might be done away with, that we should no longer be slaves to sin" (Rom 6:6). While Paul explained the "crucifixion with Christ" in connection with love in Galatians (Gal 2:20), it is connected with redemption from sin in Rom(C). The redemptive death of Christ eventually resulted in a resurrected life (Rom 6:10–12). Having argued to follow the death of Christ, Paul remained at the level of suggesting a way of redemption based on the Damascus tradition. This indicates that Paul provided a new interpretation of Christ's death for the resurrected life of the Romans.

The phrase of "raised from the dead" appears again. This is found in two places: "who was raised from the dead" (Rom 7:4) and "who raised Christ from the dead" (8:11). The phrase "from the dead" presupposes the death of Christ. While the former is used for the description of Christ with a form of passive verb, the latter is used for God with a form of active verb. The phrase "from the dead" was already used in Thess(A), Cor(B),

Galatians, and Rom(A). Thus, Paul was able to use it as an idiomatic phrase in Rom(C). It seems that Paul consistently used references to the death of Christ because it occupied an important place in his theology. This indicates that Paul relied upon the Damascus tradition rather than the Jerusalem tradition at the time of heading for Rome.

Paul emphasized the unity of the Romans with Christ in terms of death. To this end, baptism was presented as a way of uniting with Christ from a liturgical perspective. This was probably a theological answer to calm down the consistent critique of the Romans against him. The more letters Paul sent to the Romans, the more theologically significant a meaning he imposed upon the death of Christ Jesus. Accordingly, having relied on the Damascus tradition, Paul solidified the doctrine of Christianity in regard to the death of Jesus Christ.

Rom(D)

Paul also mentioned the death of Christ in Rom(D). However, no particular meaning was given to it except the introduction as the content of confession. It seems that Paul did not need to provide the Romans with a new interpretation of Christ's death anymore because of their consistent critique.

The death of Christ is presented as the contents to be believed. According to Paul, if one believes that God raised Christ from the dead, he or she will be saved (Rom 10:9). In fact, the resurrection appears more important than the death of Christ as something to be believed. This shows Paul's confidence in the death and resurrection of Christ to the end. This is reminiscent of previous statement written that those who have believed the gospel consisting of the death and resurrection of Christ would be saved as written in Cor(C) (1 Cor 15:1–5). In a sense, Paul repeated what he had already emphasized with regard to the relationship between salvation and belief in the death of Christ. This shows that Paul kept interpreting the death of Christ from a soteriological point of view in Rom(D).

It is necessary to take a look at why Paul did not impose any new meaning upon the death of Christ in Rom(D). This could be because Paul already mentioned its meaning several times in his previous letters. Or it was unnecessary to emphasize the death of Christ because there was no challenge against him under the sponsorship of the apostles of Jerusalem.

Or it could be due to the fact that Paul's instruction on the death of Christ was not strong enough to persuade the Romans. To my judgment, the third one is preferred to the first and second. Paul seems to have failed to persuade the Jewish members of the Roman church who had agreed with the idea that a dead one cannot become messiah. In consequence, it can be said that Paul gradually lost his influence over the Romans as time went by. A similar phenomenon also appeared in relations with the Corinthians during the second missionary trip.

Phil(B)

Paul praised the death of Jesus Christ on the cross in Phil(B). It is, however, described in light of humbleness and obedience. Paul seems to stop attributing the redemptive role to the death of Christ.

The cross of Jesus Christ is mentioned in the christological hymn. According to Paul, Jesus Christ "humbled himself and became obedient to death—even death on a cross! Therefore God exalted him to the highest place" (Phil 2:8–9). Paul understood the death of Jesus Christ in light of lowering oneself for the first time. Here the cross is portrayed as the pinnacle of humility before God and obedience to him. In addition, this is described as the way that led Jesus Christ to his exalted status. This kind of interpretation was already shown by mentioning the death, resurrection, and exaltation of Christ in sequence in Rom(A) (Rom 8:34). Thus, Paul was able to reveal the view that the death of Christ on cross had taken the place of turning point from self-degradation to exaltation. In this respect, Paul interpreted the death of Christ on cross anew.

Paul did not understand the death of Christ on the cross in association with redemption and salvation in Phil(B). It is probably because the Philippians stayed in the gospel Paul had preached. He attributed simply the religio-ethical meaning, humility and obedience, to the death of Christ on cross. Having written Phil(B) in the prison of Rome, Paul was careful not to use the words "cross" and "crucifixion" so that the Philippians would not be mistaken for traitors against the Roman Empire. He refrained from using them with a reference to redemption and salvation.

Paul revealed an extraordinary view on the death of Jesus Christ in Phil(B). This seems to have provided an example for Philippians to follow from a religio-ethical perspective. As a result, the cross of Jesus Christ was described in connection with humility and obedience.

Summary

Paul mentioned the death of Jesus Christ as many times as possible during his third missionary trip. He did a lot of talking about the death of Christ in Rom(C), when the critique of the Romans against him was the greatest. It is, however, noteworthy that no new meaning was given to the death of Christ on the cross other than that it was the path from humility to exaltation in the letters written during the third missionary trip. This is because there was no challenge against him under the sponsorship of the apostles of Jerusalem. Compared to the challenge of some Gentiles, it seems that the critique of the Romans was not so strong. In addition, he did not deal with the issue of the cross in order to avoid the suspicion of the Roman authorities. In this way, Paul was careful of using words such as "cross" and "crucifixion." In general, his interpretation of the death of Jesus Christ was made on the basis of the Damascus tradition. Although Paul did not enhance it much during his third missionary trip to Rome, Paul seems to have formed Christianity among the Gentiles as he stayed away from the influence of the apostles of Jerusalem.

D. CONCLUSION

Paul attributed various meanings to the death of Jesus Christ during his missionary trips to the Gentiles. It seems that no particular meaning was attributed to it during the first missionary trip except the message that God had raised Christ from the dead. Having faced the challenge of those sponsored by the apostles of Jerusalem in the middle of the second missionary trip, Paul imposed a redemptive and soteriological meaning upon the death of Jesus Christ on the cross. The stronger the challenge Paul experienced, the more theological meaning was given to the death of Christ with reliance upon the Damascus tradition. The forced death of Jesus turned into a voluntary death of Christ to heighten the sacrificial role for the salvation of people. Paul presented the death of Christ as a breakthrough for the salvation of people while being challenged by some Gentiles under the sponsorship of the apostles of Jerusalem. This seems to be the moment that Christianity was born among the Gentiles. On the other hand, during the third missionary trip, the death of Christ was given a new meaning as the way leading to the exaltation acknowledged by God. At any rate, it is definite that the theological meaning of Christ's death is closely related with a christological interpretation. Having tried to be independent from the Jerusalem church, Paul resultantly developed his instruction on the death of Christ with a reference to redemption and salvation.

4

Redemption and Salvation

PAUL COMMUNICATED VARIOUS INSTRUCTIONS on redemption and salvation in connection with his christological understanding. It seems that he adopted the Jewish concept of salvation to be delivered from wrath at the beginning of his mission to the Gentiles. While his view on redemption is rarely found, Paul delivered his soteriological instruction on the basis of the Jerusalem tradition represented by Q. There was, however, a turning point with regard to the interpretation of redemption and salvation in the middle of the second missionary trip. Paul changed his notion about the redemptive and salvific role of Jesus Christ in response to the challenge of some Gentiles sponsored by the apostles of Jerusalem. This is the granting of power to the death of Christ for redemption and salvation. In the meantime, Christianity was born among the Gentiles. Later, Paul maintained the interpretation of redemption and salvation given through Jesus Christ, but did not develop it much during the third missionary trip. This resulted in a gradual separation from the Jerusalem tradition to the Damascus tradition to be independent from the apostles of Jerusalem. Paul developed his redemptive and soteriological interpretation in response to the changed circumstances of the recipients of his letters. As a result, Christian teaching was progressively formed.

A. THE FIRST MISSIONARY TRIP

Paul definitely had a Jewish view on salvation before receiving the revelation about the Son of God. There is, however, no concrete data on this. Nevertheless, Paul, as a former Pharisee, seems to have had a Jewish view on salvation that was about being the people of God by observing the Law. However, having received the revelation, Paul learned about Jesus from Cephas on the basis of Jerusalem tradition represented by Q, and it would have had a profound effect on Paul's understanding of him in regard to the salvation of people. Based on this theological background, Paul would have proclaimed the salvation of the Gentiles during the first missionary trip.

Above all, it is necessary to take a look at what kind of concept Paul had with regard to redemption and salvation immediately after he had received the revelation about the Son of God. Without doubt, Paul was accustomed to the Jewish perspective on redemption and salvation. It has been, however, unknown whether Paul had a new concept of redemption and salvation as soon as he had received the revelation. Since he simply said that God had revealed his Son to proclaim him to the Gentiles (Gal 1:16), no implication appears with regard to their redemption and salvation. Perhaps Paul was confident of belief that a person can be incorporated into the people of God by observing the Law whether he or she is a Jew or a Gentile. It seems that Paul maintained the Jewish view on redemption and salvation because he was accustomed to Pharisaic Judaism.

Then, it seems that the religious predecessors did not exert influence on Paul in relations to redemption and salvation. The issue of redemption and salvation does not appear in the Damascus tradition that is the core of the gospel (cf. 1 Cor 15:3–5). As discussed in chapter 1, it simply lists the death of Christ according to the Scriptures, burial, resurrection on the third day, and epiphany. No connection is found between the death of Christ and the forgiveness of sins. If possible, we can find teaching on salvation in the mention of Christ's resurrection. As known in general, resurrection has been considered to be an eschatological event with a reference to the salvation of people. It is, however, noteworthy that the resurrection of Christ was mentioned in the gospel, not that of people in general. It seems that religious predecessors did not deal with the redemptive and salvific role of Christ for people at the time of transmitting the gospel to Paul.

Later, Paul received the teaching of Jesus on forgiveness from Cephas at his first visit to Jerusalem. This seems to have been limited to the first three redactions of Q. Although the words "redemption" and "salvation" do not appear there, it delivers a couple of instructions on forgiveness of sins. For instance, John asked people to repent for the forgiveness of sins and to bear the fruit worthy of repentance (Q^1 3:3, 8a). How to bear the fruit worthy of repentance is not described in detail; however, in the first redaction of Q, it seems to refer to the observance of what Jesus taught. The forgiveness of sins seems to be complete when one does the appropriate behavior after repentance; for instance, it could be loving enemies (Q^1 6:27, 29–30). In addition, the second redactor of Q also treated the issue of forgiveness in the Lord's Prayer. It is said, "Forgive us our sins, for we also forgive everyone who sins against us" (Q^2 11:4). This means that the forgiveness of sins requires proper action of the person concerned. Then, when the second redaction was over, the fruit worthy of repentance could mean forgiving the sin of a person who has sinned against him or her. At the same time, it has been taught that the disciples of Jesus had to forgive those who sinned against them seven times a day if they had repented (Q^2 17:4). As such, the effort to cleanse one's sins is emphasized in Q. However, no concept of emancipation or atonement appears at all. It is likely that Paul accepted the concept of forgiveness from Q because he, as a former Pharisee, emphasized purity in actual life rather than religious activities in the temple. It has been, however, unknown how much Paul accepted the teachings of Jesus on the basis of the Jerusalem tradition.

Paul then went on his first missionary trip. The teachings listed above seem to have been of considerable benefit when Paul preached the gospel among the Gentiles. This is because there was no need to teach them that they should attend the temple and offer sacrifices to be forgiven for their sins. Paul may have taught the Gentiles that they had to first forgive the sins of others in order to be forgiven for their sins. In addition, it is likely that Paul asked the Gentiles to keep the Law in order not to commit sins. Possibly, Paul maintained the Jewish view on the forgiveness of sins at that time. However, it seems that the concept of redemption had not yet been clearly formed. In other words, Paul asked the Gentiles to live blamelessly in their lives without committing sins.

Having finished the first missionary trip and returned to Jerusalem around 49 CE, Paul seems to have learned a new concept of forgiveness. At that time, he was acquainted with the fourth redaction of Q, which had been complete around 41 CE. It is said that although one could be forgiven for sins committed against the Son of Man, one cannot be forgiven for the blasphemy committed against the "holy spirit" (Q^4 12:10). This is the only text that mentions the forgiveness of sins in connection with Jesus the Son of Man and the spirit of God. This reveals a difference in the level of forgiveness because Jesus the Son of Man and the spirit of God were of different dimensions. In addition, no mention of the sacrifice for atonement in the temple of Jerusalem appears in Q. It seems that, having been exposed to Q, Paul still maintained the concept of forgiveness at his second visit to Jerusalem; however, no concept of redemption had been revealed. Rather, Paul's understanding did not deviate much from Pharisaic Judaism with regard to the redemption and salvation of Gentiles at that time.

A theological controversy over the Gentile table occurred in Antioch. Cephas's participation in it raised a question of whether he had violated the Law because of his withdrawal in fear of those sent by James, the Lord's brother. Having seen his withdrawal, Paul rebuked Cephas with a saying that Jews should live as Jews and Gentiles as Gentiles (Gal 2:14). On account of his rebuke, Cephas turned the back on him. This means that there was no repentance and forgiveness between them at all. The concept of atonement is unlikely to be related here. In addition, this is also related to the question of whether the Jews regard Gentiles as the people of God or not. The topic of salvation is likely to be related here. Thus, Paul would bring some change for the Gentiles even in the concept of salvation. Of course, at that time, there would not yet have been an opportunity to develop it. Nevertheless, this was an event that foreshadowed a significant change for Paul with regard to the concept of redemption and salvation.

B. THE SECOND MISSIONARY TRIP

It was not until the middle of the second missionary trip that Paul derived the concept of redemption and salvation from the Damascus and Jerusalem traditions. Before the challenge against him, salvation referred to becoming the people of God by observing the teachings of Jesus and the Law without any reference to redemption. Having faced the challenge of some Gentiles, Paul enhanced the interpretation of redemption and salvation in light of the death of Christ on cross. The stronger challenge he experienced, the more closely Paul related redemption and salvation to the death of Christ. In the meantime, Christianity was born among the Gentiles.

Thess(A)

Paul treated the issue of salvation from an apocalyptic viewpoint in Thess(A). This was made when he did not know that the apostles of Jerusalem had decided to send representatives to the Gentile churches after the theological controversy in Antioch. It seems that Paul delivered his instruction on salvation without any comment on redemption based on the Jerusalem tradition.

Jesus the Son of God is indirectly described as a transcendental figure. According to Paul, Jesus the Son of God will come from heaven and deliver people from the coming wrath (1 Thess 1:10). Hereby, the word "deliver" is used for the meaning of salvation. The deliverance from the coming wrath is reminiscent of what John proclaimed in Q (Q^1 3:7). The term "wrath" is commonly used in an eschatological context. However, there are differences between the two texts. First, while John did not introduce the agent who would make people avoid the coming wrath, Paul portrayed Jesus the Son of God as the deliverer of people from it. Second, whereas the "coming wrath" means the wrath to come in Q, it means that the wrath of God was coming at the time of writing the letter in Thess(A). This indicates that Paul had a more impending eschatological view than John. In addition, as already discussed in chapter 2, Paul presented the Son of God against the backdrop of the Son of Man appearing in the sky at the end of world as written in Q (Q^3 17:24). This indicates that Paul revealed his soteriological understanding by combining the texts originated in Q. Paul was at a level of understanding the salvation of people by the Son of God against the backdrop of Jewish concept that people should be delivered from the coming wrath by the Son of Man. Then, it can be said that although Paul had suffered a painful separation from Cephas in Antioch, he was still dependent upon the Jerusalem tradition represented by Q at the time of writing Thess(A).

Paul listed various sins committed by Jews. Having used the participle form of expression from a grammatical viewpoint, he pointed out their sins as follows: killing the Lord Jesus and the prophets, driving Paul and his companions out, displeasing God, being hostile to all men, and prohibiting Paul from speaking of salvation to the Gentiles (1 Thess 2:15–16). This indicates that Paul took their sins seriously. However, how to be forgiven is not told in this context; in addition, Paul did not even declare the forgiveness of their sins. It seems that Paul has not been theologically mature in this matter. In other words, redemption was not seriously taken into account yet. On the contrary, the sins of the Gentiles are not mentioned. Since Paul turned his back on Cephas and Barnabas in Antioch, he had to refrain from speaking unpleasantly to the Thessalonians to get them on his side. It can be said that Paul's pointing out the sins of Jews resembles that of John described in Q (Q^1 3:7). This shows that Paul still followed the Jerusalem tradition with regard to the matter of sin at the time of writing Thess(A).

The issue of salvation is mentioned in connection with the sins of the Jews. According to Paul, the Jews heaped up their sins and suffered the wrath of God because they had prohibited him from speaking of salvation to the Gentiles (1 Thess 2:16). It can be said that sin leads people to the wrath of God, which is in contrast with salvation. In this context, salvation is passively defined in that people are not subjected to the wrath of God. However, Paul did not explain how to be forgiven sins nor how to be saved in detail. It seems that there was no need for Paul to develop the concept of redemption and salvation in connection with Jesus Christ at the time of writing Thess(A).

Having not acknowledged the decision of the apostles of Jerusalem to send representatives to the Gentile churches, Paul reflected in Thess(A) what he had learned with regard to sins and salvation. Paul was dependent upon Pharisaic Judaism and the Jerusalem tradition. It seems that he did not yet face any threat severe enough to make him change his view on salvation. No concept of redemption appears in Thess(A).

Cor(A)

Paul gave a glimpse of redemption and salvation in Cor(A). This is dealt with in indirect connection with Christ from the perspective of Judaism. It seems that Paul did not develop his interpretation of redemption and salvation much in connection with Christ at the early days of the second missionary trip.

Paul showed a Jewish view of salvation. This is found in the saying that the Lord Jesus Christ would keep the Corinthians strong to the end, so that they would be blameless on his day (1 Cor 1:8). It seems that a minimal role was attributed to Christ for the blamelessness of the Corinthians. The word "blameless" refers to the condition of the Corinthians as the saved people of God. It is believed to have been described from a Jewish perspective of those who would be saved in sequence of the mentioning of deliverance from the coming wrath in Thess(A) (1 Thess 1:10). As such, Paul seems to have maintained a Jewish perspective on the state of salvation even during the early days of his second missionary trip.

Fornication is treated in association with sin. Having mentioned that the body is a member of Christ (1 Cor 6:15), Paul says, "All other sins a man commits are outside his body, but he who sins sexually sins against his own body" (6:18). The Corinthians are advised not to commit sexual immorality in their body because it is a member of Christ. This is the first case that Paul dealt with the issue of sin in connection with Christ. The spiritual unity with Christ is more precious than sexual intercourse with prostitutes. As the Law prohibits people from committing sexual immorality (Exod 20:14; Deut 5:18), Paul taught the Corinthians not to commit the sin of fornication. This indicates that he maintained the Jewish perspective on the matter of sin at the time of writing Cor(A). However, nothing is said about how to be forgiven of sins. In this respect, it seems premature to expect the concept of atonement.

Paul then presented the concept of salvation with the image of the temple. This is detected in the saying, "Do you know that your body is a temple of the Holy Spirit, who is in you, whom you have received from God? You are not your own; you were bought at a price [ἠγοράσθητε]" (1 Cor 6:19–20). As already known, Jews used to offer a sacrifice of an animal bought at a price at the temple of Jerusalem as the people of God. It seems that Paul tried to describe that the Corinthians were bought at a price to be the people of God. However, Paul was silent about what had been paid for them. The context informs readers that God offered Christ as the sacrifice by which he bought them. If my argument is acceptable, Paul presented the salvific role of Christ at a basic level. At this moment, it is also to be noted that sin offering and guilt offering could be related with the issue of "bought at a price." If Paul used the expression "bought at a price" with the sin offering or guilt offering in mind, we can catch a glimpse of the concept of forgiveness of sins here. In this regard, Paul applied the Jewish concept of atonement to the Gentile Corinthians at a basic level.[1]

There was no external shock that made Paul unfold his view on redemption and salvation at the time of writing Cor(A). It seems that he relied upon the Jewish tradition about them. Although he turned the back on Cephas in Antioch, it seems that he was not hostile to the Jewish tradition yet. Since he did not know that they had decided to send representatives to the Gentile churches, he was not nervous with the apostles of Jerusalem either.

Cor(B)

Paul dealt with sin and salvation several times in Cor(B). While redemption is scarcely mentioned, salvation is elaborated a couple of times in association with Christ. It seems that although Paul had heard of news about the visit of Cephas to Corinth, he was not aware of side effects that would result in among the Corinthians.

The salvation of a fornicator is discussed in parallel with his destruction. According to Paul, while the body [σάρξ] was destroyed, the spirit [πνεῦμα] would be saved on the day of the Lord Jesus (1 Cor 5:5). The salvation of the spirit is a new topic and offers several issues to be taken into account. First, Paul adopted the word "body" [σάρξ] in association with fornication. It was defined as sin committed in the physical body [σῶμα] in Cor(A) (6:18). The difference between them is not clear; however, it seems that Paul was in the process of developing the concept of the body [σάρξ, flesh] associated with the sin of fornication. Second, although the salvation of the spirit is mentioned in contrast with the destruction of the body, how to be forgiven sins is not mentioned in Cor(B). Third, the concept of salvation is not defined in detail yet. It seems that, based on the description written in Thess(A) (1 Thess 1:10) and Cor(A) (1 Cor 1:8), the salvation of the spirit refers to deliverance from the coming wrath on the day of the Lord Jesus Son of God on account of blamelessness. At any rate, how to be saved is not described either. Fourth, no specific role was given to Christ for the forgiveness of sins and the salvation of spirit in this context. This means that even when writing Cor(B) Paul relied

---

1. Conzelmann, *I Corinthians*, 113. Barrett argues that the concept of emancipation seems to originate from the Hebrew Bible (Exod 6:6; 13:13; Ruth 4:4f; Ps 103:4; Isa 63:1, and etc.) (*First Epistle*, 152).

on Pharisaic Judaism and the Jerusalem tradition represent by Q for the description of salvation.

Paul treated the salvation of a married couple. It was forbidden for a wife of faith to divorce her unbelieving husband, and the vice versa (1 Cor 7:12–16). Paul tried to prevent the Corinthians from divorce as much as he could because a husband or wife of faith could save his or her unbelieving spouse. No definition is described in regard to salvation, and no role is given to Christ for their salvation yet. There is only an exhortation to do according to the will of God (7:17). It can be then said that, based on the instruction of previous letters, salvation still meant the deliverance from the wrath of God on the day of the Lord Jesus due to their blamelessness. This implies that Paul was still dependent upon the Jewish tradition with regard to salvation at the time of writing Cor(B). Although Paul had heard of news about the visit of Cephas to Corinth, he apparently did not abandon the Jewish perspective of salvation.

Sin is handled in connection with married couples in an ascetic life. According to Paul, if a virgin [παρθένος] marries, she has not sinned (1 Cor 7:28, 36). Paul spoke of virgins who had pledged to maintain the ascetic life with their spouses for the sake of her sanctification of marriage.[2] If the word "marry" refers to having sexual intercourse with one's spouse, the expression of committing sin refers to breaking the vow of abstinence to keep their body holy before of God. However, Paul allowed virgins and their husbands break the vow when they were out of control with sexual desire. However, no role was assigned to Christ with regard to the forgiveness of sin in this context. This indicates that Paul did not think of redemption through Jesus Christ yet at the time of writing Cor(B). It is, however, unclear on which tradition Paul was dependent to make this kind of exhortation for the couples of holy marriage.

Paul referred to sin in association with the food offered to idols. It is said that everyone who commits sins against their brother and wounds their weak conscience commits sins against Christ (1 Cor 8:12). Paul established a relationship between Christ and the Corinthians by equating the sin against the weak with that against Christ. This reminds readers of the fourth petition of the Lord's Prayer in Q. Jesus taught that forgiving those who have sinned against "you" is the basis for asking God to forgive "your" sins (Q^2 11:4). It seems that Paul changed the relationship between God and human beings reflected in Q to that of Christ and the

---

2. Hurd defines a "virgin" [παρθένος] as a woman married without a sexual life for the preservation of purity in front of God (*Origin*, 172–78).

Corinthians in Cor(B). Paul applied it to the Gentiles with some modification. It is, however, noteworthy that no role was attributed to Christ for the forgiveness of sins yet. In addition, the concept of redemption is not found in this context. If my argument is acceptable, this shows that Paul was still dependent upon the Jerusalem tradition represented by Q with regard to the forgiveness of sins at the time of writing Cor(B).

Salvation is linked with the benefit of others. According to Paul, one should live for the benefit of others, so that they might be saved (1 Cor 10:33). It seems that salvation has come to the point of reaching a stage where a weak person can freely decide without being distracted by conscience. Salvation is simply described as taking place in relationship with others. In addition, no role was attributed to Christ with regard to the salvation of those working for the benefit of others. Paul had not developed his theological view on the salvific role of Christ yet. Salvation seems to be defined from a practical rather than a theological perspective in connection with the case of those who are weak in faith. If my argument is acceptable, it seems that Paul still had a Jewish view on salvation at the time of writing Cor(B).

Paul treated the issue of sin in connection with the resurrection of Christ. It is said, "And if Christ has not been raised, your faith is futile; you are still in your sins" (1 Cor 15:17). Paul implied that faith in the resurrection of Christ is a way that the Corinthians could be forgiven their sins. In this case, the resurrection of Christ is more focused than the person of Christ as the contents of faith. It seems that one's belief in the resurrection of Christ was the foundation upon which one can ask God for the remission of sins. This kind of instruction appears for the first time here; however, the notion of redemption does not appear. Thus, it can be concluded that the concept of redemption was not well established in connection with Christ at the time of writing Cor(B).

Paul dealt with the issues of sin and salvation in Cor(B) more frequently than in any other letters examined before. This reflects the situation that the number of those committing sins increased among the Corinthians. However, salvation is not specifically described, and the notion of redemption is absent. No specific role was assigned to Christ with regard to the forgiveness of sins and the salvation of people. Although Paul had known the division among the Corinthians that resulted from the visit of Cephas as a representative of the apostles of Jerusalem, Paul did not develop his views on redemption and salvation much in response to the Jewish instruction of Cephas at the time of writing Cor(B).

Thess(B)

Paul mentioned salvation for the first time in Thess(B). Having heard of news that the Thessalonians were shaken by those come from Jerusalem for a while but decided to stay in the gospel of Christ, he was grateful for them. So he was able to write about the salvation of being with the Lord.

The noun form of "salvation" is employed for the first time in Thess(B) among the Pauline letters. This appears in the expression of "the hope of salvation as a helmet" (1 Thess 5:8). Having set it in parallel with "faith and love as a breastplate," salvation is described in terms of soldier's gear in a militant atmosphere. It was employed for the spiritual combat between the Thessalonians and those sent by the apostles of Jerusalem (3:4–5); however, it ended with a decision that the Thessalonians would stay firmly in the gospel of Christ (3:6–7). It is, however, noteworthy that Paul did not specifically define the concept of salvation yet. Having thought of the expression of the "sons of day and light" (5:4–5), Paul used it for the saved status of the Thessalonians. This shows that Paul enhanced the expression for the saved in terms of metaphor.

Paul directly linked salvation with the Lord Jesus Christ for the first time. This is found in the saying that God appointed the Thessalonians not to suffer wrath but to receive salvation through the Lord Jesus Christ (1 Thess 5:9). "Salvation" is used in the form of a noun again in contrast with "wrath" definitely for the first time. Then, salvation refers to deliverance from the wrath that was already mentioned in Thess(A) (1:10; 2:16). In addition, it can be inferred from the context that salvation means to live together with Christ (5:10; cf. 4:14–17). It is, however, noteworthy that salvation has been given to people by the death of the Lord Jesus Christ "for us." Christ is definitely presented as an agent working on the salvation of people. If my argument is acceptable, it can be said that Paul tried to keep a distance from the Jerusalem tradition and moved toward the Damascus tradition in which the death of Christ occupies an important place. In this way, Paul developed his interpretation of salvation in response to the challenge of those sent by the apostles of Jerusalem.

The issue of salvation occupies an important place in Thess(B). This is because salvation was understood in connection with the death of the Lord Jesus Christ for the first time. Salvation refers to the life of being with him after deliverance from wrath. In this respect, Paul enhanced his soteriological interpretation. However, no concept of redemption has been established fully yet. Having known that the Thessalonians stayed firmly in the gospel in spite of the seduction of those sent by the apostles of Jerusalem, Paul began to keep a distance from the Jerusalem tradition in terms of his soteriological perspective. This shows that Christianity was conceived among the Gentiles.

Phil(A)

Paul introduced Jesus Christ as a savior for the first time in Phil(A). It is noteworthy that the transcendental aspect has been reduced in response to the challenge of those sponsored by the apostles of Jerusalem. This signaled the birth of Christianity.

The righteousness of God is mentioned in connection with Christ. Paul claimed that the righteousness of God is only "by [διά] the faith of Christ" (Phil 3:9). Since the righteousness of God is inseparable from being the people of God, it refers to the status of being saved. It is then necessary to pay attention to the phrase "faith of Christ" with a reference to the faith that Christ had and showed. While Paul used the phrase "through [διά] our Lord Jesus Christ" for the salvation of people in Thess(B) (1 Thess 5:9), it was changed to the "faith of Christ" as a means of salvation in Phil(A). In this respect, Paul specifically focused on Christ in terms of faith for the salvation of people. The observance of the Law was not presented as a way to obtain the righteousness of God anymore. This implies that Paul began to negate the Jewish tradition on account of the challenge of those sent by the apostles of Jerusalem.

Paul used the word "savior" for the first time in connection with Jesus Christ. This is manifested in the description that Paul and the Philippians were waiting for the savior coming "from there" (Phil 3:20). The savior is none other than the Lord Jesus Christ transcendentally coming from heaven. Whereas the verb "save" was adopted in Cor(B) (1 Cor 5:5; 7:16) and the noun "salvation" was used in Thess(B) (1 Thess 5:8, 9), Paul employed the word "savior" for the first time in Phil(A). The more Paul was exposed to the challenge of those sent by the apostles of Jerusalem, the more definitely Christ was portrayed as an agent working for the salvation of people. This shows that Paul enhanced his soteriological interpretation in response to the circumstances of the recipients of his letters.

A turning point was made in terms of his soteriological interpretation in Phil(A). This appears in the fact that the righteousness "by the faith of Christ" and the "savior" coming from heaven were used for the first time. This shows that although Paul maintained the Jerusalem tradition with regard to the coming of a messianic figure, he gradually focused more on the Damascus tradition with regard to the salvific role of Christ, who had died for the salvation of people. In other words, having responded to the challenge of those sent by the apostles of Jerusalem, Paul put forth Christ as the model in terms of faith for the salvation of people. It seems that the stronger the challenge against Paul was getting, the more creatively Paul attributed a soteriological role to Christ. However, no redemptive role was assigned to Christ yet. In this respect, Christianity was born to the Gentiles from a soteriological viewpoint at the time of writing Phil(A).

Cor(C)

Paul suggested the death of Christ on cross as a way of redemption and salvation in Cor(C). The redemption and salvation of people were so important that Paul explained them in various ways. They were made in response to the challenge of some Corinthians sponsored by the apostles of Jerusalem.

The cross of Christ is inseparable from salvation. According to Paul, the message of the cross is the power of God to those who are destined to be saved (1 Cor 1:18), and Christ is portrayed as the crucified one (1:23). This means that the death of Christ on the cross is the gateway to the salvation of people. Paul already linked the death of Christ to salvation in Thess(B) (1 Thess 5:9–10) and the cross of Christ indirectly with "savior" in Phil(A) (Phil 3:18, 20). Thus, Paul was able to connect the crucifixion of Christ directly with "those who are saved" in Cor(C). This is adopted for the first time here according to Paul's meticulous plan from a soteriological perspective. Paul presented the cross of Christ as an alternative for the salvation of people after he had directly faced the challenge of some Corinthians sponsored by the apostles of Jerusalem. It seems that Paul was critically getting away from the Jerusalem tradition to the Damascus tradition with regard to the interpretation of the death of Christ in terms of the salvation of people.

Paul presented Christ Jesus in connection with redemption. This is found in the saying that he became "for us" the wisdom of God—that is, righteousness, holiness, and redemption [ἀπολύτρωσις] (1 Cor 1:30). The term "redemption" appears for the first time here. A similar concept was already found with the usage of "buy at a price" [ἀγοράζω] in Cor(A) (1 Cor 6:20). Thus, Paul was able to use the word ἀπολύτρωσις in connection with Christ Jesus in Cor(C). It is, however, unclear from what or whom people were freed by Christ. In addition, the issue of sin does not appear in connection with the term "redemption" yet. It is, however, important that the cross and crucifixion of Christ Jesus were used with redemption for the first time.

Christ is related with salvation again. Having introduced the parable of a house built on a foundation of Christ and its interpretation, Paul mentioned the salvation of those who had built the house with wood, straw, or hay to be burned up (1 Cor 3:10–14). It is said, "If it is burned up, he will suffer loss; he himself will be saved, but only as one escaping through the flames" (3:15). This reminds readers of the parable of two builders written in Q (Q³ 6:48–49). The words "wise" and "house" commonly appear in both texts; in addition, the contrast of destiny is clearly shown between the survived and the destroyed. There are, however, differences in that Paul mentioned the materials used to build the house rather than the foundations upon which the houses were built. This shows Paul's modification of previous tradition into his own interpretation with regard to eschatological destiny. In this respect, Paul was getting away from the Jerusalem tradition represented by Q to the Damascus tradition since he had experienced the challenge of some Corinthians sponsored by the apostles of Jerusalem. Then, it seems that Paul defined salvation as surviving the eschatological judgment. It seems to be another expression of deliverance from the coming wrath of God.

Paul referred to the image of a sacrifice of an animal again. It is said, "You were bought at a price [ἠγοράσθητε]" (1 Cor 7:23). They were bought to be the free slaves of Christ. The image of a sacrifice of an animal was already mentioned in connection with the sin of fornication in Cor(A) (6:20). On the other hand, Paul suggested freedom from slavery by the Lord Christ in Cor(C). While Paul did not clearly portray Christ as the agent of emancipation in Cor(A), he did in Cor(C). In this respect, Paul inherited the Jewish concept of "bought at a price" and applied it to Christ. It is necessary to note that, having used the words "redemption" and "buying at a price" in sequence, Paul imposed a redemptive role upon the Lord Christ in Cor(C) (1:30; 7:23). In the meantime, Paul revealed the intention to be completely independent from the apostles of Jerusalem.

At last, salvation is described in close connection with redemption. This is found in the description that, having argued for salvation by believing the gospel, Paul presented the death of Christ "for our sins" according to the Scriptures (1 Cor 15:1–3). The concept of redemption—that is, the death of Christ for the forgiveness of sins—appears for the first time here. Having modified the death of Christ "for us" (1 Thess 5:10) to "for our sins" (1 Cor 15:3), Paul described Christ as the redeemer. This is how Paul completed his view on the death of Christ with a reference to redemption, which reminds readers of the sacrifice of the guilt offering mentioned in Isaiah 53:10. In this respect, Paul's interpretation of the death of Christ in light of redemption reaches its culmination in Cor(C) so far. It is, however, to be remembered that the nature of sin has not been elaborated.

Paul advocated the redemptive as well as salvific role of Christ in Cor(C). This is because he could not help but respond to the challenge of some Corinthians sponsored by the apostles of Jerusalem. The death of Christ on the cross was presented as an alternative to the Jewish instruction in terms of redemption and salvation. In consequence, Paul showed himself to be independent from the Jerusalem tradition represented by Q. As a result, the Christian teaching was further expanded as time went by.

Galatians

Paul critically dealt with redemption and salvation in Galatians. They were treated with a strong tone in response to the challenge of the Galatians sponsored by the apostles of Jerusalem. Having been independent from the Jerusalem tradition, Paul developed an interpretation of redemption and salvation.

First, references to redemption and salvation appear in combination. According to Paul, Christ gave himself "for our sins" to rescue "us" from this evil age according to the will of God (Gal 1:4). There are a couple of points to be compared with what was written in previous letters. First, the expression of "Christ gave himself" is another form of "Christ died" as written in Cor(C) (1 Cor 15:3). In Galatians, Paul emphasized more of the will of Christ to give himself. Second, the phrase "for our sins" is also found in Cor(C) (1 Cor 15:3). Having mentioned that Christ gave himself "for our sins," Paul referred to the redemptive death of

Christ in Galatians again. Third, the phrase "rescue us from this present evil age" reminds readers of "deliver us from the coming wrath" in Thess(A) (1 Thess 1:10). Having used the phrase "present evil age," Paul added an apocalyptic mood to the salvation of people. In this respect, Paul enhanced his theological interpretation of redemption and salvation further in Galatians than in Thess(A) and Cor(C).

Paul presented the righteousness of God by the faith of Jesus Christ. Whereas the works of the Law were declared as the way to make one a sinner, the faith of Jesus Christ was suggested as the way to make one righteous before God (Gal 2:16–17). Having mentioned the righteousness of God, Paul launched the issue of being the people of God. The righteousness of God by the faith of Christ was already argued for in Phil(A) (Phil 3:9). When the challenge of the Galatians reached its culmination, Paul heightened the salvific role of Christ for the Gentiles. In consequence, Paul enhanced a soteriological interpretation in relation to the Galatians challenging him most severely.

The issue of redemption appears again. According to Paul, Christ "bought back [ἐξαγοράζω]" people from the curse of the Law by becoming a curse for them (Gal 3:13). It is important that the active form of the verb is used here instead of the passive form adopted in Cor(A) (1 Cor 6:20) and Cor(C) (7:23). It seems that in Galatians Paul wanted to describe the active role of Christ, who had given himself for the redemption and salvation of people. In addition, Paul used a more critical term, "curse," rather than "sin," from which people should be redeemed. This shows that Paul tried to describe the redemptive role of Christ in a different way. Having relied upon the Damascus tradition that dealt with the death of Christ, Paul developed a theological interpretation in terms of redemption.

Finally, Paul portrayed the Son of God as the redeemer. This is found in the saying that God sent his Son born under the Law in order to buy back those who had been under the Law (Gal 4:4–5). It seems that, having adopted the words "buy back" and "Law" already used in Galatians 3:13, Paul tried to speak of Christ emancipating people from the curse of the Law again. Thus, it can be said that emancipation paves the way to become the "people of God," represented by the description that they received the authority to be the sons of God (4:5). In this respect, emancipation from the curse of the Law is closely related with the salvation of people in Galatians.

A significant advance was made in terms of redemption and salvation in Galatians. Paul's view on them shows a contradiction with the Jewish view in that the death of Christ was understood in contrast with the Law. The stronger the challenge Paul faced, the more focus was given to Christ the Son of God in terms of redemption and salvation. Thus, it can be said that while Paul announced the beginning of Christianity with a reference to salvation in Thess(B), Christian instruction was profoundly formed with references to the redemptive and salvific role of Christ in Galatians. This indicates Paul's independence from the apostles of Jerusalem theologically.

Cor(D)

Paul mentioned salvation twice in Cor(D). A little amount of information is found to draw its concept from the context; on the other hand, there is no mention of sin. This is because he desperately worked on the restoration of his relationship with the Corinthians.

It is necessary to take a look at two texts that include the word "salvation." First, salvation is set in parallel with consolation. This is found in the saying that Paul had been distressed for the consolation and salvation of the Corinthians (2 Cor 1:6). The parallel informs that salvation is to be understood in close connection with consolation. The reason Paul offered consolation was due to his effort to restore his relationship that had been deteriorated by the challenge of some Corinthians. This implies that Paul used the concept of salvation while taking into account the circumstances of the Corinthians.

Second, salvation is mentioned in connection with repentance. According to Paul, "Godly sorrow brings repentance that leads to salvation and leaves no regret, but worldly sorrow brings death" (2 Cor 7:10). It seems that salvation is to be understood in close connection with life contrasted with death. Life was already mentioned several times in contrast with death in the previous letters; however, it is noteworthy that salvation appears in connection with repentance in Cor(D). Of course, repentance leads one to the forgiveness of sins by God. In this respect, salvation is vaguely related to the forgiveness of sins. It seems that Paul used a fairly modest expression with regard to redemption and salvation.

It is necessary to see why Paul did not say much of salvation in Cor(D). There is no reason other than his intention to avoid a debate on it while trying to restore the relationship with the Corinthians. If he had discussed those issues, he could have been forced to deal with the Law and fall into controversy with the Corinthians. In any case, Paul could not pay attention to anything other than the restoration of his relationship with the Corinthians. This is a good case to show Paul's way of response to the changing circumstances of the recipients of his letters.

Cor(E)

Paul also referred to redemption and salvation in Cor(E). It appears in connection with his ministry. By this, he showed his pride in working for the Corinthians. This is mentioned with a hope to be reconciled with them.

The word "salvation" is used in connection with the ministry of Paul. It is said that he was the fragrance of Christ before God to those destined to be saved and those destined to be destroyed (2 Cor 2:15). In similar manner, it is said that he was the smell of life to those destined to life and that of death to those destined to death (2:16). The contrast between salvation and destruction reminds readers of Cor(C), in which the "message of cross" is defined as the means of salvation for both those destined to life and those destined to destruction (1 Cor 1:18). Then, later in Cor(D), the contrast between salvation and destruction makes readers think of eternal life contrasted with death (2 Cor 7:10). Thus, Paul was able to set salvation and life in contrast with destruction and death in Cor(E). This reveals that Paul understood salvation in light of eternal life.

Redemption appears in connection with salvation. According to Paul, God made Christ, who had been without sin, to be sin for people, so that in him they might become the righteousness of God (2 Cor 5:21). This means that the Corinthians could become the people of God through the sinless Christ. With this, Paul made readers think of the death of Christ "for our sins" as written in Cor(C) (1 Cor 15:3) and Galatians (Gal 1:4). In consequence, in Cor(E) Paul used an appeasing expression for redemption with a reference to the sinless Christ instead of his death. In addition, the phrase "righteousness of God" is used with a reference to the saved status as already mentioned in Phil(A) (Phil 3:9) and Galatians (Gal 2:16). From the fact that sin is set in confrontation with "righteousness of God," it can be inferred that Paul would like to speak of salvation given through the sinless Christ. In this respect, Paul described salvation as being accomplished after redemption at the time of writing Cor(E).

Paul then mentioned the day of salvation. It is said, "I tell you, now is the time of divine favor, now is the day of salvation" (2 Cor 6:2). Having quoted a verse from Isaiah ahead of this saying (Isa 49:8), Paul put forth the parallel between "time of divine favor" and "day of salvation." This informs that salvation is to be understood in light of divine favor. This kind of concept appears for the first time in Cor(E). It seems that Paul created the concept of salvation anew on the basis of biblical tradition. This shows that Paul was independent from the traditions inherited from Cephas and the religious predecessors. In this respect, Paul developed his own view on the salvation of people in response to the changing circumstances of the recipients of his letters.

Paul used more expressions for redemption and salvation in Cor(E). For this, the sinless Christ was introduced instead of his death on cross. Then, salvation is defined in connection with the favor of God. It seems that his concept of redemption and salvation was completely independent from the traditions that Paul had received. In this respect, Paul developed his theological interpretation with regard to redemption and salvation.

Cor(F)

Paul did not unfold the teachings on redemption and salvation in Cor(F). This seems to be because some Corinthians continued to challenge Paul. In this respect, Paul's teachings on redemption and salvation seem to have lost power for the Corinthians.

Having announced the third visit to Corinth, Paul spoke in a strong tone. He threatened to punish them; however, he made no mention of their redemption or salvation. In a situation where they constantly challenged him, Paul had to teach them about redemption and salvation. However, the Corinthians could not afford to accept it. This refers to Paul's failure to attach the meaning of atonement and salvation to the cross of Christ in Cor(F). In this way, it seems that the situation had deteriorated to the point where Paul could not bear the challenge of some Corinthians.

Paul's teachings on atonement and salvation eventually lost power for the Corinthians. They probably wanted to become the people of God by Judaization. In this respect, Paul presented a typical example of Gentiles who went to the wrong direction.

Summary

Paul referred to redemption and salvation during his second missionary trip. It seems that while he was not aware of the decision made by the apostles of Jerusalem to refute the gospel, he used to explain the issue of salvation and forgiveness of sins separately. Having relied upon the Jerusalem tradition represented by Q during the first half of the second missionary trip, Paul described the salvific role of Jesus Christ coming from heaven to deliver people from the wrath of God. On the other hand, in the second half of the second missionary trip, Paul began to get away from the Jerusalem tradition; rather, he inclined to rely upon the Damascus tradition for an explanation of redemption and salvation. As time passed, the death of Christ on the cross was getting focused more as the means of redemption and salvation. This is the time when Christianity was born. Paul developed his interpretation of redemption and salvation against the challenge of some Gentiles sponsored by the apostles of Jerusalem. However, when the Corinthians would not accept his advice and rather kept challenging him, Paul reduced the frequency of mentioning redemption and salvation. Finally, he did not mention them anymore at the end of the second missionary trip. At any rate, it can be said that as redemption and salvation were described in connection with the death of Christ, the Christian instruction expanded.

C. THE THIRD MISSIONARY TRIP

Having related with Rome, Paul expressed a strong aspiration for the salvation of people. As he strengthened his concept of redemption, his account of salvation was further elaborated. However, Paul made adjustments in his theological expression, taking into account the surveillance of the Roman authorities.

Rom(A)

Paul referred to redemption and salvation in Rom(A). Their relationship with the cross of Christ was not mentioned in order to avoid the eyes of doubts of the Roman authorities. Having taken it into consideration, Paul changed the terms used for redemption and salvation in connection with Christ.

Salvation is inseparably associated with the gospel. According to Paul, the gospel "is the power of God for the salvation of everyone who believes" (Rom 1:16). Paul linked the power of God to the gospel that leads people to salvation. This is a more advanced argument compared to the description that the message of cross is connected to the power of God in Cor(C) (1 Cor 1:18). Although the object of belief is not clearly mentioned in Rom(A), it seems to refer to the gospel Paul would proclaim. This statement is reminiscent of what he had already mentioned in Cor(C), that everyone could be saved if they believe in the gospel (1 Cor 15:1–5). It is clear that Paul handed the gospel over to Aquila and Priscilla when they stayed in Ephesus (16:19). After they had returned to Rome, they established a church and taught the gospel to the members of church. Thus, Paul revealed his intention to say more about the gospel that he had developed for the salvation of people after they returned to Rome.

Paul addressed salvation in combination with redemption. This is revealed in the saying that Christ died for "us," sinners, and they would be saved in his life (Rom 5:8–10). Paul clearly stated that Christ died for the sinners who were to be saved. After Paul had introduced redemption and salvation through the death of Christ in combination for the first time in Galatians (Gal 1:4), he mentioned them again in a more developed form in Rom(A). First, the death of Christ was described in connection with redemption. This appears in the saying that Christ died for "us," sinners (Rom 5:8). This seems to be developed following the statement that Christ died "for our sins" as written in Cor(C) (1 Cor 15:3) and Galatians (Gal 1:4). In this way, Paul continued arguing for the redemptive death of Christ in Rom(A). Second, the death of Christ was laid as the foundation upon which the salvation of people could be explained. According to Paul, people could be righteous through the "blood" of Christ and be saved from wrath (Rom 5:9). Without doubt, the "blood" is another expression of the death of Christ, and the righteousness of God refers to the status of being saved to be his people. Then, the "blood" of Christ is closely related with the salvation of the Romans. Since the righteousness of God was mentioned in association with Christ in Phil(A) (Phil 3:9) and Galatians (Gal 2:16), Paul was able to take the matter of righteousness seriously in Rom(A). Third, salvation was understood as reconciliation with God through the death of Christ his Son (Rom 5:10). Those reconciled with God were defined as those who were saved in the life of the Son of God. Reconciliation with God was already introduced in Cor(E) (2 Cor 5:18–19). However, in Rom(A) Paul described it in association with salvation with a reference to deliverance from wrath and achievement of life in Christ the Son of God. In any case, Paul significantly developed his theological interpretation linking the death and resurrection of Christ to the redemption and salvation of people. There is no mention of "cross" or "crucifixion" in Rom(A). Rather, Paul used the term "blood," lest the members of the Roman church be mistaken for traitors against the Roman Empire. This shows that Christianity had been formed on the basis of a theological interpretation of redemption and salvation through the "blood" of Christ.

Salvation is described in association with the resurrection of Christ the Son of God. According to Paul, Christ the Son has reconciled to God those who become enemies, and they will be saved because of his resurrection (Rom 5:10). Paul understood the death of Christ in connection with reconciliation and his resurrection in association with salvation. Reconciliation between God and human beings through the redemptive death of Christ was already mentioned in Cor(E) (2 Cor 5:18–21); however, in Rom(A) Paul heightened the redemptive and salvific role of Christ in connection with reconciliation between God and human beings through his resurrection. In this way, Paul enhanced his theological view on the redemption and salvation of people as time went by.

In Rom(A), Paul described the redemption and salvation through the "blood" of Christ Jesus. This seems to be the core of the gospel that Paul wanted to convey to the Romans. They received instructions on redemption and salvation from Aquila and Priscilla, who had been unable to convey more than what was recorded in Cor(C). Aquila and Priscilla encountered it while staying with Paul in Ephesus of Asia. They seem to have been unaware of his teachings about the redemption and salvation developed later; for instance, what was developed in Galatians. In this way, Paul contributed to the formation of Christian teaching on redemption and salvation.

Rom(B)

Paul also dealt with redemption in association with salvation in Rom(B). For this, the "blood" of Christ is used in connection with the "sacrifice of atonement." It seems that Paul used the Jewish tradition for the explanation of redemption at that time.

The righteousness of God is defined as the status achieved through the redemption in Christ Jesus. Paul said that although all men have sinned, they can obtain the righteousness of God by the faith of Jesus Christ; then, all will be justified freely by the grace of God that is redemption [ἀπολύτρωσις] in Jesus Christ (Rom 3:22–24). Redemption is presented as the way of leading people to the righteousness of God, which refers to the status of being the people of God. Redemption was already mentioned in connection with salvation resulted from the message of the cross of Christ, who was the wisdom of God, in Cor(C) (1 Cor 1:30). Then, the issue that all human beings are sinners was already treated in connection with the love of God by giving his Son for them in Rom(A) (Rom 5:8–10). Thus, having mentioned it in connection with sin in Rom(B), Paul was able to present redemption as the main step for the salvation of people. In this way, Paul tried to understand the righteousness of God in connection with redemption.

Paul treated redemption in connection with salvation again. This is found in the saying that God presented Jesus Christ as a "sacrifice of atonement [ἱλαστήριον]" through faith in his blood in order to demonstrate the righteousness of God, because he had left the sins committed beforehand unpunished (Rom 3:25). It is noteworthy that the term ἱλαστήριον is used for the first time in connection with sins. This is used to refer to the redemptive role of Christ, which leads people to the righteousness of God. In this way, Paul associated redemption through Christ with the salvation of people. The phrase "his [Christ's] blood" is adopted once again since its first appearance in Rom(A) (Rom 5:9). Having mentioned the "blood" instead of the death of Christ on cross or crucifixion, Paul referred to the redemptive role of Christ for the salvation of people in Rom(B). This means that Paul theologically interpreted Christ as the one who had worked on the redemption and salvation of people.

There is a reason that the redemptive role of Christ was emphasized in Rom(B). It seems that the Romans raised a question after they had read Rom(A), in which the Law was defined as an entity that brings wrath and transgression (Rom 4:15). In response, having emphasized the negative role of the Law (3:20). Paul had to deal with the issue of sin for the redemptive role of Christ. In particular, he presented the blood of Christ rather than his cross or crucifixion as a means of redemption. This statement was made so that the members of the Roman church might avoid the suspicion of the Roman authorities. They should not be regarded as the traitors against the Roman Empire. In this respect, Paul enhanced his theological interpretation of redemption and salvation on the basis of the Damascus tradition, taking into account the situation that the Romans faced.

Rom(C)

Paul dealt with the redemptive role of Christ in close connection with salvation in Rom(C). It is important to observe that the spirit of God was introduced for the description of the adopted sons of God with a reference to the status of redeemed people. Paul made a significant contribution to the interpretation of redemption and salvation.

Salvation is dealt with in connection with sin. Paul said that while sin entered the world through one man and death came to all men through sin, the righteousness and life of God were given to many people by the obedience of Jesus Christ (Rom 5:12–19). Paul made a contrast between Adam and Jesus Christ, sin and righteousness, and death and life. Paul adopted an Adamic typology for the redemptive role of Christ. Since an Adamic typology was used in Cor(B) (1 Cor 15:22) and in Cor(C) (15:45), Paul was able to focus on the life given through Jesus Christ from a perspective of Adamic typology in Rom(C). Salvation refers to the status of living without sin as Adam was sinless in the garden of Eden before the fall. In this respect, Paul described the salvation of people resulting from the obedience of Christ.

Paul once again communicated salvation in connection with sin. This is revealed in the description that God sent his Son in the likeness of sinful man to be sin in order to give life and peace not to those who had lived according to the sinful nature, but to those who lived by the spirit of God (Rom 8:3–6). Paul presented the Son of God as the one coming to the world to free people from sin. This is reminiscent of Paul's statement that God made Christ, who had no sin, to be sin "for us" in Cor(E) (2 Cor 5:21). Thus, Paul was able to present Jesus Christ the Son of God as the redeemer in Rom(C). Then, the contrast of sin with life and peace shows that they represent the status of being redeemed. Having applied Adamic typology to the redeemed in Rom(C), "life" seems to have been established itself as an element of the saved with a reference to the eternal life promised in the garden of Eden. In this respect, Paul argued for the salvation of people resulting from the redemptive role of Christ.

Salvation is described in relation to hope in pain. It is said that, having groaned inwardly, Paul, as the first fruit of the spirit of God, waited eagerly for adoption as a son of God, which refers to the redemption [ἀπολύτρωσις] of his body (Rom 8:23–24). Paul described the redemption of one's body as a condition to be adopted as a son of God. Above all, adoption as a son of God reminds readers of Paul's statement that one can be a son of God after being redeemed [ἐξαγοράζω] from the curse of the Law and receiving the spirit to be the sons of God (Gal 4:5–6). However, having used the term ἀπολύτρωσις rather than ἐξαγοράζω and substituting "being an adopted son of God" for "being a son of God," Paul made it more generalized in Rom(C) than in Galatians to describe the concept of redemption. In addition, it is necessary to pay attention to the word "redemption [ἀπολύτρωσις]," which was already used in connection with Christ in Cor(C) (1 Cor 1:30) and Rom(B) (Rom 3:24). It is to be noted that redemption appears in association with the spirit of God in Rom(C). Especially, the phrase "the first fruit of the spirit" [τὴ ἀπαρχή τοῦ πνεύματος] is reminiscent of the word "first fruit" [ἀπαρχή], used for the resurrection of Christ in Cor(B) (1 Cor 15:23). This indicates that when Paul used the phrase "the first fruit of the spirit" in Rom(C), he understood the redemption of one's body in association with "life" given through resurrection. This shows that Paul began to take into account the spirit of God for the salvation of people.

It seems that Paul dealt with the redemption and salvation of people in Rom(C) in response to the critique raised by the Romans after they had read Rom(B), in which Paul insisted that the Law makes people realize their sins (Rom 3:20). Since the Romans raised critiques against his negative view on the Law in relation to sin, he had to answer them with a reference to the redemptive role of Christ. In addition, Paul provided them with a new role of the spirit of God for the salvation of people from a perspective of Adamic typology. In this respect, Paul enhanced his interpretation of the redemptive role of Christ for the salvation of people.

Rom(D)

Paul referred to salvation most often in Rom(D). He insisted on the salvation of Jews as well as Gentiles. This reflects that Paul took into consideration the continuous critiques of the Jewish members of the Roman church against his view on the redemption and salvation of people.

Paul showed the effort to work on the salvation of both Jews and Gentiles. This is seen in the description that, having described the righteousness of God allowed to the Gentiles, Paul mentioned the salvation of Jews (Rom 9:30—10:1). This indicates Paul's intention to lead everyone to the salvation of God. Thus, he finally made a conclusion to the role of Christ with a saying that he became the end of the Law for all those saved by faith (10:4). It seems that salvation refers to "being the people of God"; that is, the children of God (Rom 9:25–26). It is, however, noteworthy that redemption is not treated at all in this context. This seems to be because the Romans would not accept Paul's sophisticated instruction on the redemption of the body as written in Rom(C). Thus, Paul seemed to have described salvation on a level that did not disturb their religious self-esteem. In this respect, Paul provided the Romans with a theological interpretation taking into account the circumstances of the recipients of his letter.

Salvation is mentioned in connection with confession. According to Paul, if one confesses with his or her mouth that "Jesus is Lord" and believes in his or her heart that God raised Jesus from the dead, he or she will be saved (Rom 10:9–10). A parallel is found between confession of Jesus as Lord and belief in God raising him from the dead. Paul already treated the confession "Jesus is Lord" according to the spirit of God in Cor(C) (1 Cor 12:3); however, in Rom(D) it is presented as a way of being saved. This is a new instruction on salvation because belief in God who raised Jesus from the dead appears in the context of how to be saved. Paul already treated the resurrection of Christ the Son of God in association with salvation in Rom(A) (Rom 5:10). However, belief in God who raised Jesus from the dead is introduced as a way of leading people to salvation in Rom(D). This shows that Paul changed his view on the way of salvation. The focus moved from the death of Christ to God's ability to raise him from death.

Paul expressed a wish for the salvation of Jews and Gentiles again. This is seen in the description that, having mentioned the salvation come to the Gentiles as the result of the fall of Israel, Paul introduced God wanting to arouse his own people to envy and to save some of them (Rom 11:11–14). Although the concept of salvation does not appear in this context, it seems to refer to maintaining the status of the people of God. Whereas Paul quit explaining the concept of salvation from an eschatological perspective in Rom(D), he continued to link the issue of faith to salvation (11:20). Finally, he wrote of a desire that all Israel would be saved (11:26). This seems to be a description to thoroughly win the hearts of the Jewish members, who made up the majority of the Roman church. It seems that Paul tried to persuade them from a soteriological perspective in response to their critique against his instruction disparaging the Law. This shows Paul's active response to the changing circumstances of the recipients of his letter.

No redemptive role is imposed upon Christ in Rom(D). While emphasizing the salvation of the Gentiles, Paul slightly mentioned salvation of the Jews. He made a narrative far from the death of Christ on the cross or his crucifixion. Rather, he delivered an instruction on salvation in connection with confession of Jesus and belief in God who had the power to raise him. This probably reflects the fact that the Jews, who made up the majority of the Roman church, did not accept Paul's view.

Phil(B)

Paul also mentioned salvation in Phil(B). However, he did not specifically describe the concept or way of salvation. This seems to be because the Philippians already knew well the teachings of Paul on salvation.

Salvation is mentioned in association with the proclamation of the gospel. This is found in the description that, having rejoiced with the successful result of proclaiming Christ, Paul turned it out for his salvation through the prayers of the Philippians and the help given by the spirit of Jesus Christ (Phil 1:18–19). This reveals that the more Paul preached the gospel of Christ, the closer he got to salvation. However, the concept of salvation is not theologically defined; in addition, the redemptive role of Christ does not appear either. On the other hand, Paul was able to describe the spirit of Jesus Christ as an entity that could help people to reach salvation. This kind of description was possible for Paul because he already mentioned the spirit of God as working out the redemption and salvation of people in Rom(C). This means that as time passed Paul came to focus on what Christ was doing for the salvation of people. In this way, Paul presented a new interpretation of redemption and salvation in Phil(B).

Paul then explained how the Philippians had lived according to the gospel of Christ in connection with salvation. This is revealed in the description that standing "firm in one spirit, contending as one man for the faith of the gospel without being frightened in any way by those who oppose" is a sign for their salvation (Phil 1:27–28). The meaning of salvation is not defined in detail here; however, it seems to be described in opposition to destruction. Although it was difficult for Paul to win over a number of people by overcoming the challenge of opponents in the prison of Rome, he tried to build up people with the gospel of Christ. In this respect, salvation is characterized in contrast with destruction.

Finally, a wish for the salvation of the Philippians is revealed. According to Paul, they had to continue to work out their salvation with fear and trembling (Phil 2:12). The terms "fear" and "trembling" are used to describe the obedience to God. This makes readers think of Jesus Christ's obedience even to death on cross (2:8). The Philippians should have taken after the life of Jesus Christ shown to them. In this respect, the crucifixion of Jesus Christ is indirectly presented as a way of leading people to salvation.

Paul did not attribute any redemptive or salvific role to the crucifixion of Christ in Phil(B). This is because it was supposed to have been written in the prison of Rome and would have to pass through the surveillance of the Roman authorities. Rather, it seems that Paul was confident that the Philippians had stayed in the gospel.

Summary

Paul continued dealing with redemption and salvation during his third missionary trip. It is, however, noteworthy that, compared with what had been written during his second missionary trip, the concepts of redemption and salvation were not developed much. Above all, this is found in the fact that the cross or crucifixion of Christ Jesus does not appear as the means of redemption and salvation. Although the coming of Christ as a sinful man to the world for the forgiveness of sins of people was mentioned, his redemptive role was significantly reduced. In addition, salvation is to be understood in connection with life given after the resurrection of Christ. Having taken into account the Jewish members of the Roman church, Paul often dealt with the righteousness of God as the status of being saved. At any rate, Paul avoided using words that could make the Romans mistaken for traitors against the Roman Empire. Paul developed the teachings on redemption and salvation differently taking into account the changing circumstances of the recipients of his letters.

D. CONCLUSION

While preaching the gospel to the Gentiles, Paul spoke of redemption and salvation. The redemption and salvation of people were the most important element of the gospel he had preached. It seems that he communicated the instruction on salvation from a Jewish perspective at the beginning of his mission to the Gentiles. A typical example is found in the concept of judgment and reward on the day of the Lord Jesus Christ as reflected in Thess(A), Cor(A), and Cor(B). As such, Paul seems to have used it well without abandoning what he learned from Judaism. However, when the apostles of Jerusalem sent representatives to the Gentile churches and made the Gentiles challenge Paul, he presented the teaching that one can be righteous in front of God by the faith of Jesus Christ, who had died on cross for the remission of sins. Redemption leads people to salvation, which is being the people of God. This is getting stronger as reflected in Thess(B), Phil(A), Cor(C), Galatians, and Cor(E). Meanwhile, Christianity was born and began to grow among the Gentiles. For the Romans and Philippians, Paul described salvation from a wider perspective in that the salvation of people was connected with the resurrection of Jesus Christ in the letters written during the third missionary trip. In general, as the challenge against him grew, Paul showed a tendency to deviate from the Jerusalem tradition and relied more on the Damascus tradition to develop the concepts of redemption and salvation. Paul developed the concept of salvation into what he wanted to teach, having taken into account the circumstances of the recipients of his letters. In this respect, Christian instruction on redemption and salvation was expanded as time went by.

5

The Law

A GREAT NUMBER OF scholars have studied Paul's view on the Law for centuries. However, it has been a complicate matter that has not yet come to a definite conclusion. No one has provided a satisfactory answer with regard to his understanding of the Law. Nevertheless, how Paul's perception of the Law changed becomes evident when we go through the descriptions of it in chronological order. As we know, Paul was a Pharisee who had been faithful to the Law. However, something happened that made him change his view on it. As some Gentiles challenged him under the sponsorship of the apostles of Jerusalem, Paul changed his view from a positive attitude to a negative one. It is at that time that Christianity seems to have been born to the Gentiles. At any rate, Paul's negative view on the Law reached its peak in the second half of his second missionary trip. A similar phenomenon also appeared during his third missionary trip, when the critique of the Romans kept increasing. In the meantime, Christian instruction on the Law expanded.

A. THE FIRST MISSIONARY TRIP

Paul maintained a Jewish view on the Law at the beginning of the mission to the Gentiles. This is revealed by the fact that he retained the Pharisaic tradition even after receiving the revelation about the Son of God. It seems that Paul adhered to the Law while preaching the gospel under the influence of the apostles of Jerusalem, who had been in charge of composition of Q.

The Law was life itself to the Jews in that they tried to live according to the Law. It is clear that Paul located the reason for living in the Law as he confessed that he had been a faultless Pharisee by the Law (Phil 3:5–6). In addition, he was more enthusiastic about the traditions of his ancestors than any of those in his own age (Gal 1:14). These sayings signify that he had exerted all his might for the Law before he received the revelation of God. Without doubt, Paul had a positive view on the Law at that time.

Paul respected the Law even after he had received the revelation of God. This is supported by the fact that he went up to Jerusalem to meet Cephas around 38 CE, three years after he had received the revelation (Gal 1:16–19). It is reasonable to assume that Cephas delivered instruction on how to keep the core of the Law as written in Q; for instance, it was related with ritual cleansing and tithing (Q^3 11:39–42). The third redactor of Q criticized the Pharisees for not doing what they had taught. The redactor did not deny the Law; rather, he asked them to observe and interpret it correctly. Thus, the disciples of Jesus were willing to observe the Law sincerely. At that time, Paul would have accepted and tried to keep it. Even more, he was willing to keep the Law better than the disciples of Jesus.

What Paul taught about the Law during his first missionary trip is reflected in his letters. Although he delivered teachings on the Law with a favorable attitude, he seems to have exempted the Gentiles from circumcision. This is supported by the fact that having gone up to Jerusalem with Titus, a Greek, after the first missionary trip around 49 CE (Gal 2:3), he did not make him get circumcised. Although Paul asked the apostles of Jerusalem to allow the Gentiles to be exempted from circumcision, this does not mean that Paul wanted to make them free from the Law. Since Paul was passionate about the Law at the time of his second visit to Jerusalem, he did not change his view that the Gentiles should keep the Law in general. He simply petitioned for their exemption from circumcision and was able to obtain the consent of the apostles. If Paul had taken a negative position on the Law, they would not have allowed the Gentiles to be exempted from circumcision.

There was an opportunity for Paul to reaffirm his position on the Law during his stay in Jerusalem around 49 CE. There was a chance for Paul to learn more about the Law from the fourth redaction of Q, which is supposed to have been composed during the time of resistance against the Roman emperor Gaius Caligula's attempt to erect his statue in the temple of Jerusalem around 40–41 CE. As mentioned in chapter 1, this is reflected in the temptation story of Jesus, where three verses were quoted from Deuteronomy as the answer to the devil (Q^4 4:4, 8, 12; cf. Deut 6:13, 16; 8:3). This indicates that the fourth redactor of Q had put forth the observance of the Law. In addition, there are two more verses that introduce the articles of the Law (Q^4 14:5; 16:18) and a verse that includes the word "Law" (16:16–17). They provide readers with a reasonable assumption that the apostles of Jerusalem emphasized the observance of the Law more as time went by. For this reason, Paul must have pledged to be more loyal to the Law during his second stay in Jerusalem. This would have allowed Paul to gain more trust from the apostles of Jerusalem.

The theological controversy over the Gentile table in Antioch shows Paul's position on the Law. Cephas took part in the Gentile table; however, it is not clear whether he knew that Gentile food would be provided (Gal 2:12–13). When some people sent by James, the Lord's brother, arrived at the Antiochene church, Cephas stepped away from the table in fear of them. This is probably because he did not want to be criticized by James, who was a hard-liner with regard to the Law. This means that Cephas admitted to himself that he had violated the Law by participating in the Gentile table. However, having seen his withdrawal, Paul rebuked him for not following the gospel. This indicates that Paul prioritized the gospel as a standard of faith over the Law. It seems that Paul took a reserved position on the Law in relation to the Gentiles. Having heard the rebuke of Paul, Cephas was upset for two reasons. First, Paul was not authoritative enough to rebuke Cephas, who was one of the twelve apostles of Jerusalem. Second, Cephas seemed to think that by allowing the Gentiles to be exempted from circumcision Paul ignored the Law as a whole. This means that Paul prioritized the Gentiles over the apostles of Jerusalem. As a result, Cephas turned his back on Paul and left for Jerusalem. In this way, Paul and Cephas showed a different position on the Law in relation to the Gentiles in Antioch around 50 CE.

It seems that the apostles of Jerusalem followed up with sanctions against Paul. They decided to ask the Gentiles to observe the Law and to be circumcised. The apostles of Jerusalem seem to have been concerned about Paul's teaching that the Gentiles might not have to obey the Law. In addition, the Gentiles were asked to refuse the gospel that Paul had preached. Accordingly, the apostles of Jerusalem sent representatives to the Gentile churches that Paul had established in order to make the

Gentiles be Jewish. Without knowing of their decision, Paul set out on his second missionary trip. This made him suffer from some Gentiles.

B. THE SECOND MISSIONARY TRIP

Paul had taken a friendly position on the Law until the challenge of some Gentiles erupted against him in the middle of the second missionary trip. Having heard of news that those sent by the apostles of Jerusalem asked the Gentiles to keep the Law and made them stand against him, Paul began to take a negative posture toward the Law. This culminated in Galatians because the Galatians made him the most pained. Then, Paul continued to take a negative position on the Law in general.

Cor(A)

Having not mentioned the Law in Thess(A), Paul referred to it two times in Cor(A). It seems that Paul held a broad-range view on the Law and a friendly attitude toward it. Without knowing the decision that the apostles of Jerusalem asked the Gentiles to refute the gospel and his authority, Paul sent Cor(A) ahead of his second visit to Corinth.

The Law is mentioned for the first time in relation to tongues. According to Paul, "In the Law it is written: 'Through men of strange tongues and through the lips of foreigners I will speak to this people, but even then they will not listen to me'" (1 Cor 14:21). It seems to be quoted from Isaiah, which has been generally considered to belong to the Prophets (Isa 28:11). Nevertheless, Paul mentioned Isaiah as part of the Law. Then, a question arises whether Isaiah belongs to the Law or not. It seems that Paul thought of the term "Law" as a substitute for the Hebrew Scriptures. This implies that he treated the Law in a wide range of positive perspectives even at the time of writing Cor(A). As Paul had spiritual authority as the founder of the Corinthian church, he was able to deliver the lessons he had wanted. In this respect, Paul seems to have interpreted the Law as he wished at the beginning of his second missionary trip.

Paul once again referred to the Law in a broad sense. This is found in the saying, "As in all the congregations of the saints, women should remain silent in the churches. They are not allowed to speak, but must be in submission, as the law says" (1 Cor 14:34). The verse quoted here is not actually found in the Hebrew Scriptures. However, it has been believed to be written against the backdrop of Genesis (Gen 3:16). Of course, Genesis is the first book of the Torah, which means the Law. However, doubts arise as to whether the quoted phrase can be considered a legal provision or not. Nevertheless, Paul applied the word "Law" to it. This means that Paul portrayed a wide range of perspectives on the Law at the time of writing Cor(A).

Paul took a friendly attitude toward the Law at the beginning of his second missionary trip. He would have taken this position on his first missionary journey, too. This shows that his concept of the Law was not so rigid; rather, it seems to have been a little vague. At that time, there was no one who had challenged him against his teachings on the Law. In addition, it is noteworthy that Paul did not mention anything about the Law in Thess(A), written earlier than Cor(A). This indicates that Paul did not put much weight on the Law at the beginning of his second missionary trip.

Cor(B) and Thess(B)

Paul was silent about the Law in Cor(B) and Thess(B), written later than Cor(A). A common factor in the two letters is that references to those sent by the apostles of Jerusalem appear. However, it is noteworthy that the members of the two churches took different positions toward them.

The Law is not treated in Cor(B) at all. At that time, Paul heard the news from the people of Chloe that Cephas had visited Corinth as a representative of the apostles of Jerusalem (1 Cor 1:11–12). Cephas baptized some Corinthians; in addition, he seems to have taught them to keep the Law and to be circumcised. Some members followed his teachings, but others did not. It seems that Paul was cautious of mentioning the Law for two reasons. First, this is the first case of Paul hearing the news after the theological controversy in connection with Cephas. Second, Paul was concerned about the impact of the teachings that Cephas had given to the Corinthians. In response, Paul would need to organize his concept of the Law in his own way. This may have been why he did not mention the Law in Cor(B).

Paul did not mention the Law even in Thess(B). It is clear that a certain number of people, called the "tempter," visited the Thessalonian church (1 Thess 3:5). They were those sent by the apostles of Jerusalem to make the Thessalonians keep the Law and stay away from the instruction of Paul. While Paul mentioned the visit of Cephas to Corinth in Cor(B), he did not present any names of those who came to the Thessalonian church. Without doubt, the "tempter" would have been people of the same class as Cephas. However, just as Paul did not mention the Law in Cor(B), so was it in Thess(B). As the Thessalonians decided to stay in the gospel that Paul had preached, he seems to have been more cautious about how to approach the Law.

Paul apparently was shocked when he heard of news that the apostles of Jerusalem had sent representatives to the Gentile churches. They were sent in response to Paul's rebuke of Cephas at the theological controversy over the Gentile table in Antioch. Thus, Paul could not help but be allergic to their instruction that the Gentiles should observe the Law and be circumcised. It seems that Paul had to be silent about the Law because he needed time to clear up his concept of it at the time of writing Cor(B) and Thess(B).

Phil(A)

Paul mentioned the Law in connection with righteousness in Phil(A). However, the concept of the Law is not clear. Nevertheless, Paul began to show an unfavorable view on the Law on account of those sent by the apostles of Jerusalem.

The word "Law" appears two times in connection with righteousness. On the one hand, it appears in the statement that Paul was flawless as for righteousness in the Law (Phil 3:6); on the other hand, the righteousness of God is not by the Law but by the faith of Christ (3:9). In both cases, the Law appears in relation to righteousness. Although Paul did not describe the concept or scope of the Law in detail, it is definite that he changed his position on the Law in terms of how to become the people of God. In consequence, it can be said that Paul adopted the Law in a narrower sense in Phil(A) than in Cor(A).

It is clear that Paul changed his view on the Law in Phil(A). Although he did not provide a definite reason, it can be deduced from the changing circumstances around him. This is related to the apostles of Jerusalem, who sent representatives to the Gentile churches Paul had established. They demanded that the Philippians should observe the Law and be circumcised. As a result, some Philippians were shaken for a while but remained in the gospel Paul had proclaimed. The challenge of those sent by the apostles of Jerusalem made Paul turn to a negative position on the Law. In response, Paul began to insist that the Gentiles could be righteous by the faith of Christ, not by the Law.

A turning point is found in Phil(A) in terms of Paul's view on the Law. Having argued that the Law does not make people righteous before God, Paul offered the faith of Christ as an alternative. In this way, Paul was getting independent from the Jerusalem tradition in his attitude toward the Law. This is the moment that Christianity was born among the Gentiles. It seems that Paul had to insist on righteousness by the faith of Christ in order to protect the Gentiles from Judaization.

Cor(C)

Paul dealt with the Law in earnest in Cor(C). As the letter progressed, his negative view on the Law became stronger. Having been challenged by some Corinthians sponsored by the apostles of Jerusalem, Paul had to defend the gospel by refuting the role of the Law.

The Law is mentioned in connection with the issue of salary. According to Paul, the Law of Moses says that those who do the work of God must eat and live for it (1 Cor 9:8–9). This seems to be quoted from Deut 25:4. Then, it can be said that Paul identified the Law as the books written by Moses. This is the first case where Paul defined the range of the Law. Then, it is necessary to discuss the issue of salary promised according to the Law of Moses. It seems to be connected with Cephas in that he asked the Corinthians for a salary on the basis of instruction of Moses and Jesus (1 Cor 9:13–14; Lev 2:3; Q^2 10:7). Paul also acknowledged the right to ask for it; however, he refrained from using that right because he himself believed he had already received great grace from God (1 Cor 9:15–18). Paul did not demand remuneration from the Corinthians. In this respect, the Law of Moses was stipulated in that it could not precede the grace of God.

Paul presented the Law in association with the religious status of people. This is found in the description that to those under the Law Paul became like one under the Law, though he himself was not under the Law, and that to those not having the Law he became like one not having the Law, though he was not free from the Law in Christ (1 Cor 9:20–21). This means that Paul could change his attitude of treating Jews or Gentiles in connection with the observance of the Law. The reason Paul took this kind of attitude is because he wanted to bring salvation to both those under the Law and those without the Law. As much as possible, Paul tried to embrace those who challenged him under the sponsorship of the apostles of Jerusalem, who had relied on the Law as reflected in Q (Q^4 4:1–13; 14:5; 16:16–18; etc.). This shows Paul's neutral position toward the Law up to that point. In consequence, it can be said that Paul provided his theological interpretation in response to the changing circumstances of the recipients of his letters.

A more negative view on the Law is found in association with its nature. According to Paul, "The sting of death is sin, and the power of sin is the law" (1 Cor 15:56). This shows Paul's negative view on the Law. Having mentioned death, sin, and the Law in sequence, Paul made the Law understood in light of death and sin. This is another case that the Law is mentioned from a negative point of view. It would have had a tremendous impact on some Corinthians who wanted to become the people of God by the Law. In this way, Paul presented a new interpretation of the Law in order to give proper instruction in response to the challenge of some Corinthians sponsored by the apostles of Jerusalem.

In Cor(C), Paul began to show in earnest a negative view on the Law. This is stronger than that mentioned in Phil(A). When Cephas encouraged the Corinthians to challenge Paul, he began to present a negative view on the Law. In other words, his negative perspective was revealed in earnest after Paul was directly challenged by some Corinthians under the sponsorship of the apostles of Jerusalem. As a result, Paul was getting more independent from them and made Christianity grow among the Gentiles. Perhaps, having been acquainted with this kind of instruction, Aquila and Priscilla returned to Rome later and established a church there on the basis of what they had learned from Paul in Ephesus (1 Cor 16:19). However, it is not clear how much they agreed with the instructions of Paul on the Law.

Galatians

Paul was the most negative on the Law in Galatians. It is because the Galatians challenged Paul by observing the Law according to the instruction of those sent by the apostles of Jerusalem. Thus, Paul was forced to criticize the Law most severely in order to bring the Galatians back to the gospel.

The Law is presented in contrast with the faith of Christ. According to Paul, the Gentiles could be righteous not by the works of the Law but by the faith of Jesus Christ (Gal 2:16; cf. 5:4–5). The contrast between the Law and the faith of Christ was already presented in connection with righteousness in Phil(A) (Phil 3:9). However, in Galatians, Paul changed it into the contrast between the works of the Law and the faith of Jesus Christ. This is an expression of Paul's response to the instruction of those sent by the apostle of Jerusalem, who asked the Galatians to observe the Law and to be circumcised. Here, the Law refers to all the commandments, including the provision of circumcision, because Paul used the plural term "works" in connection with the Law. In this regard, Paul made the concept of the Law more concrete in Galatians than in his previous letters.

Paul once again described the Law from a negative viewpoint. This is found in the statement that Paul died through the Law to it in order to live for God (Gal 2:19). After the Law was linked to death in Cor(C) (1 Cor 15:56), it appears in association with death again in Galatians. This is the first case that Paul presented the contrast between death and life in terms of the Law. It seems that, while those sent by the apostles of Jerusalem taught the Galatians the Law as a means of living for God, Paul denied such teaching with an implication that the Law leads people to death. This means a break from the Law. As Paul progressed in writing Galatians, he made negative comments on the Law more and more.

The Law is once again expressed negatively in contrast with the spirit of God. This appears in the rhetorical question of whether the Galatians received the spirit of God by observing the Law or by believing what they heard (Gal 3:2, 5). Paul spoke of receiving the spirit of God not by the Law but by belief in what they had heard. The Law stands in opposition to the faith of Christ as well as the spirit of God. This is the first case that the spirit of God is mentioned in contrast with the Law. According to Paul, the experience of the spirit of God had nothing to do with the observance of the Law at all. In this regard, Paul kept revealing a negative view on the Law. This also indicates that he made progress in his interpretation of the Law.

Paul understood the Law in light of curse. It is said, "All who rely on observing the law are under a curse"; in addition, "Christ redeemed us from the curse of the law by becoming a curse for us" (Gal 3:10, 13). Paul took a position negative enough to see the Law as a source of curse. This was a warning to the Galatians, who tried to be the people of God by observing the Law according to the instruction of those sent by the apostles of Jerusalem. Without doubt, they taught the Galatians to keep the Law so that they might not be cursed. Accordingly, Paul argued that they would be cursed on account of their obedience to the Law. Rather, they had to be redeemed by Christ, who had become a curse for them. In this regard, Paul presented a more critical view on the Law as Galatians progressed.

The Law is described in contrast with the promise of God. According to Paul, the Law was given four hundred and thirty years later than the promise given to Abraham and God gave the inheritance in his grace through a promise, not by the Law (Gal 3:17–18). This conveys the instruction that the Law is less authoritative than promises in terms of chronological order. With a reference to Abraham and his descendants, Paul pointed out the inferiority of the Law. This reflects the fact that those sent by the apostles of Jerusalem taught the Galatians that they could be the descendants of Abraham by observing the Law. In response, Paul presented the promise of God as the basis on which they could be the people of God. In this respect, a negative view on the Law was given them with an emphasis that it was inferior to the promise of God.

Paul described the characteristics of the Law in four ways. It was added for transgressions [παράβασις], effective until the offspring to whom the promise referred would come, put into effect through angels, and given by a mediator (Gal 3:19). All of these show corrupted, inferior, and temporary characteristics of the Law. They are a collection of elements that show the negative aspect of the Law. Those sent by the apostles of Jerusalem probably told the Galatians that the Law was given through angels by a mediator to protect people from committing transgressions. However, while criticizing this, Paul made the opposite interpretation with an emphasis on the inferiority of the Law. In this respect, Paul's negative statement on the Law reached its peak.

Eventually, the Law was placed in opposition to the Son of God. According to Paul, God sent his Son Jesus Christ and redeemed those under the Law (Gal 4:4–5). Paul argued that the Law was not a way of leading people to redemption, but rather an entity binding them. This implies that those sent by the apostles of Jerusalem taught the Galatians that the role of the Law is to redeem people. In response, Paul portrayed the Son of God as the one to redeem those under the Law from its curse. In this way, Paul kept describing the negative aspect of the Law.

Paul came to a conclusion about the Law. It is said, "The entire law is summed up in a single command, 'Love your neighbor as yourself'" (Gal 5:14; Lev 19:18). Without doubt, the "entire Law" mentioned above refers to every article written in the Law; however, Paul taught the Galatians to keep the core nature of the Law rather than every article of it. With a somewhat negative view on the Law, Paul conveyed how to keep the entire Law. This could be a reflection on Paul's attitude toward the Law, which had been too much negative up to that point. In this way, Paul demanded the Galatians to stay in the gospel rather than to observe the Law.

Finally, the Law is mentioned in association with Christ. Paul asked the Galatians to keep another command, "Carry each other's burdens," in order to fulfill the Law of Christ (Gal 6:2). This is accordant with the command, "Love your neighbor as yourself." In this way, Paul tried to suggest how to faithfully keep the Law at the ending of Galatians. It is important to observe that Paul already used the phrase "Law of Christ" in Cor(C) (1 Cor 9:21) and mentioned the love of Christ the Son of God for him in Galatians (Gal 2:20). This means that the Law is meaningful when it is carried out with the love that Christ showed. Thus, loving neighbors is the top priority for the completion of the Law. Paul showed a positive view in relation to loving neighbors to the completion of the Law in Christ.

Paul described the Law more often and negatively in Galatians than in other letters. When the challenge of the Galatians against the gospel reached its peak, Paul provided the reasons that the Law should be downgraded in connection with a redemptive role. Since the Galatians challenged him on the basis of the Jewish instruction of those sent by the apostles of Jerusalem, Paul had to defeat their arguments by arguing for the inferiority of the Law to the spirit of God, the promise of God, and the Son of God. Rather, Paul encouraged the Galatians to fulfill the Law in Christ. In the meantime, Christian teaching reached its peak in connection with the Law.

Cor(D), Cor(E), and Cor(F)

Paul was silent about the Law in Cor(D), Cor(E), and Cor(F). There are various reasons for it. This indicates that Paul interpreted the Law according to his relationship with the recipients of his letters.

Each of Cor(D), Cor(E), and Cor(F) has its own reason that the Law is not dealt with in it. First, the Law is not mentioned in Cor(D). It seems that Paul could not afford to pay attention to the Law because his priority was on the comfort of the Corinthians to improve his relationship with them. In other words, he did not want to reveal his negative view on the Law. Second, the word "letter" is used instead of the "Law" in Cor(E) (2 Cor 3:6–7). Having used this euphemism, Paul did not want to be in confrontation with the Corinthians on account of his view on the Law. He did all he could to reconcile with them. Third, Paul kept silent with regard to the Law in Cor(F). This is probably because the consistent challenge of the Corinthians was finally revealed. In other words, Paul realized that he could no longer keep them in the gospel by teaching them a negative view on the Law. Perhaps Paul was frustrated with the Corinthians who had not accepted his negative view on the Law.

The Law was a sensitive issue to some Corinthians who had challenged Paul. They were deeply influenced by the apostles of Jerusalem, who tried to deliver the Jewish teachings. In any case, Paul did not deal with the issue of the Law in Cor(D), Cor(E), and Cor(F), taking into account the circumstances of the recipients of his letters.

Summary

Paul expressed his view on the Law in his letters written during his second missionary trip. A progressive change is found in that while he had taken a friendly position before the challenge of some Gentiles, he turned to a negative position after the challenge. This reflects the fact that they challenged Paul on the basis of the Jewish view on the Law delivered by those who came from the Jerusalem church. Thus, Paul had to respond to it and provided an alternative with regard to the Law. Meanwhile, Christianity was born to the Gentiles. Paul showed changes in the range and concept of the Law according to the circumstances that he faced. This shows that Paul presented his theological interpretations in relation to the recipients of his letters.

C. THE THIRD MISSIONARY TRIP

Having sent four letters to the Roman church, Paul took a negative view on the Law in general. He associated the Law with wrath and transgression in Rom(A). Accordingly, it seems that some Romans, especially the Jewish members, who made up the majority of the Roman church, asked him for an explanation. Having answered them, Paul significantly developed a negative view on the Law. The more questions and critiques they raised, the more negative a view on the Law Paul revealed. Paul interpreted it in a way to persuade the Romans while maintaining his basic view on the Law.

Rom(A)

It seems that in Rom(A) Paul delivered what he had concluded about the Law during his second missionary trip. The Law was presented with a negative stance in that Paul linked the Law to wrath and transgression. Despite that Paul should have considered the position of the Jewish members of the Roman church more, he seems to have overlooked it.

The Law is set in contrast with the righteousness of faith. This is manifested in the expression of God's promise not of the Law but of the righteousness of faith (Rom 4:13). Paul set the Law in contrast with the righteousness of faith in terms of God's promise. The Law was already set in contrast with the faith of the Galatians and the promise of God in Galatians (Gal 3:2, 17–18). However, the difference is clear in that Paul modified the contrast between the Law and the promise of God to that between the Law and the righteousness of faith in Rom(A). This indicates that Paul made a theological contribution to the interpretation of the Law. This would have been a shock to the Romans, especially the Jewish members, because they had never heard such a view. Then, a subtle tension would have formed between Paul and the Romans.

Paul then made a more negative statement about the Law. According to him, the Law brings wrath [ὀργή], and where there is no Law there is no transgression [παράβασις] (Rom 4:15). Paul revealed a negative view on the Law. The term "transgression" was already used in association with the Law in Galatians (Gal 3:19). Thus, Paul was able to link it to the Law in Rom(A). At any rate, Paul presented the Law in connection with wrath and transgression. Having constituted a parallel, wrath and transgression exacerbate the mess with regard to the effects of the Law. Such a declaration would have been a shock to the Jewish members of the Roman church because it was completely different from the traditional interpretation.

Paul outlined what he was trying to convey to the Romans about the Law in Rom(A). This was the cornerstone for him to communicate in more detail later. They probably had already heard of his view on the Law from Aquila and Priscilla, who had spent a certain period of time with him in Ephesus (1 Cor 16:19). At that time, Paul defined the Law as the power of death and sin from a negative view as written in Cor(C) (1 Cor 15:56). However, it seems that Aquila and Priscilla had returned to Rome from Ephesus before Galatians was written. Having established a church in Rome, they taught the members to respect the Law because it was Jews who mostly joined the church. Thus, it seems that the Romans were not well aware of the fact that Paul had an extremely negative position on the Law as written in Galatians. So it seems that Aquila and Priscilla had nothing to say to them when Paul spoke of his negative view on the Law in relation to wrath and transgression.

It seems that the Romans, especially the Jewish members, were quite resentful after they became acquainted with Paul's negative comments on the Law as written in Rom(A). Naturally, they seem to have asked Paul to explain his view on the Law. They would not have accepted Paul until hearing his explanation.

Rom(B)

Paul had to answer the question of the Romans in Rom(B). Accordingly, Paul offered an interpretation, having linked the Law with sin anew. Thereby, Paul developed his interpretation of the Law in a direction that made the Romans more annoyed.

Paul presented his view on the Law and wrath. This is revealed in his account of wrath (Rom 1:18—2:11) and the Law (2:12—3:31). This seems to be an answer to the question that the Romans raised after reading Paul's negative view on the Law in Rom(A) (4:15). First of all, Paul presented a critique against the Jews in connection with the Law. Paul criticized their crimes despite that they had the Law (2:17–19). This implies that Paul was well aware of the situation of the Romans because he already knew many members as reflected in Rom(A) (16:3–16). It is, however, important that Paul admitted the worth of the Law, insisting that it should be kept. This shows that Paul was stifled for a moment with his negative view on the Law at the time of writing Rom(B).

Paul described his negative view on the Law. Having associated the Law with sin, Paul came up with a new interpretation that nobody can obtain the righteousness of God by works of the Law; rather, he or she can only be convicted of sin (Rom 3:20). This is more critical than his previous declaration in that while the Law was connected with transgression in Rom(A), it was associated with sin in Rom(B). Paul still maintained his negative view on the Law. In this respect, Paul raised a critique against the Romans for committing crimes while still having the Law.

The relationship between the Law and faith is discussed. Paul emphasized once again that people would eventually be led to the righteousness of God by the faith of Christ, not by the works of the Law (Rom 3:28). This was already argued for in Galatians (Gal 3:2, 5). In Rom(B), Paul portrayed Christ as an example of faith, having broken the relationship with the Law. In addition, Paul said, "Do we, then, nullify the law by this faith? Not at all! Rather, we uphold the law" (3:31). This reveals Paul's positive view on the Law, which coincides with the description of fulfilling the Law of Christ in Galatians (Gal 6:2). Paul insisted that the Romans should approach the Law from the perspective of the faith of Christ.

Paul presented a theological interpretation of the Law with a negative view in Rom(B). The Law that convicts of sin could be fulfilled if the Roman treat it with faith. Thus, Paul explained the issue that the righteous must live by faith in order to fulfill the Law. In this way, Paul came up with a theological interpretation of the Law having taken into account the situation of the Romans. This was the answer of Paul to the questions raised by the Jewish members of the Roman church who had observed the Law. In this respect, Paul provided them with an alternative from a theological perspective. Such an answer is believed to have gone beyond what Aquila and Priscilla could speak of Paul's negative view on the Law.

It seems that the Romans, especially the Jewish members, were outraged by Paul's explanation. This is because Paul explained the Law in connection with sin. Their question seems to have developed into a critique against him. And they seem to have given Paul another chance to explain with regard to his negative view on the Law. It is not difficult to assume that they would not accept him until they heard his answer.

Rom(C)

Paul once again had to make an apology for his view on the Law in Rom(C). Having explained the relationship between the Law and sin in detail, Paul gave the Romans an answer to their critique against his negative view on the Law delivered in Rom(B). It seems that Paul had refrained to some extent from a negative position on the Law while writing Rom(C).

There is a provocative statement on the Law. According to Paul, the Law was added so that the trespass [παράπτωμα] might increase (Rom 5:20). Having reflected Paul's negative view on the Law, this shows no difference from the previous interpretation of the Law in connection with transgression [παράβασις] in Galatians (Gal 3:19) and in Rom(A) (Rom 4:15). It seems that Paul used "transgression" and "trespass" as interchangeable words in Rom(C) (Rom 5:14, 20). Although Paul used them to emphasize the grace of Christ, the Jewish members of the Roman church may not have yet been able to erase their uncomfortable feelings about his negative view on the Law.

The Law is described in connection with sin. According to Paul, sin cannot claim people because they are not under the Law but under grace (Rom 6:14). Having set the Law in sharp contrast with the grace of God, Paul alluded to the close relationship between the Law and sin. In this way, Paul seems to have further developed the declaration that people become conscious of sin through the Law as written in Rom(B) (3:20). This indicates that the more questions and critiques the Romans raised, the more negative a view on the Law Paul presented to them. It seems that this negative stance reached its peak when he presented the sharp contrast between the Law and the grace of God in Rom(C).

Paul elaborated on the relationship of the Law to sin. This is found in the claim that the Law leads people to death because of the lust of sin (Rom 7:5). Paul presented a new interpretation that sin, personified, manipulates the Law. Whereas the Law was already dealt with in direct relationship with sin in Galatians (Gal 3:21–22), a negative role was attributed to the lust of sin rather than to the Law in Rom(C). On the other hand, Paul argued that sin took advantage of the commandments of the Law by taking the opportunity (Rom 7:8, 11). This implies Paul's slight retreat from attributing a negative role to the Law. In other words, Paul gave an interpretation that the sin hidden in the nature of human beings was more responsible than the Law itself for the trespass. Paul used a more periphrastic expression in Rom(C) than in Cor(C), where the Law was defined as the power of sin (1 Cor 15:56). It seems that, having taken into account the Romans, especially the Jewish members, Paul refrained from applying a negative view to the Law to some extent. In this way, Paul seems to have avoided the critique against him.

The formal stance against the Law appears. According to Paul, the Law is holy, good, and spiritual; thus, the responsibility for sin was attributed to those who want good but cannot do it (Rom 7:12–20). In this way, Paul released the Law from the responsibility of causing sin. This is a more developed interpretation than a somewhat positive expression of the Law in Galatians (Gal 6:2) and Rom(B) (Rom 3:31). In this way, Paul described the Law as an entity increasingly far from sin in Rom(C). It is, however, to be noted that his negative view on the Law has not yet been abandoned. This is how Paul asked the Romans to accept the gospel he was trying to preach. However, it is still unclear whether they accepted his instruction or not.

Paul described the importance of positioning with a couple of contrasts related to the Law. This appears in the contrast between the Law of God and the law of sin, and between the Law of the spirit of life in Christ and the law of sin and death (Rom 7:21–25; 8:2). Paul put them in sharp contrast in order to emphasize by whose initiative the Law should be kept. It is, then, important to observe that the spirit of God is connected with the Law. This shows Paul withdrawing from an extremely negative attitude toward it. In this way, having taken into account the position of the Romans, Paul revealed his theological view on the Law. It seems that he wanted to be in close relationship with them.

The fulfillment of the Law is also mentioned. According to Paul, the righteous requirement of the Law can be fully met by those who live according to the spirit of God (Rom 8:4). This is a teaching that if people live according to the spirit of God they can keep the Law completely. It is then necessary to discuss the issue of the spirit of God and the fulfillment of the Law. First, Paul dealt with the intervention of the spirit of God. This reminds readers of Paul's statement that the Galatians experienced the spirit of God in opposition to the works of the Law in Galatians (Gal 3:2, 5). However, in Rom(C) the spirit of God is described as an agent taking the lead in people's lives to fulfill the Law. Second, the fulfillment of the Law matters. Whereas Paul stated to fulfill the Law of Christ in Galatians (Gal 6:2), he paid attention to the fulfillment of the Law with the guidance of the spirit of God in Rom(C). This shows Paul's effort to fulfill the Law increasingly as the critique of the Romans against his view on the Law became stronger.

Paul referred to the Law in relation to the ethics that the saints should observe. This is found in the description that the Law is fulfilled by loving others (Rom 13:8, 10). This means that love is required by the Law. This reminds readers of the previous statement that the Law of Christ would be fulfilled by loving neighbors and carrying the burden of others as written in Galatians (Gal 5:14; 6:2). In Rom(C), however, Paul emphasized the active action of loving to fulfill the Law. In this way, a friendly view on the Law appears in connection with the issue of loving others. This is the answer of Paul given to the Romans who raised critiques against his negative view on the Law.

Paul took to some extent a position of reserving the Law in Rom(C). Having mentioned that sin inflicted the Law on people's mind, Paul imposed a negative role upon sin rather than the Law. This is what Paul wrote in a direction that would acceptable to the Romans without changing his negative view on the Law. Having associated the Law with God, Christ, and the spirit, Paul presented a new interpretation of it to the Romans, especially the Jewish members. This is how Paul considered the position of the Romans without changing his stance toward the Law.

It seems that the Romans fully understood Paul's position on the Law. However, he seems to have noticed that he had a fundamentally negative attitude toward the Law. As a result, the Romans no longer questioned or criticized his view on it. It seems that Paul no longer needed to explain to the Romans in relation to the Law.

Rom(D)

Paul did not mention the Law much in Rom(D). This means that the Romans no longer raised questions about it or that Paul lost the confidence in the possibility of persuading the Romans. It seems that Paul described the Law with a somewhat benign view.

Various aspects of the Law are written about from a theological perspective. First, Paul mentioned the Law in the list of benefits that the Israelites enjoyed (Rom 9:4). The Law is listed along with the issue of adoption as sons of God, glory, covenants, worship, and promises. However, Paul did not mention the function of the Law anymore. Thereby, Paul no longer made statements of the Law. Second, the Law is mentioned in connection with Christ. According to Paul, Christ became the end of the Law to accomplish the righteousness of God for people (Rom 10:4). This reminds readers of his previous instruction to fulfill the Law of Christ as written in Galatians (Gal 6:2). Paul substituted "the end of the Law" for "to fulfill the Law of Christ" used in Galatians. This means that Paul no longer wanted to make comments on the validity of the Law. Third, Paul put faith in parallel with the Law in terms of righteousness (Rom 10:5–6). Although Paul did not think that the Law and faith were at the same level, he thought of the Law with a little more friendly position. In this way, Paul refrained from describing an extremely negative view on the Law.

Paul gave a benign interpretation of the Law to some extent in Rom(D). It seems that the Romans did not criticize him anymore after reading Rom(C). It is not clear whether they accepted Paul's view or they no longer needed to respond to his view. In my opinion, perhaps the latter case should be preferred.

Phil(B)

Paul did not treat the Law in Phil(B). The reason that he did not deal with it has not been known. However, it can be surmised that there was no need to write on the Law because the Philippians stayed firmly in the gospel Paul had proclaimed.

There is no allusion even to the Law in Phil(B). Paul did not need to mention the Law to the Philippians because they had overcome the challenge of those sponsored by the apostles of Jerusalem. In addition, the Philippians provided financial aid to him. For this, he was so pleased that he only offered compliments to them. After his request for financial assistance had been turned down by the Romans, he received financial help from the Philippian church in the prison of Rome. They showed love for Paul, which was the most important provision of the Law.

Paul stopped talking about the Law while writing Phil(B) at the end of his third missionary trip. Although a similar phenomenon had already appeared during the second missionary trip while writing Cor(D), Cor(E), and Cor(F), the reasons were completely different. As such, Paul seems to have changed his description of the Law in response to the changing circumstances.

Summary

Having sent four letters to the Romans during the third missionary trip, Paul had a lot of communication with them about the Law. It began with Paul's negative narrative of the Law in Rom(A), and then he gave theological interpretations as an answer to their questions in Rom(B). Paul did not change his negative view on the Law in Rom(C); however, he refrained a little bit from a critical view on it by attributing the negative role to sin more than the Law. It seems that Paul was not able to convince them in the end as reflected in Rom(D). On the other hand, in Phil(B), sent to the Philippians, who had been in good relations with him, Paul did not mention the Law at all. This is opposite to the relationship Paul had with the Corinthians during his second missionary trip. It seems that the Law was not described anymore. Meanwhile, his theological interpretation of the Law developed. This seems to have made Paul expand Christianity even to Rome.

D. CONCLUSION

Paul showed various understandings of the Law. This is expressed in a way to convey his view on it in response to the changing circumstances of the recipients of his letters. At the beginning, Paul, a former Pharisee, was zealous for the Law. Having received the revelation from God about his Son, he did not need to change his view on the Law. The apostles, including James, the Lord's brother, who had the hegemony in the Jerusalem church, were in the position of emphasizing the observance of the Law, and Paul seems to take it for granted until the end of his first missionary trip. However, everything changed after the theological controversy over the Gentile table in Antioch. The apostles of Jerusalem decided to deny the gospel Paul had proclaimed to the Gentiles and sent representatives to ask them to observe the Law in addition to the instruction of Jesus. Under their sponsorship, some Gentiles began to challenge Paul against the gospel and his authority. In response, Paul started revealing a negative view on the Law. In the meantime, Christianity was born to the Gentiles. The stronger the challenge became, the more negative a view on the Law he presented until the end of his second missionary trip. However, Paul took a slightly different attitude toward the Law during his third missionary trip to Rome. Although he criticized the Law, he admitted that it was given for good purposes. As a result, Paul adjusted his view on the Law and turned to a benign position on it. In consequence, it can be said that Paul developed his theological interpretation of the Law in response to the changing circumstances of the recipients of his letters. Eventually, an interpretation of the Law developed in connection with Christianity.

6

The End of World

PAUL WAS INTERESTED IN the end of world. However, he did not mention it as consistently as we usually think. It seems that he presented an eschatological instruction on the basis of Jewish tradition at the beginning of his mission to the Gentiles. There was, however, a turning point that changed his view on the end of world. As the challenge against him became stronger, Paul elaborated his eschatological instruction for a while. On the other hand, the amount of eschatological instruction was radically reduced when the challenge reached its peak in the middle of the second missionary trip. It is, however, unfortunate that there is no clear connection between eschatological teaching and the birth of Christianity. Then, Paul dealt with eschatological instruction to a minimal degree without any apocalyptic reference during his third missionary trip. In this way, Paul changed his eschatological view in response to the circumstances of the recipients of his letters. It is then necessary to trace how Paul developed his eschatological view over time.

A. THE FIRST MISSIONARY TRIP

It seems that Paul delivered eschatological instruction from a Jewish perspective during his first missionary trip. Since there is no record of this, what he taught to the Gentiles has not been known exactly. However, it can be inferred to some extent from his biographical past.

Above all, Paul was familiar with the Pharisaic tradition. This requires a broad scope of discussion; however, perhaps the most prominent element in relation to an eschatological view is the belief in the resurrection of people. Since the Pharisees understood the resurrection as an eschatological event, Paul must have believed in the judgment of God that would follow the resurrection at the end of world. In addition, he was confident in the coming of Gentiles to Jerusalem with abundant amount of gifts given to God (Mic 4:1–2). A greater amount of Jewish teaching had been given to Paul with regard to what would happen at the end of world.

An event occurred to Paul that encouraged his eschatological understanding. God revealed his Son to Paul so as to proclaim him to the Gentiles around 35 CE (Gal 1:16). Paul seems to have taken it as an eschatological event from a Jewish perspective at that time. In other words, the proclamation of God to the Gentiles would have been believed to take place in the end of world. Thus, Paul seems to have thought that the end would come soon when he proclaimed the Son of God to the Gentiles. A decision was made to dedicate himself to work on the eschatological mission according to the will of God.

It seems that Paul received eschatological instruction a little from the religious predecessors in Damascus. They informed him of Christ resurrected according to the Scriptures (1 Cor 15:4). It is likely that they were also of the Pharisees in that they believed in resurrection. Paul accepted the instruction on the resurrection of Christ with a reference to realized eschatology. However, it would have been a tremendous shock to him. Then, he would have expected that other eschatological events would happen soon. This understanding would have given Paul a motive to proclaim the resurrection of Christ as well as of Gentiles with enthusiasm.

There was a chance for Paul to learn more about eschatological instruction from Cephas. When he went up to Jerusalem to meet Cephas around 38 CE (Gal 1:16–18), there were many teachings on what would happen at the end of world in Q. First, the unexpected coming of Jesus the Son of Man has been written in comparison with a thief (Q^3 12:39–40). The disciples of Jesus were admonished to be ready for the sudden coming of Jesus the Son of Man, described against the backdrop of "one like a son of man" (Dan 7:13). Then, Paul also accepted the instruction on the coming of the Son of Man at the end of world. The Son of Man will come as lightning strikes flashes and lights up the sky from one end to the other (Q^3 17:23–24). This reveals the transcendental and apocalyptic coming of the Son of Man. In addition, Paul learned an instruction that people will not be ready for the end of world. They will enjoy eating and drinking, marrying and giving in marriage, as those of days of Noah did (Q^3 17:26–27, 30). This refers to their preoccupation in their greed without any precaution about the end of world. Moreover, Paul learned an instruction on the judgment of "this generation" by the Gentiles (Q^3 11:31–32). There was also a metaphor about the eschatological judgment that the grain would be piled up in a barn but the tares would be thrown into the unquenched fire (Q^3 3:17); in addition, an ax had been lying at the root of tree (Q^1 3:9). The urgency of eschatological judgment appears among the sayings listed above. This is part of what Paul learned from Cephas on the basis of the Jerusalem tradition represented by Q. It seems that Paul was fascinated with the eschatological instruction delivered in the name of Jesus. This reflects the fact that Paul was equipped with the eschatological view on the impending end of world during his first visit to Jerusalem.

At last, Paul set on the first missionary trip after he had met Cephas. The journey began in Antioch of Syria and went all the way down to Corinth of Achaia. It seems that he had spoken of the imminent end of world. However, there is no record of this; thus, we cannot know exactly about it. It is likely that Paul preached the resurrection of saints on the basis of the Pharisaic tradition, the resurrection of Christ inherited from the religious predecessors in Damascus, and various eschatological instructions learned from Cephas on the basis of the Jerusalem tradition. He is likely to have mentioned the advent of a messianic figure. His eschatological instruction seems to have been close to that of Judaism. Paul would have given an eschatological instruction having taken into account the circumstances of the Gentile audience. Paul would have carefully spoken of an eschatological lesson because he was not familiar with their religious preferences in the area he was visiting for the first time. However, he would have preached eschatological lessons with religious authority. As his teachings to the Gentiles had great repercussions, he was able to establish churches in many places.

Paul returned to Jerusalem accompanied with Titus, a Greek, after the first missionary trip around 49 CE. Titus seems to have accompanied him to Jerusalem as an eschatological appreciation (Gal 2:1–4). Jews believed that the Gentiles would come up to Jerusalem with gifts at the end of world (Mic 4:1–2; Zech 14:14). Thus, Paul took Titus to Jerusalem to show that the end of world had come. "It accentuates the inclusion of Gentile believers in the eschatological people of God."[1] This reflects the fact that during the first outreach to the Gentiles Paul enthusiastically cried out the instruction on the impending end of world and it was accepted by some Gentiles. This seems to have made Paul more confident in the eschatological teachings that he had proclaimed.

There was another chance for Paul to learn more about the end of world during the second visit to Jerusalem around 49 CE. At that time, he was exposed to the fourth redaction of Q, which had been complete around 41 CE. From it, Paul learned about the eschatological instruction. There are some eschatological places such as Gehenna and the kingdom of God where people will go after the judgment at the end of world (Q^4 12:5; 13:28–30). They seem to be transcendental places where people go after death. Then, Paul learned something more about the eschatological judgment embedded in the Parable of the Talents (Q^4 19:12–26). The eschatological reward and punishment are well described there. He was subordinate to the authority of the twelve apostles of Jerusalem, entrusted with the role of eschatological judge (Q^4 22:30). This informed him of the eschatological judgment against the twelve tribes. At that time, Paul was in a position to accept the eschatological teachings delivered by the apostles of Jerusalem because he was subordinate to their authority.

Later, Paul was in a theological controversy over the Gentile table in Antioch. It seems that Barnabas thought Gentiles could share food with Jews from an eschatological viewpoint (Gal 2:11–14). Thus, the Antiochene congregation invited Cephas in gratitude for the exemption of the Gentiles from circumcision and provided him with Gentile food. However, having heard the news of the arrival of those sent by James, the Lord's brother, Cephas withdrew from fellowship with the Gentiles. Having seen his withdrawal, Paul understood it as an action of breaking the confidence that Jews as well as Gentiles were the people of God from an eschatological perspective. Thus, having known that Cephas did not abandon religious discrimination against the Gentiles, Paul rebuked him for hypocrisy against the truth of the gospel. As a result, they turned their backs on each other. Nevertheless, Paul did not seem to give up confidence in the eschatological belief that he should make the Gentiles the people of God.

---

1. Lüdemann, *Paul*, loc. 184 of 3299.

After returning to Jerusalem, Cephas apparently discussed the matter of the Gentiles with the apostles. Having thought that Paul had taught that Gentiles have equal rights with Jews from an eschatological point of view, they might have decided to revise this. The apostles of Jerusalem demanded circumcision and observance of the Law from the Gentiles. Accordingly, a certain number of representatives were sent to the Gentile churches Paul had established during his first missionary trip. This was an event contrary to Paul's eschatological conviction that God had allowed the Gentiles to be his people.

B. THE SECOND MISSIONARY TRIP

After the theological controversy in Antioch, Paul left for the region of the Gentiles again. This was the second missionary trip. The eschatological issue was treated in his letters sent to the churches he had established during the first missionary trip. However, Paul stopped delivering eschatological instruction when the challenge against him reached its peak at the time of writing Galatians. It is, however, somewhat ambiguous to point out the birth of Christianity in connection with eschatological instruction.

Thess(A)

Paul described what would happen at the end of world in Thess(A). As for this, the coming of Jesus the Son of God was the top priority in his eschatological instruction. This implies that Paul maintained the Jewish viewpoint at the beginning of his second missionary trip.

First, Paul focused on the coming of the Son of God. It is said that the Thessalonians were waiting for the Son of God from heaven, whom God had raised from the dead (1 Thess 1:10). Hereby, Paul focused on the coming of the Son of God more than his death and resurrection. This seems to be described against the backdrop of the Son of Man coming at the end of world as written in Q (Q^3 17:23–24). The phrase "coming of the Son of Man like the lightning" was changed to "the coming of the Son of God from heaven" in Thess(A). In addition, as discussed chapter 2, Paul substituted the title "Son of God" for "Son of Man" so that the messianic figure might be understandable to the Gentiles. It seems that Paul applied to Jesus the Son of God the Jewish tradition inherited from

Q that a heavenly figure would come at the end of world. This indicates that Paul relied on the Jerusalem tradition even in the early days of his second missionary trip.

Second, deliverance from wrath comes to fore as the reason that the Son of God will come from heaven. Paul defined Jesus the Son of God as the one coming from heaven to deliver people from wrath (1 Thess 1:10). Then, the term "wrath" is used again in the description that, having forbidden the salvation of Gentiles, the Jews had been filled with sins and God's wrath (2:16). The wrath of God seems to refer to the juridical verdict given to those who did not accept the gospel. In this way, Paul paid attention to the coming wrath while writing Thess(A). Paul's instruction reminds readers of John's rebuke to the crowd to be baptized and to flee from the coming wrath (Q^1 3:7). Paul's dependence upon Q is supported by the fact that the word "wrath" and the eschatological judgment appear commonly in both texts. On the other hand, a difference is found in that while the word "flee" was used in Q to emphasize what people should do, Paul emphasized the role of Jesus, who would deliver them from the coming wrath. From the description above, it can be said that Paul transformed John's eschatological proclamation described in Q into the work of Jesus in Thess(A). Thus, it can be said that the lessons presented above may reflect what Paul proclaimed during the first half of his second missionary trip.

Paul did not mention instruction on the end of world much in Thess(A). This seems to have been unfamiliar to the Thessalonians, who were accustomed to Greek culture. However, Paul relied on Q to convey the eschatological instruction that Jesus the Son of God from heaven would deliver them from the coming wrath. This implies that even in the early days of the second missionary trip, Paul delivered eschatological teachings from a Jewish perspective.

Cor(A)

Paul continued to describe the end of world in Cor(A). The Lord Jesus Christ was portrayed as an eschatological judge. However, Paul did not pay much attention to eschatological matters in the early days of his second missionary trip.

The manifestation of the Lord Jesus Christ is mentioned. According to Paul, the Corinthians did not lack any spiritual gift as they had eagerly waited for the appearance [ἀποκάλυψις] of Christ (1 Cor 1:7). This reminds readers of God revealing [ἀποκαλύψαι] his Son to Paul (Gal 1:16). The word of same root is used commonly in both texts. If Paul understood the revelation of God as an eschatological event, then the appearance of the Lord Jesus Christ should also be understood from an eschatological perspective. However, Paul did not elaborate on it further.

Paul presented the day of the Lord Jesus Christ in an eschatological context. It is said that Jesus Christ would keep the Corinthians strong to the end, so that they might be blameless on the day of the Lord Jesus Christ (1 Cor 1:8). This refers to the eschatological judgment in that the phrase "to the end" was adopted. The day of the Lord Jesus Christ reminds readers of "the day of YHWH" mentioned by the prophets in the Hebrew Scriptures (Isa 2:12; Ezek 30:3; Joel 2:1, etc.). This is the day of eschatological judgment by God (YHWH). It seems that Paul substituted "the day of the Lord Jesus Christ" for "the day of YHWH." In addition, the eschatological judgment is mentioned in Q that would be passed at the time when the Son of Man comes (Q^3 12:42–46). The servants will be rewarded or punished according to how much they have completed what the household asked for. This kind of eschatological judgment turned into the description in Cor(A) that the Corinthians would be rewarded or punished according to whether they were blameless or not. This means that Paul developed his interpretation of eschatological judgment as time passed. It seems that even at the time of writing Cor(A) Paul relied on the Jerusalem tradition with regard to his eschatological view on the role of the Lord Jesus Christ.

The resurrection of people is dealt with in an eschatological context. According to Paul, God raised the Lord and will also raise the Corinthians (1 Cor 6:14). The general resurrection is mentioned for the first time in Cor(A). Although the phrase "end of the world" does not appear in the immediate context, the general resurrection has been believed to be an eschatological event according to the Pharisaic Judaism. Having mentioned the resurrection of Christ learned from the religious predecessors in Damascus, Paul was able to deal with the resurrection of saints inherited from the Pharisaic tradition as well in Cor(A). This indicates that Paul applied the Pharisaic concept of general resurrection to the Gentiles.

With regard to eschatological teachings, Paul seems to have stayed at a basic level while writing Cor(A). They may have been the driving force behind the Corinthians maintaining their faith in God. In any case,

Paul delivered eschatological lessons based on what he had learned from Judaism, including the Jerusalem tradition.

Cor(B)

Paul suggested an elaborated schedule with regard to eschatological events in Cor(B). This lists what would happen after the resurrection of Christ in detail. Having heard of news about the Corinthians from the people of Chloe, Paul developed his eschatological instruction further, especially the eschatological timetable.

"The day of the Lord" is presented from an eschatological point of view. According to Paul, the fornicator should be given up to Satan in order that the sinful nature [σάρξ, flesh] might be destroyed, while his spirit [πνεῦμα] should be saved on the day of the Lord (1 Cor 5:5). The phrase "day of the Lord" is a short duplication of "day of the Lord Jesus Christ" used in Cor(A) (1 Cor 1:8). It is adopted with a reference to the time of eschatological judgment. In addition, Paul set the destruction of "flesh" in contrast with the salvation of "spirit." Paul replaced the blameless condition written in Cor(A) by the contrast between the destruction of flesh and the salvation of spirit in Cor(B). In this way, Paul changed his counsel based on realistic evaluation. This means that Paul heard of news about the crimes that had taken place among the Corinthians before writing Cor(B). In response, Paul gave them the instruction on the basis of the Jerusalem tradition that there will be eschatological judgment when Jesus the Son of Man comes (Q^3 12:42–46).

Paul had a view on the imminence of the end of world. This is reflected in expressions such as "impending crisis," "time is short," and "this world in its present form is passing away" (1 Cor 7:26, 29, 31). Having been used for the first time in Cor(B), they point to the imminent coming of the end of world. The expectation of imminence reminds readers of the unexpected coming of the Son of Man like a thief as written in Q (Q^3 12:39–40). The difference between unexpectedness and imminence shows how Paul understood the end of world. In other words, Paul made a contribution to eschatological interpretation with an emphasis on the imminence of the end of world in Cor(B) compared to the unexpectedness written in Q.

The resurrection of Christ is described in connection with that of saints. According to Paul, the resurrection of Christ is impossible without that of saints, and vice versa (1 Cor 15:12–19). This was an answer to the question that the Corinthians raised after reading the instruction on the resurrection of Christ and saints written in Cor(A) (6:14). This means that Paul's previous instruction on resurrection was not so persuasive that the Corinthians would believe. Accordingly, Paul was compelled to come up with a circular interpretation of the resurrection of Christ and saints in Cor(B). As for this, Beker argues:

> Thus, Paul treats the warrant as an axiomatic premise because the very question of the Corinthians is taken for granted by Paul, that is, the necessary connection between the resurrection of Christ (which they affirm) and the futurity and materiality of a general resurrection (which they deny). "The apocalyptic connection," then, constitutes the basis of Paul's argument (15:20–28).[2]

As Beker points out, Paul failed in explaining the relationship between the resurrection of Christ and that of saints. It seems that Paul persisted in arguing for their resurrection without any theological basis of cause and effect.[3] There had been a theoretical barrier between the resurrection of Christ as the theological event and the general resurrection of the Corinthians from a practical point of view. However, in Cor(B), Paul did his best to make the argument persuasive enough to the Corinthians with regard to the issue of resurrection. In this respect, Paul made a significant advance in the interpretation of resurrection based on the Pharisaic tradition and the Damascus tradition.

An elaborate timetable is presented in connection with the events that would happen at the end of world. According to Paul, Christ was raised first, then those who belong to him will be raised, and finally the end will come with the result that everything will be subjected to him (1 Cor 15:23–28). Paul described what would happen at the end of world after the resurrection of Christ in detail. Hereby, the word "advent" [παρουσία] is used for the first time. The advent of Christ with those belonging to him is believed to be a combination of the two events described in Q: the coming of the Son of Man and the selection of people (Q^3 17:24, 34–35). In other words, Jesus the Son of Man will come to take those who have been chosen. It seems that, having inherited these

---

2. Beker, *Paul*, 168.

3. Conzelmann already said, "For theological reasons, Paul sets out not from the fact, but from proclamation and faith" (*I Corinthians*, 265).

instructions, Paul combined them to describe Christ coming with those who belong to him. In addition, Paul introduced another concept, that at the end of world Christ will hand over the kingdom to God after he destroys the final enemy, "death," in addition to all dominion, authority, and power—namely, the heavenly beings.[4] As for this, Beker says, "On the one hand, the resurrection of Christ is a sign of the impending kingdom (1 Cor 15:24); on the other hand, the general resurrection of the dead is the completion of the resurrection of Christ."[5] This means that the resurrection of Christ is the pinnacle from an eschatological point of view. Finally, God will put everything under Christ because God is all in all. This indicates that Christ will enjoy transcendent authority. In this way, Paul imposed an enhanced role upon Christ from an eschatological standpoint in Cor(B). It seems that, having described the eschatological schedule, Paul relied on all the traditions inherited from the Pharisees, the religious predecessors, and the apostles of Jerusalem in combination.

It is necessary to answer why Paul elaborated the eschatological schedule. To my judgment, the visit of Cephas to Corinth should be taken into account (1 Cor 1:12). Having visited the Corinthian church as a representative of the apostles of Jerusalem, he persuaded the Corinthians to refuse the gospel that Paul had preached. Not knowing about his visit, Paul sent Cor(A) with an instruction on the resurrection of Christ and saints (6:14). Without doubt, the Corinthians read it and then asked Cephas about the resurrection of the Lord Christ. The only answer returned from him was that the messianic figure neither dies nor rises from the dead according to the Jewish tradition. In reality, the death and resurrection of Jesus is not been mentioned in Q. which is supposed to have been finally complete in charge of the apostles of Jerusalem, including Cephas. Thus, the Corinthians could not help but ask the people of Chloe to inform Paul of their question about the resurrection of Christ and saints. In response, Paul explained the resurrection of Christ and saints as well as the eschatological schedule in Cor(B) (15:12–28). It seems that Paul tried to make the Corinthians convinced about the resurrection of Christ and saints as well as the eschatological schedule.

---

4. Barrett, *First Epistle*, 357.
5. Beker, *Paul*, 177.

Thess(B)

Paul provided a more elaborated instruction on what would happen at the end of world in Thess(B). After Paul heard of news that the Thessalonians had been shaken a little bit by those from the Jerusalem church, but had remained in the gospel, he delivered eschatological lessons as an answer to their questions. Having heavily relied on the Jerusalem tradition represented by Q, Paul presented the Jewish perspective on eschatological events.

Above all, the advent of the Lord Jesus Christ is mentioned four times. For this, Paul used the Greek word παρουσία (1 Thess 2:19; 3:13; 4:15-16; 5:23), which had already been adopted in Cor(B). The frequent use of it refers to his special interest in the coming of the Lord Jesus Christ in Thess(B). As shown before, the advent of Christ was described against the backdrop of the coming of the Son of Man written about in Q (Q^3 17:23-24, 30). Their relationship was already discussed in Thess(A) and Cor(B). Then, this indicates Paul's heavy reliance on the Jerusalem tradition represented by Q with regard to the eschatological coming of the Lord Jesus Christ. It seems that, having based his view on the teachings of Q, Paul tried to defeat the teachings of those sent by the apostles of Jerusalem. This indicates that Paul looked at eschatological events from a Jewish perspective even when writing Thess(B).

Paul mentioned the achievements to be presented at the advent of Christ. This is found in the description that the Thessalonians would be his hope, joy, or crown at the coming of the Lord Jesus (1 Thess 2:19). This means that they were the trophy of his spiritual warfare. In this way, Paul taught the Thessalonians that there would be merit to be presented before the Lord Jesus. It seems to be described against the backdrop of Q, in which the steward was portrayed as the one who had to present what he had done for the master at the time of accounting (Q^3 12:42-46; Q^4 19:12-26). This means that Paul was dependent upon the Jerusalem tradition with regard to his eschatological view. In other words, Paul maintained the Jewish perspective even at the time of writing Thess(B).

An instruction was given with regard to readiness for the coming of the Lord Jesus. According to Paul, the Thessalonians should be faultless and holy in the presence of God when Christ comes with all the saints (1 Thess 3:13). This is reminiscent of what Paul said in Cor(A) that the Corinthians should be blameless on the day of the Lord Jesus Christ. This would mean that the Thessalonians should also be faultless and holy by observing the Law and the instruction of Jesus embedded in Q. Blamelessness in holiness refers to the status that the people of God should maintain. In this way, Paul relied on the Jewish tradition for eschatological instruction at the time of writing Thess(B).

Paul prescribed the timetable of eschatological events again. This is found in the description that the Lord Jesus, risen from the dead, will come from heaven with a loud command, the voice of the archangel, and the trumpet call of God; then the dead will rise first and those alive and left will be caught up together with them in the clouds to meet the Lord in the air in order to be with him forever (1 Thess 4:14–18). This timetable is focused on the destiny of saints both dead and alive. It seems to be an advanced version of the eschatological schedule in Cor(B). It addition, it is a more advanced form of what was written in Q, according to which the Son of Man will appear in lightning and the chosen will be taken to somewhere (Q^3 14:23–25; 17:34–35). It seems that Paul used all the traditions he had inherited in combination; for instance, while the general resurrection originated in the Pharisaic tradition, the resurrection of Christ was based on the Damascus tradition, and the advent of Christ was described against the coming of the Son of Man in the Jerusalem tradition.

The instruction on the end of world is continued in the form of parable. According to Paul, the day of the Lord will come like a thief in the night and destruction will come suddenly as labor pains for a pregnant woman (1 Thess 5:2–3). The day of the Lord was already mentioned in Cor(A) and in Cor(B). In addition, the term "thief" and the theme of unexpected coming remind readers of those appeared in Q: "If the owner of the house had known at what hour the thief was coming, he would not have let his house be broken into" (Q^3 12:39–40). Moreover, the issue of destruction coming suddenly as labor pains on a pregnant woman seems to derive from the destruction occurring to people at the coming of the Son of Man (Q^3 17:26–27). Moreover, the pair between a male thief and a female pregnant woman reminds readers of three pairs between male and female in Q (Q^3 11:31–32; 13:18–21; 17:34–35). This shows Paul's dependence upon the Jerusalem tradition represented by Q at the time of writing Thess(B).

Paul described the transcendent aspect of eschatological events in Thess(B). This seems to be a more advanced version of eschatological instruction than that written in Cor(B). Having known that the Thessalonians were shaken for a while by those from the Jerusalem church but that they stayed in the gospel, Paul delivered eschatological instruction intermingled with the Pharisaic, Jerusalem, and Damascus traditions in Thess(B). In the meantime, he still maintained a Jewish view on the eschatological timetable.

Phil(A)

Paul reduced the amount of eschatological instruction in Phil(A). Having heard of news that the Philippians had been shaken by those come from Jerusalem but stayed in the gospel, Paul encouraged them with eschatological lessons. For this, having relied on the Jerusalem tradition, he also presented new teachings.

The coming of the Lord Jesus Christ from heaven is introduced in connection with the heavenly citizenship of the Philippians. According to Paul, their citizenship is in heaven, and they have to wait for the savior Lord Jesus Christ from there (Phil 3:20). Here Paul alludes to heaven, the place where the Lord Jesus Christ is staying before coming to the world. However, unlike the cases of Cor(B) and Thess(B), the companionship of saints with Christ has been omitted in Phil(A). This means that attachment to the members of church has decreased from an eschatological perspective. In addition, there is no interest in the eschatological timetable. This implies that his confidence in eschatological events diminished. Moreover, Paul did not use the word παρουσία anymore. This brought his theological understanding to the level of speculation about the coming of the Lord Jesus Christ. This means that, having been a little dependent upon the Jerusalem tradition represented by Q, Paul reduced the weight on eschatological instruction in Phil(A) in comparison with Cor(B) and Thess(B).

The transformation of the body is treated for the first time. According to Paul, by the power of God, the Lord Jesus Christ will bring everything under his control and transform the lowly bodies of people so that they will live like his glorious one (Phil 3:21). Two points must be considered here. First, whereas it was stated that all things would be put under the feet of Christ in Cor(B), the authority of Christ to control everything is presented in Phil(A). However, Paul had greatly lessened the detail of description in Phil(A) in comparison with Cor(B). Second, Paul described the Lord Jesus Christ as the one who can transform the mortal body to the glorious one. This is not mentioned in the eschatological schedule described in Cor(B) and Thess(B). Thus, in Phil(A) Paul added a new instruction on the transformed body that is worthy of living in heaven. In this respect, the Lord Jesus Christ was presented as the savior. At that time, it seems that a Christian view of eschatological lesson has emerged. However, it should be admitted that, compared to the topics addressed in the previous chapters—that is, the christological issue, the death of the Lord Jesus Christ, his redemptive and salvific role, and the Law—the moment of the beginning of Christian teaching is unclear with regard to eschatological instruction.

When the Philippians were momentarily shaken by the Jewish teachings of those sent by the apostles of Jerusalem but soon stayed firmly in the gospel, Paul encouraged them with eschatological teaching. However, the description of the eschatological schedule was considerably reduced in Phil(A) compared to that described in Cor(B) and Thess(B). On the other hand, the salvific role of the Lord Jesus Christ was emphasized with the transformation of the mortal body to the glorious one. Paul gradually stayed away from the influence of the apostles of Jerusalem.

Cor(C)

Paul revealed the expectation of the coming of the Lord Jesus Christ in Cor(C). It is, however, noteworthy that the amount of eschatological instruction rapidly reduced in response to the challenge of some Corinthians sponsored by the apostles of Jerusalem. His dependence upon the Jerusalem tradition was getting less when he had faced the challenge directly.

The coming of the Lord is mentioned in connection with the disclosure of hidden things. According to Paul, the Corinthians had to wait until the Lord comes in order that he will bring to light what was hidden in darkness and would expose the motives of men's hearts (1 Cor 4:5). The coming of the Lord was already mentioned in Thess(A), Cor(B), Thess(B), and Phil(A) against the backdrop of the Son of Man written in Q (Q^3 17:23–24). In addition, the description that the Lord will bring to light what was hidden in darkness also reminds readers of the saying in Q: "There is nothing concealed that will not be disclosed, or hidden that will not be made known" (Q^4 12:2–3). Having inherited the instruction from Q, Paul applied it to the coming of the Lord in Cor(C). This means that Paul was dependent upon the Jerusalem tradition represented by Q with regard to eschatological instruction at the time of writing Cor(C).

Paul dealt with the transformation of the body that would occur at the end of world. This is found in the saying, "We will not all sleep, but we will all be changed—in a flash, in the twinkling of an eye, at the last trumpet. For the trumpet will sound, the dead will be raised imperishable, and we will be changed" (1 Cor 15:51–52). This should be discussed in three ways. First, Paul mentioned the transformation of the dead to resurrection at the end of world. This refers to the discontinuity between the mortal body and the imperishable one in order to show "the miraculous character of the future life."[6] At any rate, the imperishable is reminiscent of what was described in Phil(A), that Christ would change the lowly body to a glorious one of Christ (Phil 3:21). This indicates that Paul enhanced his description of the transformed body as time passed. In this way, Paul developed his eschatological lesson in Cor(C) a little more than in Phil(A). Second, Paul referred to the sound of a trumpet in Cor(C). This is one of the three described in Thess(B): a loud command, the voice of the archangel, and the trumpet of God (1 Thess 4:16). There is a difference in the frequency of narratives for eschatological elements. The difference shows that Paul's interest in the end of world declined in Cor(C) compared to Thess(B). Third, the change of those alive is to be focused. Whereas Paul described those alive as being caught up into the air and meeting Christ there in Thess(B) (1 Thess 5:17), only the transformation of body is mentioned in Cor(C). The difference between the two letters shows again that Paul's interest in eschatological events diminished. Nevertheless, Paul continued to describe the eschatological transformation of the mortal body with an apocalyptic mode in Cor(C).

The coming of the Lord is mentioned once again. This is found in the saying "Come, O Lord!" (1 Cor 16:22). The petition appears in the form of the optative mood for the first time in regard to the eschatological coming of the Lord. It seems that Paul was still convinced of the coming of the Lord to the extent that he expressed it with an imperative verb form. This is how Paul attracted the attention of the Corinthians and made them long for the promised coming of the Lord Jesus Christ at the end of world. As discussed before, the wish for his coming is reminiscent of the Son of Man coming at the end of world (Q^3 17:23–24). In this respect, Paul showed a basic reliance upon the Jerusalem tradition

---

6. Conzelmann, *I Corinthians*, 282–83.

represented by Q with regard to eschatological instruction at the time of writing Cor(C).

It is necessary to see the reason that Paul reduced the frequency and intensity of eschatological instruction in Cor(C). As shown before, several elements of eschatological phenomena disappeared in relation to Christ. Paul showed only a basic level of dependence upon the Jerusalem tradition in association with the coming of the Lord. Having faced the challenge of some Corinthians, Paul seems to have thought that it was no longer possible to make them return to the gospel from an eschatological standpoint. As Paul increasingly developed the instruction of Christianity, it seems that he adopted the eschatological lesson less.

Galatians

Paul made a brief comment on eschatological events at the beginning of Galatians. On the other hand, no eschatological teaching appears in the main text. It seems that Paul refrained from mentioning the eschatological issue when the challenge against the gospel and his authority reached its culmination.

There are two references to eschatological matters. One is that God raised Jesus Christ, and the other is the purpose of rescuing people from the evil age (Gal 1:4). The former was already mentioned several times as a standardized expression in the letters written earlier than Galatians. On the other hand, the latter is a soteriological lesson that contains an eschatological aspect with a reference to the evil age. However, since this actually reflects the apocalyptic tradition, the eschatological aspect is quite weak. If so, Paul actually gave less eschatological instruction in Galatians than we would expect.

There is a reason that Paul almost abandoned eschatological instruction in Galatians. This is because he faced the most severe challenge of the Galatians. Perhaps, having been busy refuting the Law, he had no more energy to describe the eschatological lessons. In addition, Paul thought that eschatological instruction was meaningless to them. It seems that Paul slightly relied on the Damascus tradition for the resurrection of Christ; on the other hand, he no longer relied on the Jerusalem tradition for eschatological teaching in Galatians. Paul made little contribution to the development of Christianity from an eschatological point of view because he almost gave up delivering eschatological instruction in Galatians.

Cor(D)

Paul showed the least interest in the end of world in Cor(D). The day of the Lord Jesus is the only topic mentioned in association with it. Having known that it was difficult to make the Corinthians return to the gospel with eschatological instruction, Paul seems to do his best here to restore his relationship with them.

The day of the Lord Jesus is mentioned in an eschatological context. According to Paul, as the Corinthians understood him in part, they will understand fully that they can boast of him just as he will boast of them on the day of the Lord Jesus (2 Cor 1:14). The day of the Lord Jesus appears in the context of what will be revealed at the end of world. The expression related to the day of the Lord Jesus Christ was already used in Cor(A), Cor(B), and Thess(B). Paul mentions the "day of the Lord Jesus" with a reference to the eschatological judgment in Cor(D). In addition, the statement that as the Corinthians understood Paul in part they will come to understand fully on the day of the Lord Jesus reminds readers of what was written in Cor(C): the Lord "will bring to light what is hidden in darkness" (1 Cor 4:5; cf. Q^4 12:2–3). Paul applied the statement written in Cor(C) to his relationship with the Corinthians in Cor(D). This indicates that Paul used eschatological instruction to restore his relationship with them.

Paul significantly reduced his interest in the eschatological issue in Cor(D). Having tried to restore his relationship with the Corinthians, he could not devote himself to the eschatological issue. His reliance on the Jewish tradition appears to be at a minimal level. This is because Paul's resentment toward the apostles of Jerusalem increased due to the consistent challenge of some Corinthians sponsored by them. It is, however, important to observe that Paul kept delivering instruction on the eschatological issue to a minimum in Cor(D) after he had rarely mentioned it in Galatians. In this way, Paul refrained from delivering eschatological instruction while working on the restoration of his relationship with the Corinthians.

Cor(E)

Paul reduced the frequency of describing eschatological matters in Cor(E). Except general resurrection and eschatological judgment, Paul did not deal with it. He was more interested in reconciliation with the Corinthians.

The resurrection of people in the future is mentioned in an eschatological context. According to Paul, God, who raised the Lord Jesus from the dead, will also raise Paul and the Corinthians, and God will present them in front of him (2 Cor 4:14). The resurrection of the Lord Christ and the saints was already mentioned in Cor(A) (1 Cor 6:14) and Cor(B) (1 Cor 15:12–24); then, it reaches the culmination in Thess(B) (1 Thess 4:16–17). However, in Cor(E), Paul put an emphasis on the presence of people in front of God after their resurrection. This seems to have been presented as a follow-up to the description of Thess(B) that the resurrected will welcome Christ in the air. It seems that the eschatological interpretation was given in connection with the compensation for belief in the gospel Paul had proclaimed.

Paul described the resurrection with a parable of a dwelling place. It is said, "If the earthly tent we live in is destroyed, we have a building from God, an eternal house in heaven" (2 Cor 5:1). Then, Paul defined resurrection as living in the heavenly dwelling (5:2). It seems to refer to the resurrected body clothed with heavenly dwelling (5:4). This reminds readers of the transformation of lowly bodies to the glorious ones as written in Phil(A) (Phil 3:21) and that of the perishable to the imperishable as written in Cor(C) (1 Cor 15:53). Accordingly, Paul was able to describe the transformation of the body with a metaphor in Cor(E). This shows Paul's development of a particular subject from an eschatological point of view. Nevertheless, he avoided treating other eschatological issues here. In consequence, it can be said that Paul's interest in the eschatological issue decreased in Cor(E).

The eschatological judgment is dealt with in connection with personal witness before God. According to Paul, people must all appear before the judgment seat of Christ and each one will receive what is due them for the things done while in the body, whether good or bad (2 Cor 5:10). The phrase "judgment seat of Christ" appears for the first time here with a reference to a new instruction that Christ was regarded as the eschatological judge (cf. Q 22:30). In addition, the phrase "each one may receive what is due him for the things done while in the body, whether good or bad" is also used for the first time here. This is an eschatological teaching that typically shows a Jewish perspective. In this way, Paul applied to the Corinthians the eschatological perspective used among the Jews when he tried to reconcile with them.

No eschatological issue is dealt with except the general resurrection of saints and the eschatological judgment in Cor(E). This indicates that Paul's interest in the eschatological issue diminished while he tried to be reconciled with the Corinthians. The challenge of some Corinthians seems to have made Paul feel skeptical of eschatological teachings. However, Paul still maintained a basic belief in the resurrection and judgment from a Jewish viewpoint.

Cor(F)

Paul dealt with eschatological matters little in Cor(F). This is probably because its usefulness was denied. Paul was probably forced to focus on the practical matter of the Corinthians, who constantly challenged him.

It could be said that eschatological teaching is found in only one place. According to Paul, "Their end will be what their actions deserve" (2 Cor 11:15). This may reveal an eschatological character. However, even if it is not conveyed from a Christian point of view, it is a level of content that can be delivered from an ethical one. This shows that Paul almost gave up teaching from an eschatological perspective. This is supported by the fact that there is no longer any teaching from an eschatological point of view in the rest of Cor(F).

Paul stopped preaching from an eschatological point of view as the Corinthians continued to challenge him. This phenomenon was also observed at the time of writing Galatians earlier. Paul probably gave up the belief that eschatological teachings could bring the Corinthians back to the gospel.

Summary

Paul frequently dealt with the eschatological issue during his second missionary trip. In particular, he expressed most the coming of the Lord Jesus Christ on the basis of Q representing the Jerusalem tradition. The general resurrection of saints was consistently mentioned on the basis of the Pharisaic tradition. Without doubt, Paul based his eschatological teaching on the resurrection of Christ handed down from the Damascus tradition. However, as the challenge against him grew, Paul began to convey eschatological lessons more elaborately. Nevertheless, when the challenge reached its peak, he refrained from delivering eschatological instruction. Then, at the end of the second missionary trip, eschatological teachings rarely appeared. Perhaps Paul thought that his eschatological instruction was not powerful enough to make those who followed the Jewish instruction return to the gospel. It was not easy for Paul to persuade them by explaining eschatological events he had never experienced. In any case, Paul showed ups and downs in connection with eschatological lessons during his second missionary trip. However, the birth of Christianity is somewhat unclear in connection with the eschatological instruction when compared to other topics treated in the previous chapters.

C. THE THIRD MISSIONARY TRIP

Paul delivered eschatological teachings during his third missionary trip. However, his interest in it was getting less in the letters sent to or from Rome than in previous ones. Even if he was interested, Paul stayed at a level of repeating what he had already taught.

Rom(A)

Paul continued cutting down on eschatological matters in Rom(A). The eschatological lessons were carefully delivered from a Jewish perspective because there was no challenge among the Romans, whose majority was supposedly Jews. Paul stayed at the level of dealing with the eschatological judgment that would be at the end of world.

First, the seat of eschatological judgment is mentioned in connection with God. According to Paul, everyone will stand before the judgment seat of God (Rom 14:10). The term "seat" is used a second time since it appeared in Cor(E) (2 Cor 5:10; cf. Q 22:30). The difference is found in that while it was connected with Christ in Cor(E), it is with God in Rom(A). Paul substituted God for Christ in Rom(A) because the majority of the Roman church were supposedly Jews. In this way, Paul put forth the juridical role of God from a Jewish perspective.

Second, the eschatological accounting of each one to God was mentioned. Paul seems to have put an emphasis on the responsibility of each one from an eschatological point of view (Rom 14:12). This makes people think of the statement written in Cor(E) that "each one may receive what is due him for the things done while in the body, whether good or bad" (2 Cor 5:10). It seems that Paul used it in a summarized form in Rom(A). As discussed before, the eschatological accounting was one of the important topics in Q (Q^3 12:42–46; Q^4 19:12–26). Without doubt, the topic of eschatological accounting originated in the Jewish tradition. In this respect, Paul put forth the eschatological judgment and its result from a Jewish perspective.

Paul put an emphasis on the eschatological judgment of God upon the Romans according to what they had done, whether good or bad. This shows a typical aspect of Judaism. The reason that Paul was dependent upon the Jewish tradition for eschatological instruction is that the majority of the Romans were supposedly Jews. However, eschatological teaching was not the main theme in Rom(A). Paul described an eschatological way that the Romans should have to abide ethically in their religious life. It seems that Paul did not want to give the Romans pressure with regard to eschatological instruction.

Rom(B)

Paul briefly mentioned the wrath of God from an eschatological perspective in Rom(B). This is the answer of Paul to the question that the Romans raised about his statement that the Law brings wrath as written in Rom(A). However, Paul only dealt with it quite a bit in relation to the eschatological subject in Rom(B).

Wrath appears in connection with the righteous judgment of God. According to Paul, people were storing up wrath against themselves for the day of God when his righteous judgment would be revealed (Rom 2:5). The wrath of God will be given to those of stubborn and unrepentant heart at the righteous judgment of God. This means that the wrath of God results from what a man has done before God. Paul already gave an instruction on retribution for works in Cor(E) (2 Cor 5:10) and Rom(A) (Rom 14:12). This is a lesson typically found in Judaism. Therefore, everyone should take responsibility for what they have done. As such, Paul dealt with the eschatological judgment from a Jewish perspective. Meanwhile, he enhanced his eschatological interpretation a little.

Paul continued to deal with the issue of wrath. It is said, "Do not take revenge, my friends, but leave room for God's wrath" (Rom 12:19). Paul tried to say that God is the one who finally judges and punishes. The wrath of God began to be dealt with in Q (Q^1 3:7), and then appeared in Thess(A) (1 Thess 1:10) through to Rom(A) (Rom 4:15). After all, Paul regarded the wrath of God as one of eschatological punishment. This shows again that the wrath of God must be understood in the context of eschatological judgment. Then, it seems that Paul understood God's revenge on behalf of his people in light of vindication for them. This implies Paul's dependence upon the Jerusalem tradition while writing Rom(B) to the Romans, whose majority was supposedly Jews.

There is a reason that the wrath of God is presented from an eschatological perspective in Rom(B). Since Paul presented the Law as an entity that would bring wrath in Rom(A) (Rom 4:15), the Romans objected to it and raised a question about the relationship between the Law and wrath. Thus, Paul was compelled to answer them from an eschatological point of view on the wrath of God. This reflects the fact that there was tension in his relationship with the Jewish members who made up the majority of the Roman church. Thus, Paul warned them about the wrath of God from an eschatological point of view. In this way, Paul gave an appropriate interpretation from an eschatological perspective in response to the changing circumstances in his relationship with the Romans.

Rom(C)

Paul treated the eschatological issue least in Rom(C). This is found only in the description that the spirit of God will give life to the mortal body. It seems that Paul reduced the frequency of dealing with eschatological instruction as the critique of the Romans against him increased.

The general resurrection of saints is mentioned in connection with the spirit of God. According to Paul, if the spirit of God was living in the Romans, God, who had raised Christ from the dead, would also give life to their mortal bodies through his spirit, who lives among them (Rom 8:11). Two points should be considered here. First, Paul was assuring them of the resurrection of saints to be fulfilled at the end. This is the first case that Paul mentioned the spirit of God in connection with the general resurrection. Paul once talked about the spirit of God intervening for eternal life in Galatians, which had been written at the peak of their challenge against him (Gal 6:8). The intervention of the spirit of God for the life of the mortal body is also mentioned in Rom(C), which was written at the peak of the critique against him by the Romans, especially the Jewish members. In this way, Paul tended to depend on the spirit of God with an eschatological instruction whenever he was challenged or criticized. Second, the mortal body needs to be studied. Paul mentioned the transformation of the lowly body into the glorious one of Christ in Phil(A) (Phil 3:21) and then to the imperishable body in Cor(C) (1 Cor 15:52). The mortal body is in parallel with the lowly body but in contrast with the glorious and imperishable body. In this way, Paul showed that he developed his interpretation of the resurrected body from an eschatological point of view.

It seems that Paul radically reduced the amount of eschatological description in Rom(C). This was due to the serious inquiries and critiques of the Romans against his view on the relationship between the Law and sin as written in Rom(B) (Rom 3:20). Thus, it seems that Paul felt a great sense of disparity and accordingly judged that his eschatological lesson could not make the Romans accept the gospel he would preach in more detail. This kind of tendency was already shown in the second half of his second missionary trip. The more Paul wrote to the Romans, the less he presented the eschatological lesson. This is also supported by the fact that no eschatological statement appears in Rom(D).

Phil(B)

Paul referred to the eschatological issue in a minimum in Phil(B). It appears only with references to the day of Christ and the end of world coming near. Paul exhorted the Philippians with eschatological lessons.

The day of Christ is mentioned two times. First, the Philippians were admonished to discern what was best to be pure and blameless until the day of Christ (Phil 1:10). This reminds readers of what was written in Cor(A) that the Corinthians should be blameless on the day of the Lord Jesus Christ (1 Cor 1:8). However, in Phil(B) Paul referred to the ability to discern the inadequacy of others and taught them not to be sinful. In addition, it is necessary to look at the phrase "until the day of Christ" used with a reference to persistence. Paul advised the Philippians to avoid their transgressions until that day. Second, Paul revealed the desire to boast on the day of Christ because of his own work (Phil 2:16). This reflects the fact that he maintained a good relationship with the Philippians, having waited for a reward at the end of world. This makes readers think of Paul's boasting of the Corinthians on the day of the Lord Jesus as written in Cor(D) (2 Cor 1:14; 7:4). However, when Paul had a good relationship with the Philippians, he expressed his wish to boast on the day of Christ about what he had done well. This indicates that Paul described things differently according to his relationship with the recipients of his letters. At any rate, Paul continued to describe what would happen on the day of Christ. It is, however, to be remembered that instruction on the end of world was not developed much in Phil(B).

A brief mentioning of the end of world appears again. According to Paul, "The Lord is near" (Phil 4:5). This reminds readers of the plea for the coming of the Lord written in Cor(C) (1 Cor 16:22). Then, it was possible for Paul to proclaim the nearness of the Lord in Phil(B). It is, however, to be noted that it is not clear wether the day of the coming of the Lord was near or the Lord was at a place near to the Philippians. It seems that the former is preferred to the latter because the issue of time was usually connected with the Lord in the previous letters. Nevertheless, its meaning is ambiguous in comparison with the petition for the coming of the Lord in Cor(C). This shows that Paul's interest in the eschatological issue had decreased over time.

Paul did not add anything new to Phil(B) in regard to the eschatological issue. It seems that Paul did not want to make the Philippians nervous with it because he had a good relationship with them staying in the gospel. Paul simply repeated what he had already taught the Gentiles of other churches. Paul did not develop his eschatological lesson further in Phil(B), written at the end of his life in Rome.

Summary

Paul provided a certain amount of eschatological instruction in the letters written on the way to Rome or there. However, as he had shown during his second missionary trip, he was getting less interested in eschatological lessons due to the increasing critique of the Romans against him during his third missionary trip. This is supported by the fact that no eschatological instruction appears in Rom(D) and that a small amount of it does later in Phil(B). Paul seems to have lost confidence in eschatological lessons when the critique against him was fierce in the middle of the third missionary trip. In the end, Paul was not welcomed by the Romans and apparently was imprisoned for unknown reasons.

D. CONCLUSION

Paul had been a Pharisee. He was accustomed to an eschatological worldview. His past made him accept the teaching of the resurrection of Christ handed down from the religious predecessors in Damascus and the eschatological events learned from Cephas in Jerusalem. Therefore, he seems to have proclaimed eschatological teachings on the basis of the traditions mentioned above during his first missionary trip to the Gentiles. However, a new aspect unfolded during his second missionary trip. He developed an eschatological interpretation of his own when some Gentiles sponsored by the apostles of Jerusalem challenged him. This culminated in Phil(A), where Jesus Christ is described as the savior who transformed the mortal bodies of people into glorious ones. Christianity is believed to have been born as eschatological teachings grew stronger. However, when the challenge reached its extreme at the time of writing Galatians, he almost stopped delivering eschatological teachings to them. This is probably because Paul thought that the interpretation of the end of world was no longer convincing to them. Accordingly, Paul occasionally conveyed eschatological teachings among his letters written later than Galatians, but these remained at the basic level of theological interpretation. This shows that Paul adjusted the level of eschatological instruction as he responded to the changing circumstances of the recipients of his letters. A similar phenomenon appears in the letters written during the third missionary trip. Meanwhile, eschatological lessons showed ups and downs in their own way.

7

The Spirit of God

PAUL WAS INTERESTED IN the spirit of God from a theological viewpoint. It was an important element among Jews in their religious life. Thus, Paul was already familiar with the spirit of God from a Jewish perspective. Then, after he had received the revelation, there was a chance to learn more about it from Cephas in connection with Jesus on the basis of the Jerusalem tradition represented by Q. This made Paul have his own concept of the spirit of God. However, no one knows how much Paul dealt with the issue of the spirit of God during his first missionary trip because no record has been left. On the other hand, having been challenged by some Gentiles in the middle of his second missionary trip, Paul began to emphasize the role of the spirit of God in contrast with "flesh." This reached its peak at the time of writing Galatians. A similar phenomenon is found among letters sent to Rome during his third missionary trip. This is reflected in the fact that references to the spirit of God most appear when Paul was most criticized by the Romans. The spirit of God must be understood in terms of power, not from a Trinitarian perspective.

A. THE FIRST MISSIONARY TRIP

Paul had his own knowledge of the spirit of God that he learned from the Hebrew Scriptures and Pharisaic tradition when he had been in Judaism. In addition, Paul learned more about the spirit of God from Cephas on the basis of the first three redactions of Q. It seems that Paul would have delivered an instruction on the spirit of God based on Jewish tradition during his first missionary trip.

What Paul learned about the spirit of God from the Pharisaic tradition has not been known in detail. He stated that he was a Pharisee; however, it is not clear what he had inherited in relation to the spirit of God since no clue to this has been left. Nevertheless, it is important to admit that Paul learned about the spirit of God from the Pharisees because they would have passed on the knowledge of the spirit of God written of in the Hebrew Scriptures. The spirit of God is mentioned at the beginning of Genesis (Gen 1:2). The spirit of God is primarily portrayed as an agent for carrying out God's commands in the Hebrew Scriptures. Without doubt, Paul was familiar with this concept.

It seems that the revelation of God about his Son had little to do with the spirit of God. This is evident in that there is no mention of the spirit of God in association with the revelation. In a similar manner, the gospel of Christ seems to have had little to do with the spirit of God. The religious predecessors of Damascus mentioned nothing other than the death, burial, resurrection, and appearance of Christ. From this, it can be known that the theological interpretation of the spirit of God had not been developed even immediately after Paul had received the revelation in Damascus.

Paul seems to have learned more about the spirit of God from Cephas on the basis of the Jerusalem tradition. When he went up to Jerusalem around 38 CE, he had a chance to be acquainted with Q, in which John had talked about the baptism of Jesus with "spirit" [πνεῦμα] and "fire" [πῦρ] (Q^3 3:16). The Greek term πνεῦμα literally means "wind," which is in parallel with "fire." Thus, the spirit seems to be defined as a being that exerts power like invisible wind as well as visible fire. Without doubt, the term "spirit" appears with the concept inherited from the Hebrew Scriptures and Jewish tradition. Thus, Paul could have accepted the concept of the spirit of God working with Jesus without difficulty.

The spirit is presented again in association with Jesus. According to Q, the spirit of God descended from heaven upon the baptized Jesus in the form of a dove (Q^3 3:21–22). The spirit is considered to be a substitute for God working through it. In addition, the descent of the spirit refers to the presence of God with Jesus. The spirit is introduced as a medium of communication between God and human beings. This instruction would have made Paul think deeply about the presence of God through the spirit, so that he might change his view on the temple of God.

It is necessary to discuss the theological background with regard to the spirit of God. The Greek word for "dove" is περιστερά, which refers to יונה [Jonah] in Hebrew. This was used for the prophet Jonah. Thus, the spirit that came down upon the baptized Jesus in the form of a dove could refer to the spirit of Jonah, who declared a judgment on the Gentile Ninevites (Jon 1:2; 3:4). The "spirit" descending upon Jesus could mean the "spirit of judgment upon the Gentiles" in this context.[1] This is supported by the fact that in the third redaction of Q the Gentiles are often mentioned in connection with the eschatological judgment (Q^3 7:1–10; 10:13–14; 11:31). If so, Paul would have learned that the spirit of God exists for judgment upon the Gentiles.

There is another meaning for the spirit. The spirit that came down from heaven upon the baptized Jesus in the image of a dove seems to have been described against the backdrop of Genesis. It is said that the spirit of God was hovering on water (Gen 1:2). The word "hovering" refers to an image of a bird spreading her wings to protect her young (Deut 32:11).[2] It is important that the dove is a type of bird that can be described against the backdrop of the hovering spirit of God. Thus, Jesus should be understood as the one who came to the world for a new creation. His baptism signifies the end of this world and the beginning of a new world. In this respect, the spirit of God should be seen from an eschatological point of view. If so, Paul would have understood that the spirit came for eschatological judgment.

Paul seems to have learned a lot about the spirit of God from Cephas on the basis of Q. The spirit of God was given for the eschatological judgment against the Gentiles. This may have made Paul proclaim Jesus the Son of God to the Gentiles. His understanding fits well with the purpose for which he received the revelation of God about his Son (Gal 1:16). For this reason, Paul must have been more passionate about the mission to the Gentiles. This interpretation will help readers to discuss what Paul said about the spirit of God in his letters.

When Paul went on his first missionary trip, he would have talked about the spirit of God to the Gentiles. However, he did not leave any data on what he taught in detail. Perhaps it is likely that he delivered instructions on the basis of what he had learned from the Pharisaic tradition and Q. At that time, it seems that the Gentiles experienced the spirit of God.

---

1. Ra, Q, 100–101.
2. Westermann, *Genesis*, 107.

This is reflected in Thess(A) describing that the gospel was preached by the "holy" spirit of God (1 Thess 1:6). From the fact that Thess(A) is the first letter to the Gentiles during Paul's second missionary trip, it can be inferred that Paul preached the gospel and the Thessalonians experienced the presence of the spirit of God during his first missionary trip. Perhaps Paul believed that the spirit of God worked with him.

Paul returned to Jerusalem after he had finished his first missionary trip. Having met the apostles around 49 CE, he had a chance to be acquainted with the fourth redaction of Q, which is supposed to have been completed around 41 CE. This made Paul learn a little more about the spirit of God. First, the fourth redactor described the spirit of God leading Jesus to the devil in the wilderness (Q^4 4:1–2). The spirit of God appears as a personified agent in that he led Jesus. This is quite different from the spirit of God described as a tool of eschatological judgment in the third redaction of Q (Q^3 3:21). Moreover, the spirit of God appears in opposition to the devil. The fourth redactor thus revealed a deep interest in spiritual beings. This narrative reflects the fact that the apostles of Jerusalem, who had been in charge of the fourth redaction of Q, had great interest in spiritual beings. Anyway, having learned this, Paul would have identified the "spirit" descended from heaven in the image of a dove with the "spirit of God" leading Jesus to the devil in the wilderness.

Then, Paul was exposed to the issue of blasphemy against the spirit of God. It is revealed in the saying that while anyone who rebels against the Son of Man can be forgiven, whoever blasphemes the "holy" spirit of God cannot be forgiven (Q^4 12:10). The spirit of God is portrayed as a personified being and described as an agent superior to Jesus the Son of Man. The superiority of the spirit of God to Jesus is mentioned again following the story of temptation. This implies that the twelve apostles of Jerusalem, including Cephas, emphasized the role of the spirit of God at the time of the apostolic meeting. In this way, Paul would have received teaching on the spirit of God and formed a concept that the spirit of God was superior to Jesus. He would have gone on his second missionary trip with more knowledge of the spirit of God.

In conclusion, Paul had more knowledge of the spirit of God over time. Although how he got to know about the spirit of God has not been well reflected in his letters, Paul would have learned about it from the Hebrew Scriptures, the Pharisaic tradition, the Jerusalem tradition represented by Q, and his experience during the first missionary trip. The spirit of God is described as a means of eschatological judgment and a personified agent superior to Jesus. It seems that Paul also went on his second missionary trip with a broader concept of the spirit of God.

B. THE SECOND MISSIONARY TRIP

During his second missionary trip, Paul faced a case that made him change his perception of the spirit of God. He seems to have introduced the spirit as a certain entity that enabled Gentiles to live holy. When Paul faced the challenge of some Gentiles sponsored by the apostles of Jerusalem, he changed the notion of the spirit of God. Having set it in contrast with "flesh," which refers to human nature against God, Paul presented the spirit of God as an entity that made the Gentiles the people of God. In this respect, Paul made a significant contribution to the understanding of the spirit of God.

Thess(A)

Paul referred to the spirit in Thess(A). He applied the adjective "holy" to the spirit. The "holy" spirit is portrayed as an entity that led the Thessalonians to the life of the people of God.

The "holy" spirit is presented in connection with the gospel. According to Paul, the Thessalonians received the gospel not simply with "word" [λόγος] but also with power, the "holy" spirit, and deep conviction (1 Thess 1:5). This means that when Paul preached the gospel in words during the first visit to Thessalonica, power, the "holy" spirit, and deep conviction accompanied. It is noteworthy that the terms "word" and the "holy spirit" were also used in Q. The term "word" appears as a means to rebel against the Son of Man or to blaspheme the "holy" spirit in Q (Q^4 12:10). Although he omitted the issue of blasphemy, Paul seems to have adopted the words and applied them to the Thessalonians in Thess(A). Thus, it can be said that Q plays the role of source for the description of the "holy" spirit in Thess(A). It is presumed here that the spirit worked on the Thessalonians as a whole. As such, it seems that the relationship with the "holy" spirit was generally established from a positive standpoint even in the early days of the second missionary trip.

Paul presented the "holy" spirit in connection with "word." It is said that the Thessalonians received the "word" [λόγος] with the joy of the "holy" spirit in the midst of troubles (1 Thess 1:6). The "word" here refers to the message that Paul delivered to the Thessalonians during the first visit to Thessalonica. The "holy" spirit was portrayed as an entity that could make the Thessalonians filled with joy in spite of troublesome circumstances. This reminds readers of Q, in which the "holy" spirit is described as an entity to teach the disciples of Jesus when they were anxious about what to say before synagogue (Q^4 12:12). Although outwardly the two verses of Paul and Q show a lot of difference, there is a common element in that the words/messages [λόγος] were given through the "holy" spirit in difficult situations. Moreover, Paul used an allusion to Q 12:10, 12 in sequence in Thess(A) (1 Thess 1:5–6). It is then possible that Paul took the lesson from Q and applied it to the life of the Thessalonians with some modification.

God is portrayed as the one giving the "holy" spirit. According to Paul, God gave the Thessalonians the "holy" spirit (1 Thess 4:8). Having applied the adjective "holy" to the spirit, Paul regarded the "holy" spirit as a being that made the Thessalonians live holy. This becomes even more evident when it is associated with the purpose of God for calling men to be sanctified as described in the previous text (4:3–7). God is the one who gives the spirit to sanctify those called to be his people. It is important here that the spirit is presupposed to be given to the Thessalonians as a whole. This shows that Paul maintained a friendly view of the Thessalonians at the time of writing Thess(A).

Paul consistently used the title "holy spirit" in Thess(A). The adjective "holy" is attached to the spirit because he wanted to show the role of making the Thessalonians live holy from a Jewish viewpoint. Having inherited the "holy" spirit from Q, Paul tried to deliver the lesson that God gave the word/message through the "holy" spirit and made his people sanctified. The spirit was presupposed to be given to the Thessalonians regardless of their spiritual state. It is likely that Paul stayed at the level of delivering the Jewish concept of the spirit at the time of writing Thess(A).

Cor(A)

Paul referred to the spirit of God for the first time in Cor(A). The spirit of God turns out to be a personified agent who dwells among people and sanctifies them. In this regard, Paul seems to have kept relying upon the Jerusalem tradition with regard to the role of the spirit of God in the early days of mission.

Paul mentioned the spirit of God dwelling in human beings. This is found in the description that the spirit of God dwelled among the Corinthians (1 Cor 3:16). Paul defined the Corinthians as the temple because the spirit of God had dwelled among them. It is important that the term "dwell" is used to make a close relationship between the spirit of God and the Corinthians. This reminds readers of the personified aspect of the spirit of God already expressed in Q (Q^4 4:1–2; 12:10). It is possible that Paul inherited and applied it to the relationship of the Corinthians to the spirit of God in Cor(A). This is the contribution that Paul made for the interpretation of the spirit of God on the basis of the Jerusalem tradition represented by Q. Here, it is necessary to see that Paul once again described the spirit of God as dwelling among the Corinthians regardless of their spiritual state. This shows that Paul maintained a friendly view of the Corinthians at the time of writing Cor(A).

Then, the spirit of God is described as an entity working on the sanctification of people. According to Paul, the Corinthians were washed, sanctified, and justified in the name of the Lord Jesus Christ and the spirit of God (1 Cor 6:11). Paul described that the spirit of God had worked on the cleansing, sanctification, and righteousness of people. The spirit of God is set in parallel with the name of the Lord Jesus Christ. This is different from Q, which describes the spirit of God as an agent superior to Jesus (Q^4 4:1–2; 12:10). If so, it seems that while writing Cor(A) Paul put the position of the Lord Jesus Christ equal to the spirit of God. In this respect, Paul enhanced theological interpretation with regard to the status of the spirit of God.

Paul referred to the "holy" spirit once again. This appears in the saying that the body of the Corinthians is the temple of the "holy" spirit dwelling among them (1 Cor 6:19). Paul described it against the backdrop of the temple of Jerusalem, in which God had been believed to dwell. This shows Paul's view on the temple of the "holy" spirit from a Jewish perspective. In other words, just as the Jews believed God's dwelling in the most holy place of temple, Paul taught that the "holy" spirit of God dwelled among the Corinthians. In addition, the dwelling of the spirit of God seems to be described against the backdrop of the presence of it upon the baptized Jesus (Q^3 3:21). In other words, Paul applied to the Corinthians what he had inherited from Q with regard to the presence of the spirit of God. If my argument is acceptable, Paul enhanced his theological interpretation of the role of the "holy" spirit of God over time.

Paul used the term "spirit of God" and "holy spirit" together in Cor(A). They were used to inform that God makes people holy with his spirit. It is important that the spirit of God was personified as an entity dwelling among the Corinthians to make them the temple of God. It seems that Paul used the term "holy spirit" because he thought he had authority as the founder of the Corinthian church and had a good relationship with the Corinthians. Without doubt, Paul was dependent upon the Jewish tradition in general with regard to the role of the spirit of God at the time of writing Cor(A).

Cor(B)

Paul described the spirit of God as the source of everything necessary for the life of faith in Cor(B). This appears in Paul's answer to the questions related to the religious life of the Corinthians. It is given based on his opinion rather than relying on any particular tradition.

The term "spirit" is mentioned in Paul's answer to a question about the "virgins." The spirit of God is mentioned after he taught how to treat the matter of "virgins" (1 Cor 7:40). As discussed in chapter 4, the "virgins" are supposed to be those who maintained a sexless life with their husbands to keep their holiness before God. Paul spoke of the spirit to support his claim for the first time. In other words, he was confident that he had taught a proper lesson with regard to holy marriage. This implies that Paul made his own interpretation because he had received no tradition about the virgins. In this regard, Paul claimed that the couples in holy marriage had to be obedient to what the spirit had told him. Thus, the spirit was used to impose authority upon the instruction of Paul about the virgins. In consequence, it can be said that Paul unfolded an interpretation of the spirit of God in consideration of the exceptional case of the Corinthians.

Paul associated the spirit of God with gifts. This is seen in the expression that there are many gifts but the spirit is the same (1 Cor 12:4). Paul taught that the spirit of God is the source of all gifts. Paul argued for the unity among the Corinthians divided by conflict on account of the spiritual gifts.[3] In this way, practical matters are dealt with in connection with the spirit of God. Again, Paul presented the spirit of God

---

3. Conzelmann, *I Corinthians*, 208. Unity in diversity was the top priority for the divided Corinthians (1 Cor 1:11–17; 11:17–29).

to the Corinthians as a way of solving the practical matter regardless of their spiritual condition. This kind of interpretation was made creatively without any dependence upon a certain tradition at the time of writing Cor(B).

Finally, the reason that the spirit was given is presented. According to Paul, the spirit of God was manifested for the benefit the Corinthians (1 Cor 12:7). Paul noted the good influence exerted on the Corinthians by the spirit of God. Then, various gifts are introduced that were given for their benefit (12:8–11). This benefit is to be understood as for the community rather than the individual person. As such, the spirit of God was presented as an entity to provide the Corinthians with something beneficial in their religious life. In other words, the spirit of God was described as an essential element for the life of faith. In this way, while describing the role of the spirit of God, Paul seriously considered the benefits of the Corinthians. The emphasis on their benefit indicates that Paul was in a somewhat tense relationship with the Corinthians at the time of writing Cor(B).

Paul mentioned the "spirit" three times in Cor(B). It is, however, noteworthy that the adjective "holy" was not applied to the "spirit." This reflects Paul's thought that the Corinthians did not live holy. However, Paul seems to have admitted that the spirit of God exists for the benefit of the Corinthians as a whole. It seems that the visit of Cephas to Corinth resulted in the division among them and made Paul step back from the Jerusalem tradition for his interpretation of the spirit of God.

Thess(B)

Paul mentioned the spirit of God only once in Thess(B). One's attitude toward the spirit of God is focused. Paul preached this kind of instruction without relying on any tradition.

The word "spirit" is used in two places with different meaning. The one is found in the advice not to annihilate the spirit of God (1 Thess 5:19), and the other is in parallel with "body" and "soul" of human beings (5:23). The spirit of God is used only once without the adjective "holy" in Thess(B), as in the case of Cor(B). This reflects the fact that Paul did not view the Thessalonians as holy people at the time of writing Thess(B). This is supported by the saying that Paul wanted them to be without defect in holiness at the advent of Christ (3:13; 5:23). This means that although the Thessalonians did not generally follow the instruction of those sponsored by the apostles of Jerusalem, they were still flawed. In this respect, the reason that the adjective "holy" was not applied to the spirit of God is to be suggested.

The annihilation of the spirit of God is mentioned for the first time. This reflects the fact that among the Thessalonians there were some who stayed away from the spirit of God. It seems to be understood in association with what happened to the Thessalonians. As Paul pointed out, a certain number of Thessalonians were shaken by the "tempter" but soon decided to stay in the gospel that Paul had proclaimed (1 Thess 3:5–6). Then, it can be said that the annihilation of the spirit of God means forsaking the gospel. In this respect, Paul encouraged the Thessalonians to make the right decisions from a spiritual viewpoint.

Paul concentrated on describing one's attitude toward the spirit of God in Thess(B). This is somewhat different from what was described with regard to the spirit of God in Thess(A). Paul seems to have dealt with the reality of the Thessalonians in Thess(B). This kind of tendency already appeared in Cor(B). It seems that Paul entered a situation where he could not only praise the Gentiles. Accordingly, Paul suggested a lesson that they must live according to the spirit of God. This indicates that Paul came up with his theological answers to the changing circumstances of the Thessalonians without dependence upon any traditions.

Phil(A)

Paul mentioned the spirit of God once in Phil(A). The spirit of God is closely related with the issue of worship. This implies that Paul paid attention to one's attitude toward the spirit of God in the middle of the situation that those sent by the apostles of Jerusalem asked the Philippians to refuse the gospel.

One's attitude toward the spirit of God is mentioned in connection with the liturgical service. The Philippians were advised to worship God in the spirit of God (Phil 3:3). It seems that Paul taught them to worship God following the spirit of God. This implies that there were some who did not worship God in the spirit of God. This kind of instruction is similar with what Paul taught the Thessalonians not to annihilate the spirit of God as written in Thess(B) (1 Thess 5:19). Everyone was encouraged to decide his or her position in relation to the spirit of God in Phil(A).

In this respect, the spirit of God is described as an agent who works differently according to each one's decision. This is different from what is described as an entity working for all the members of church as a whole as written in Thess(A), Cor(A), and Cor(B). This shows that, having faced the changed circumstances of the Thessalonians, Paul changed his view on the relationship with the spirit of God.

Paul mentioned the spirit of God in a controversial context. This is revealed in that worship in the "spirit" [πνεῦμα] of God appears in parallel with boasting of Christ Jesus and distrust of reliance on "flesh" [σάρξ] (Phil 3:3). The contrast between the "spirit" and "flesh" is reminiscent of that found in Cor(B) (1 Cor 5:5). Then, the contrast between "spirit" and "flesh" appears a second time in Phil(A). However, a difference is definite between them; in Phil(A), the word "spirit" is adopted to identify the real people of God, while "flesh" refers to those who relied upon the Jewish instruction delivered by the apostles of Jerusalem. In this way, Paul put the spirit of God in contrast with "flesh" for contentious purposes. In this respect, Paul was staying away from the Jewish tradition with regard to his view on the spirit of God.

A change is seen in the description of the spirit of God in Phil(A). While Paul used to describe the spirit of God working on the benefit of Gentiles as a whole in letters written earlier, he began to focus on one's attitude toward the spirit in Thess(B) and in Phil(A). This shows Paul's efforts to make the Philippians have a right relationship with God from a spiritual standpoint. Although this kind of theological advance is not directly related with the birth of Christianity, it can be said to be a significant change.

Cor(C)

Paul dealt with the spirit of God with a reference to personification in Cor(C). The spirit of God was described as an entity that influenced something religious to the Corinthians. Having faced the direct challenge of some Corinthians, Paul put forth the power of the spirit of God for their salvation. In this respect, Paul presented the Christian view on the spirit of God.

The "spirit" is set in parallel with "power." According to Paul, his proclamation was not with wise and persuasive words, but with a demonstration of power and the spirit of God (1 Cor 2:4). The parallel between the spirit of God and power informs that the spirit is none other than the divine power itself. Paul had already combined the "holy" spirit and power with words in Thess(A) (1 Thess 1:5). However, Paul put the spirit and power in contrast with the wise and persuasive words of the world in Cor(C). It seems that the Corinthians experienced power that refers to something spiritual enough to be regarded as the work of the spirit of God at the time of receiving the gospel. The Corinthians were advised to choose their position in relationship to the spirit of God. Paul asked them to decide to choose between the spirit of God and the words of the world.

Paul described the spirit of God as a messenger. This is seen in the description that the spirit of God informs people of the divine plan for their salvation (1 Cor 2:10–13). Paul imposed the role of messenger upon the spirit of God from a soteriological viewpoint. This reminds readers of Q, in which Jesus declared that only those chosen by him could know God (Q^3 10:22). However, having applied the role of messenger to the spirit of God in Cor(C), Paul paid more attention to the spirit of God than Jesus in connection with the issue of revealing the divine plan. Thus, each person should decide whether he or she accepts the divine plan revealed by the spirit of God. Now, the spirit of God is no longer described as a being who works the same regardless of the spiritual state of people.

The "holy" spirit of God appears in connection with the confession of Jesus. According to Paul, no one who is speaking by the spirit of God says "Jesus be cursed," and no one can say "Jesus is Lord" except by the "holy" spirit (1 Cor 12:3). Here, the term "spirit" appears in two different forms: "spirit of God" and "holy spirit." Paul seems to emphasize that the confession of the Lord Jesus is possible only by the "holy" spirit. In other words, the "holy" spirit makes a person make a right confession of Jesus. In this way, the matter of whether one lives with the spirit of God comes to the fore in Cor(C).

Finally, Paul linked the spirit of God with baptism. This is seen in the saying that everyone was baptized by one spirit into one body and was given the one spirit to drink (1 Cor 12:13). Paul presented baptism by one spirit as a way to overcome diversity. This was of a different level from the baptism by Cephas that had been described in Cor(B) (1 Cor 1:12–17). The combination of spirit and baptism was already shown in Q, where Jesus was introduced as a baptizer with the spirit and described as the one baptized with it (Q^3 3:16, 21). However, in Cor(C) Paul presented baptism in one spirit for the Corinthians. It is believed that Paul interpreted and applied the tradition of Q in a new dimension. As such, Paul developed his interpretation of baptism with the spirit of God, having been away from the Jerusalem tradition.

In Cor(C), Paul presented a new interpretation of the spirit of God after he had been directly challenged by some Corinthians under the sponsorship of the apostles of Jerusalem. The spirit is related with power to refer to the experience of something spiritual at the time of receiving the gospel. As a result, Paul portrayed the spirit as a messenger working on the deliverance of the divine plan, a trigger for the confession of Jesus, and a worker for the alliance among the Corinthians. In this way, the spirit of God was described as an entity working on the spirituality of human beings. In the meantime, Christian teaching about the spirit of God was expanded.

Galatians

Paul referred to the spirit of God most in Galatians. Having been contrasted with "flesh," the spirit of God is portrayed as an entity that made the Galatians the people of God. While the challenge against him reached its culmination, Paul strengthened the role of the spirit of God.

The Galatians seems to have experienced the spirit of God. This is detected from the rhetorical question of whether they received the "spirit" by the works of the Law or by the faith of hearing (Gal 3:2). Paul never emphasized the experience of it as much as in Galatians, having compared with the cases mentioned in Thess(A) (1 Thess 1:5; 4:8), Cor(A) (1 Cor 6:19), and Cor(C) (2:4). In any case, it has been alleged that the Galatians received the spirit by the faith of hearing the gospel, not by the works of the Law. This is the first case that the spirit of God is set in contrast with the works of the Law. If so, it seems that Paul made the Galatians remember the experience of the spirit of God to prevent them from keeping the Law; rather, they were advised to remain in the gospel. In consequence, the experience of the spirit of God was presented as a cornerstone for the Galatians to be the people of God. This shows how Paul stayed away from the Jewish perspective with regard to the theological interpretation of the spirit of God.

The "spirit" [πνεῦμα] of God is set in contrast to "flesh" [σάρξ]. Paul said, "After beginning with the spirit [πνεύματι], are you now trying to attain your goal by human effort [σάρκι]?" (Gal 3:3). Paul set the spirit of God in sharp contrast with "flesh" again. The contrast between them was found in Phil(A) (Phil 3:3), and then they were applied to the contrast between the "spiritual people" [πνευματικός] and the "worldly ones" [σάρκινος] in Cor(C) (1 Cor 3:1–3). The sharp contrast between the spirit of God and "flesh" reflects the struggle among the Galatians in terms of religious position. Without doubt, "flesh" is closely related with the works of the Law taught by those from the Jerusalem church. Then, Paul mentioned the spirit of God in order to prevent the Galatians from following the instruction delivered by those under the sponsorship of the apostles of Jerusalem. The spirit of God is an essential being that everyone should follow. Galatians is the first letter in which the spirit of God prevails over "flesh."

Paul put the spirit of God in parallel with "power." This is found in the rhetoric question of whether God gave the Galatians his "spirit" and "power" by the works of the Law or by belief in what they had heard (Gal 3:5). Paul already mentioned the "spirit" in parallel with "power" in Cor(C) (1 Cor 2:4; cf. 1 Thess 1:5). However, when the "spirit" was put in parallel with "power" in Galatians, the "spirit" of God seems to refer to a powerful miracle occurred among the Galatians. On the other hand, having mentioned the contrast between "faith" and the Law twice (Gal 3:2, 5), Paul put forth the experience of the spirit of God by the faith of hearing the gospel, not by observance of the Law. In this way, Paul described the spirit of God in a state far from the Jewish perspective.

The spirit was mentioned in connection with the promise of God. According to Paul, the Galatians might receive the promise of the spirit by faith (Gal 3:14). He associated the spirit with promise for the first time. This shows Paul's emphasis on the role of the spirit in terms of promise. In addition, faith plays a role of making the promise of the spirit fulfilled. This means that the spirit of God was the driving force that made the Galatians the people of God. The role of the spirit of God was getting expanded as Galatians progressed. Paul probably conveyed this kind of instruction so as to make the Galatians defeat the teachings of the apostles of Jerusalem, who had asked them to observe the Law for the fulfillment of promise. This also shows that Paul was getting separated from the Jewish perspective on how to fulfill the promise of God.

Paul treated the issue of sonship in connection with the spirit of God. It is said that God sent the spirit of his Son into the hearts of people (Gal 4:6). Paul presented the spirit of God as the driving force to make the Galatians the sons of God. This is another expression of being the people of God, written for the first time here. The issue of sonship reminds readers of Q, which describes that Jesus became the Son of God by receiving the spirit and hearing the heavenly announcement (Q^3 3:21–22). Perhaps Paul tried to insist that the Galatians had become the sons of God by the experience of the spirit of God against the backdrop of Q. Thus, having used the Jerusalem tradition, Paul insisted that the Galatians should be the sons of God by the spirit of God, not by the Law. This is how Paul emulated the Jewish tradition in his own way.

The spirit was extremely contrasted with "flesh." According to Paul, a man who followed the "flesh" persecuted the one who was born of the "spirit" (Gal 4:29). Paul presented the contrast between the "spirit" and "flesh" against the backdrop of Isaac and Ishmael (Gen 21:8–21). Perhaps, those sent by the apostles of Jerusalem to the Galatians preached that Jews had been the promised children of Isaac born of the "spirit," while the Gentiles had been the children of Ishmael according to "flesh." However, Paul gave an opposite interpretation with a reference that while a man who followed "flesh" is to be compared to Ishmael, the one born of the "spirit" is the descendant of Isaac. In turn, the former refers to those sent by the apostles of Jerusalem, who insisted on the compliance of the Gentiles with the Law; on the other hand, the latter refers to the Gentiles who lived according to the spirit of God. This indicates that Paul was creative enough to interpret the spirit with regard to the issue of being the promised people of God. In this way, Paul tried to make the Galatians stay away from the Jewish instruction delivered by those who had come from the Jerusalem church.

Paul presented the contrast between the "spirit" of God and "flesh" again. This is found in the description that the Galatians would not gratify the desires of flesh when living by the spirit of God, that the desires of flesh were contrary to that of the spirit, and that those who had been led by the spirit of God were not under the Law (Gal 5:16–18). This shows again that the spirit of God is in opposition to "flesh." Paul then presented the fruit of the spirit in contrast to the work of the flesh (5:19–23). This shows a sharp contrast between the "spirit" of God and "flesh." In this respect, the Galatians were advised to live according to the spirit of God, which prevails over "flesh."

The spirit of God appears in connection with life. According to Paul, those who live by the spirit of God should keep in step with it and those who live for the spirit will have eternal life from it (Gal 5:25; 6:8). Paul taught that living in the spirit of God is the way to eternal life. This is the first case that Paul described the spirit of God in connection with eternal life. An active and positive role is given to the spirit of God. In this respect, Paul expanded the role of the spirit of God as Galatians progressed.

Paul described the spirit of God in various ways in Galatians. Among them, the most attractive is the contrast between the "spirit" of God and "flesh." The sharp contrast between them was made when the challenge against Paul reached its peak. As a result, the spirit of God is portrayed as an entity that made the Galatians the people of God. Paul created various interpretations of the spirit of God in response to the Jewish teachings of those sent by the apostles of Jerusalem to the Galatians. Having presented this kind of interpretation, Paul wanted the Galatians to be the promised people of God from a spiritual point of view. Meanwhile, Christian teaching expanded.

Cor(D)

Paul presented the spirit of God two times in Cor(D). It was used for the support of his claim in the midst of his effort to restore his relationship with the Corinthians. Although Paul attributed a new role to the spirit of God, no significant advance was made with regard to it.

The spirit is portrayed as an entity that guaranteed what Paul had told. According to him, God put the spirit in the hearts of people as a deposit so as to guarantee what Paul had said (2 Cor 1:22). This presents the role of the spirit of God in assuring that what Paul had said to the Corinthians was certain. He once spoke of the spirit of God to support his teaching in Cor(B) (1 Cor 7:40). In any case, Paul mentioned the spirit in Cor(D) as an excuse for failing to keep his promise to visit Corinth again. Paul was sensitive to his failure to keep his promises because this was closely linked to whether he was a true apostle.[4] In this respect, Paul mentioned the spirit of God to strengthen his effort to restore the relationship with the Corinthians.

The "holy" spirit is mentioned in the benediction. The fellowship of the "holy" spirit is in parallel with the grace of the Lord Jesus Christ and the love of God (2 Cor 13:13). Paul thought of the "holy" spirit having fellowship with people. This shows the personified aspect of the "holy" spirit to some extent. The adjective "holy" had already been applied to the spirit in Thess(A) (1 Thess 1:5-6; 4:8), Cor(A) (1 Cor 6:19), and Cor(C) (12:3). However, in Cor(D) the adjective "holy" was linked to the spirit

---

4. Furnish, *II Corinthians*, 141.

in regard to the issue of fellowship. This shows Paul's effort to show a friendly attitude toward the Corinthians so as to enjoy a restored relationship with them in addition to a wish that they should be the holy people of God by accepting the gospel.

Paul mentioned the spirit of God while trying to restore his relationship with the Corinthians. To this end, Paul spoke of the spirit of God to convey his sincerity and enjoy holy fellowship. This is an interpretation that Paul gave in his own way. Regarding the theological interpretation of the role of the spirit of God, he seems to have been almost independent from the Jewish tradition.

Cor(E)

Paul mentioned the spirit of God in various ways in Cor(E). It was used in affirming his office for the ministry of reconciliation. Paul thus used the spirit of God to justify his ministry.

The spirit was used to support Paul's argument. According to him, the Corinthians were Christ's letters, not written with ink but with the spirit of the living God, not on tablets of stone but on tablets of "human hearts" [σάρκινος] (2 Cor 3:3). Here, having set the "spirit" of God in parallel with the "human hearts," Paul argued that the former should dominate the latter. This is a more advanced expression than the saying that the spirit of God guaranteed what Paul had said as written in Cor(D) (1:22). Likewise, in Cor(E) Paul described the spirit as an entity who testified to his sincerity. This appeared in the midst of his struggle for reconciliation with the Corinthians. This shows Paul interpreting the role of the spirit of God anew to strengthen his relationship with them.

Paul then linked the spirit of God to his office. It is said that God made Paul a minister of a new covenant, not of "letter" [γράμμα] but of the "spirit" [πνεῦμα] of God, because it gave the Corinthians life (2 Cor 3:6). Paul had self-consciousness as a minister of a new covenant in the spirit of God. Here the "spirit" of God appears as an entity more powerful than the "letter." Using the term "letter," which was a substitute for the Law, Paul would not provoke the Corinthians who had followed the Jewish instruction by observing it. In the end, Paul stressed that the spirit of God was superior to the Law with regard to the matter of making them the people of God.

The spirit appears in connection with the Lord. According to Paul, the Lord is the spirit, and where the spirit of the Lord is, there is freedom (2 Cor 3:17). Having defined the Lord as the "spirit," Paul would like to mention the presence of the Lord in spirit with a reference to Christ. In addition, he wanted to refer to freedom from "the written Law."[5] This informs readers of Paul's intention to make the Corinthians free from the apostles of Jerusalem, who had asked them to observe the Law. There is no other way to be free from it except by following the spirit of Christ. In this respect, Paul presented a new interpretation of the spirit of God, taking into account the circumstances that he had faced in relations to the Corinthians.

Paul once again referred to the "holy" spirit. The "holy" spirit is found in the list of what Paul had experienced during his mission to the Gentiles (2 Cor 6:6). It is, however, not clear whether the phrase "in the holy spirit" should be treated independently or connected to the previous word "kindness." To my judgment, the latter is preferred to the former because Paul tried to speak of kindness in the "holy" spirit. In other words, the "holy" spirit seemed to be described as an entity that produces kindness. It seems that no great role was given to the spirit of God when the Corinthians did not quit challenging Paul against the gospel and his authority at the time of writing Cor(E).

Paul referred to the spirit of God in connection with his office for reconciliation with the Corinthians. Having put an emphasis on his office of ministry given by God, Paul mentioned the spirit of God for the justification of reconciliation with them. This implies that Paul also recognized his relationship with them getting deteriorated. In the meantime, Paul showed his independence from the Jerusalem tradition in connection with the interpretation of the spirit of God.

Cor(F)

Paul linked the spirit of God to personal ministry in Cor(F). This means that the spirit transcends the boundary of space and works equally to the coworker. Paul stopped interpreting the spirit in connection with the Corinthians when the restoration of his relationship with them was no longer possible.

---

5. Barrett, *Second Epistle*, 123.

The spirit is mentioned in Paul's excuse for Titus. It is said that Paul and Titus worked in the same spirit (2 Cor 12:18). This means that even if Paul and Titus worked in different places, the spirit of God would work the same. Paul mentioned the spirit of God in the sense of fully trusting Titus. In other words, when the Corinthians accused Titus, Paul defended him. This kind of instruction reminds readers of what Paul said in Cor(B) that while he was apart from the Corinthians in the body he was together with them in spirit (1 Cor 5:3). However, there is a difference in that while the spirit of a human being was focused in Cor(B), the spirit of God working between Paul and Titus was mentioned in Cor(F). Paul emphasized the work of the spirit of God rather than the human spirit. In consequence, it can be said that Paul showed dependence more on the spirit of God when it was no longer possible for the Corinthians to return to the gospel he had proclaimed.

Paul did not mention the spirit of God working for the Corinthians in Cor(F). This is because he knew that the Corinthians had kept refusing him and the gospel. It seems that Paul thought they would not return to the gospel he had preached. Thus, he stopped mentioning the spirit of God working for the Corinthians. Rather, the spirit of God was applied to Paul and his coworkers to justify his ministry. In this respect, Paul delivere instruction on the spirit of God taking into account the circumstances of the Corinthians. At that time, Paul seems to have been completely independent from the Jerusalem tradition.

Summary

Paul's instructions on the spirit of God went through ups and downs during his second missionary trip. In the early period of it, Paul described the spirit of God as an agent leading the Gentiles as a whole to a better state. The spirit of God made them accept the gospel, live holy, and overcome severe suffering; in addition, the spirit of God was portrayed as the source of spiritual gifts. All of these roles seem to have been closely related to Paul's wish that the Gentiles might live according to the gospel he had proclaimed. On the other hand, in the middle of his second missionary trip, Paul began to face the challenge of some Gentiles sponsored by the apostles of Jerusalem. He then presented the spirit of God as an entity to be with personally. The climax is seen in that the spirit of God was described in opposition to the "flesh," which refers to human nature disobedient to God. Thus, Paul argued that he had worked according to the spirit of God in general; on the other hand, he accused challengers who had tried to live according to the Law of following the desire of the "flesh." In this respect, Paul began to be independent from the apostles of Jerusalem. In the meantime, Christianity was born and expanded.

C. THE THIRD MISSIONARY TRIP

Paul sent four letters to Rome and a letter to Philippi during his third missionary trip. His theological interpretation of the spirit of God varied according to his relationship with the recipients of his letters. Paul mentioned the spirit of God most when the critique against him was greatest. In the meantime, Paul offered new interpretations of the spirit of God.

Rom(A)

Paul mentioned the holy aspect of the spirit of God in Rom(A). This reveals that Paul wanted the Romans to be holy by the spirit of God. The "holy" spirit seems to have been described as an entity that carries out the work of God.

A holy aspect was applied to the spirit of God. According to Paul, through the spirit of "holiness" [ἁγιωσύνης] Jesus Christ was declared with power to be the Son of God by his resurrection from the dead (Rom 1:4). This is the first case that mentions the spirit of "holiness" involved in the resurrection of Jesus Christ and his sonship. First, the spirit of "holiness" is to be regarded as another expression of the "holy" spirit. It is likely that Paul invented it for the emphasis on the holy aspect of the spirit of God. Second, the role of the spirit of God is to be examined. It was described in Q that Jesus was proclaimed to be the Son of God after the "spirit" had descended upon him at his baptism (Q^3 3:21–22); on the other hand, Paul stated that the spirit was involved in the resurrection of Jesus Christ and made him the Son of God. The spirit of God has been given the role of making Jesus the Son of God. The moment of being the Son of God has been shifted from baptism in Q to resurrection in Rom(A). Third, the relationship between the spirit of God and "power" reminds readers of previous cases found in Thess(A) (1 Thess 1:5), Cor(C) (1 Cor 2:4), and Galatians (Gal 3:5). It seems that Paul tried to put forth the miraculous and powerful role of the spirit of God. In this respect, Paul made a significant contribution to the interpretation of the spirit of God in connection with the sonship of Jesus Christ.

Paul presented the "holy" spirit in connection with the love of God. According to him, it is the "holy" spirit of God that pours love into the hearts of human beings (Rom 5:5). Paul connected the "holy" spirit with the love of God for the first time. While the "holy" spirit was mentioned in association with love in Cor(D) (2 Cor 13:13) and Cor(E) (6:6), the spirit of God was personified as the deliverer of God's love in Rom(A). The ministry of the "holy" spirit has an inseparable relationship with the love of God through the death of his Son Christ (Rom 5:8). In this respect, Paul described the "holy" spirit of God as an entity active enough to love people, including Paul. This indicates that Paul further expanded the role of the spirit of God in relation to love.

Paul expanded the role of the spirit of God in Rom(A) on the basis of what he had already dealt with in previous letters. Above all, he put an emphasis on the holy aspect of the spirit. This is similar to the friendly attitude he had taken toward the Gentiles during the first half of his second missionary trip before a challenge arose against him. Since the majority of the Roman church was made up of Jews, it seems that Paul referred to the spirit of God from a Jewish perspective with an allusion to what had been described in Q. In this respect, Paul put them in his mind when writing Rom(A).

Rom(B)

Paul spoke of the spirit of God to exhort the Romans in Rom(B). The spirit is revealed in connection with the love of God and his kingdom. This shows Paul's wish to keep a good relationship with the Romans.

The "holy" spirit is mentioned for the life in the kingdom of God. According to Paul, the kingdom is not a matter of eating and drinking, but of righteousness, peace, and joy in the "holy" spirit (Rom 14:17). Paul explained the nature of the kingdom of God enjoyed in the "holy" spirit. The kingdom of God was indirectly related with the spirit of God in regard to its inheritance in Cor(A) (1 Cor 6:9–11) and Galatians (Gal 5:16–24); on the other hand, Paul directly connected the "holy" spirit to the kingdom of God in Rom(B). In this way, Paul expressed his wish that the Romans might live holy. This implies that Paul was concerned about the spirit of God for life in the kingdom of God.

Paul mentioned the spirit of God for exhortation. It is said that Paul urged the Romans by the Lord Jesus Christ and the love of the spirit of God (Rom 15:30). Paul mentioned the love of the spirit of God after he connected the "holy" spirit with the love of God in Rom(A) (Rom 5:5). It seems that the spirit of God was defined as a supplier of love to people. Then, it is definite that the subject of love has been handed over from God to the spirit of God in Rom(B). This indicates that Paul enhanced his interpretation of the role of the spirit in response to the changing circumstances of the Romans.

Paul tried to express favor with the Romans by referring to the spirit of God in Rom(B). Although they raised questions about his negative view on the Law, Paul did not deal with the role of the spirit of God in relation to it. Rather, he tried to win their favor by mentioning the role of the spirit for a mature life of faith. Regardless of their doubt, Paul sincerely wanted the Romans to be the people of God and live as holy as possible in the spirit of God.

Rom(C)

Paul referred to the spirit of God frequently in Rom(C). In the first half of it, the spirit of God appears in contrast with negative entities such as the Law, sin, and death; on the other hand, in the second half of it, the spirit of God appears for the edification of the Romans. Paul presented the spirit of God to make the Romans the people of God.

The spirit of God appears in contrast with the "letter" [γράμμα]. According to Paul, people should serve the spirit in a new way, not in the old way of the "letter" (Rom 7:6). The contrast between the "spirit" of God and the "letter" informs readers of the unreliable relationship between Paul and the Romans. Paul already wrote that the spirit of God gives life but the "letter" kills in Cor(E), written at the time of potential challenge of some Corinthians against him (2 Cor 3:6). The contrast between the "spirit" of God and the "letter" shows a similar situation that the Romans consistently raised critiques against his negative view on the Law as written in Rom(B) (Rom 3:20). Thus, Paul could not help but defend himself against their critique by referring to the spirit of God.

Paul described the spirit of God as an entity against sin and death. This is found in the contrast between the Law of the spirit of life and the law of sin and death (Rom 8:2). Paul put the spirit of life in contrast with sin and death. Whereas the "spirit" was contrasted with the "flesh" in Galatians (Gal 3:2, 5; 5:18) and with the "letter" in Cor(E) (2 Cor 3:6), the spirit is in opposition to sin and death in Rom(C). This reflects the fact that there were critiques of the Romans against Paul, who defined the Law as the origin of sin in Rom(B) (Rom 3:20). Thus, having linked the spirit of God to life, Paul had to explain what he thought of the Law in connection with the "spirit" of God, which is in contrast with sin that results in death in Rom(C). He wanted to teach them life in the spirit of God to be the true people of God. This also shows Paul's effort to enhance the understanding of the spirit of God in contrast with sin and death.

The spirit of God is portrayed as an entity leading people to resurrection. For this, Paul presented a contrast between the "spirit" of God and the "flesh" in terms of dwelling. This is found in the saying that if the spirit of God dwelled among the Romans, they would have been not in the "flesh" but in the spirit of God (Rom 8:9). Paul exhorted them to live according to the spirit of God. The dwelling of the "holy" spirit among the Corinthians was dealt with in Cor(A) (1 Cor 3:16–17; 6:19). Thus, Paul was able to deliver the instruction on the dwelling of the spirit of God among the Romans in Rom(C). The spirit of God is portrayed as an entity that leads people to life claimed to be given through Christ (Rom 8:9–10). In particular, the spirit of "Christ" is mentioned here for the first time. Although the data is not sufficient enough to determine their relationship, it seems that the spirit of God and the spirit of Christ "are used interchangeably to describe what dwells within Christians."[6] Then, Paul wished the Romans a blessing to be resurrected from the dead with the spirit of God; in other words, their mortal bodies will get the eternal life (8:11). Whereas Paul once asserted that Jesus Christ the Son of God was resurrected from death by the power of the spirit of "holiness" in Rom(A) (1:4), he applied it to the Romans in Rom(C). In this respect, Paul enhanced his theological understanding of the spirit of God in terms of dwelling and resurrection.

Paul mentioned the sonship of people in connection with the spirit of God. Having been in contrast with the "flesh," the spirit of God is portrayed as a being that provided the Romans with life and divine sonship (Rom 8:13–14). The contrast between "spirit" and "flesh" was mentioned for the first time in Cor(A) (1 Cor 5:5), used from a theological perspective in Phil(A) (Phil 3:3), applied to the Corinthians in Cor(C) (1 Cor

---

6. Lüdemann, *Paul*, loc. 2023 of 3299.

3:1–3), and adopted for the life in Galatians (Gal 5:2–24). Thus, Paul was able to put the spirit of God in contrast with the "flesh" in Rom(C). In particular, the issue of divine sonship started to be described in Galatians (Gal 4:4–6). However, Paul changed it into the adopted sonship in Rom(C). Although Paul weakened the status of sonship, the right to call God "daddy" [ἀββά] was maintained. Finally, according to Paul, the spirit of God, along with the spirit of human beings, proves that they are children of God (Rom 8:16). In this way, the spirit of God was personified, having been distinguished from the spirit of human beings. In this way, Paul made a contribution to the interpretation of the role of the spirit of God from positive standpoint.

The spirit is described as the one working on the redemption [ἀπολύτρωσις] of the body. According to Paul, the Romans were the first fruit of the spirit of God and they had to wait eagerly for their adoption as the sons of God through the redemption of their bodies (Rom 8:23). This informs that the spirit of God works on the redemption of people. The phrase "first fruit of the spirit" is reminiscent of the "first fruits" referring to the resurrected Christ as mentioned in Cor(B) (1 Cor 15:23). However, in Rom(C) Paul applied it to the Romans and claimed their resurrection by the spirit of God. This shows that Paul expanded the range of the spirit of God working on the redemption of people.

Paul defined the spirit of God as a mediator. It is said that the spirit sought for the Romans with an unspeakable lament in helping their weakness (Rom 8:26–27). Paul attributed the role of mediator to the spirit of God. This means that God knows what the spirit thinks and that the spirit prays for the saints according to the will of God. This reminds readers of Paul's previous teaching that the spirit is found in the depths of God and is known to people as written in Cor(C) (1 Cor 2:10) and that Jesus Christ plays the role of mediator at the right of God as written in Rom(A) (Rom 8:34). It seems that Paul combined them and attributed the intercessory role to the spirit of God in Rom(C). This shows that Paul enhanced his interpretation of the role of the spirit of God as circumstances changed.

The "holy" spirit is mentioned in connection with the issue of hope. According to Paul, the Romans should be in the power of the "holy" spirit to make their hopes more abundant (Rom 15:13). Having mentioned the "power of the holy spirit," Paul seems to expect a miraculous result. The parallel between the "spirit" of God and "power" was already found in Cor(C) (1 Cor 2:4) and Galatians (Gal 3:5), which are supposed to have been written under the severe challenge against Paul. On the other hand, the phrase "power of the holy spirit" is used in Rom(C). It seems that the power of the "holy" spirit of God was mentioned in the absence of hope among the Romans. As they continued criticizing Paul against his negative view on the Law, he had no hope that they would receive the gospel. Accordingly, Paul hoped for a remarkable change to occur in the "holy" spirit. This seems to have been the exhortation as Paul's last scream.

Paul treated the spirit of God with various issues in Rom(C). The spirit has been contrasted with sin, death, and the "flesh"; has been portrayed as an entity that leads people to life; and has been described as the one playing a role in conferring the divine sonship. These are the theological interpretations presented in the context of Paul being criticized by the Romans with regard to his negative view on the Law. In this way, Paul took into account the circumstances of the Romans and provided them with answers in connection with the spirit of God. At that time, Paul did not show any reliance upon the Jerusalem tradition for his interpretation of the spirit of God.

Rom(D)

Paul referred to the "holy" spirit two times in Rom(D). Having sent the last letter to the Romans, Paul wanted them to live holy. Paul made a theological interpretation of the spirit to the end in order to convince them that his office was for them.

The "holy" spirit is mentioned in connection with conscience. According to Paul, his conscience confirmed the truth in the "holy" spirit of God with great sorrow and unceasing anguish (Rom 9:1–2). Paul mentioned the "holy" spirit to convey the credibility of his words. The phrase "conscience in the holy spirit" is used for the first time here. Having connected the "holy" spirit with conscience, Paul tried to reveal his honesty and sincerity. This reminds readers of Paul's saying in Cor(D) that the spirit of God was given as a deposit to guarantee his words (2 Cor 1:22). While the word "testimony" [συμμαρτυρέω] was used to describe the role of the spirit that made the Romans the adopted sons of God in Rom(C) (Rom 8:16), Paul used it to develop the idea of the "holy" spirit and to support his conscience in Rom(D). This means that Paul did not act according to his own will, but rather according to the "holy" spirit of God. In this respect, Paul made a contribution to the interpretation of the spirit of God with regard to its role.

Paul also linked the "holy" spirit to his office. It is said that he was a priestly minister of Christ Jesus to proclaim the gospel to the Gentiles, so that they might become an offering acceptable to God and sanctified by the "holy" spirit (Rom 15:16). Having mentioned the offering acceptable to God, Paul declared that his office was to make them the people of God in the "holy" spirit. This kind of argument was already made in connection with the ministry of a new covenant in Cor(E) (2 Cor 3:6–8). Having revealed his confidence in his ministry in Rom(D), Paul claimed to work for the Romans. This is believed to have been given as a result of their continuous critique against him. In other words, Paul wanted them to be the people of God who were wholly obedient like sacrifices offered to God. This is the final exhortation of Paul regarding the "holy" spirit.

Paul referred to the "holy" spirit two times in Rom(D). It was used to reveal his confidence that his ministry was for the Romans. Paul mentioned the "holy" spirit to apologize for himself when the Romans criticized his negative view on the Law and refused the gospel he wanted to deliver. He really wanted them to be the people of God in the "holy" spirit. It has been unknown how much the Romans accepted what Paul taught about the spirit of God. In the meantime, his teachings related to the spirit of God developed over time. As a result, Christian teaching was added to.

Phil(B)

Paul also mentioned the spirit in Phil(B). It is, however, noteworthy that the spirit of "Christ" appears in connection with salvation. This shows that as time went by Paul focused more on the role of Christ. In this regard, Paul presented a new theological interpretation to the Philippians, with whom he had the best relationship.

The spirit of "Jesus Christ" is presented in connection with salvation. This appears in the explanation that Paul was able to preach and rejoiced in Christ because the spirit of Jesus Christ helped him to salvation (Phil 1:19). Paul introduced the "spirit of Jesus Christ" for the first time here. Whereas the "spirit of the Lord" was mentioned in Cor(E) (2 Cor 3:17), the "spirit of Christ" was presented to make his people in Rom(C) (Rom 8:9). Thus, Paul was able to mention the "spirit of Jesus Christ" in connection with the salvation of people in Phil(B). We are not sure of whether the "spirit of Jesus Christ" is to be identified with the "spirit of

God." If Paul wanted to understand the spirit from a new perspective, they could be interchangeable. In this respect, Paul expanded his range of interpretation of the spirit as time passed.

Paul dealt with the fellowship of the spirit. This appears in a statement that if the Philippians had fellowship of the spirit, they would share the same heart (Phil 2:1–2). It is, however, unclear whose spirit is referred to in this case. It could be the spirit of God, Christ, or human beings. From the context, the "spirit" is to be related to the phrase "in Christ" described earlier. Thus, it seems to refer to the "spirit of Christ" here. This is supported by the fact that Paul already mentioned the "spirit of Jesus Christ" (1:19). Whereas Paul once mentioned the fellowship of the "holy" spirit in Cor(D) (2 Cor 13:13), the fellowship in the spirit of Christ is introduced anew in Phil(B). This shows Paul getting focused more on the role of Christ. In consequence, it can be said that Paul always looked for new interpretations with regard to the role of the spirit.

The spirit was presented from a favorable point of view in Phil(B). This is probably because the Philippians maintained a good relationship with Paul to the end. They even supported him financially while being imprisoned in Rome. All that Paul could give them in the prison of Rome were words of comfort, encouragement, and joy. Having referred to the help and fellowship of the spirit of Christ, he expressed the desire to be with them in spite of his imprisonment. In this way, Paul tried a whole new interpretation of the spirit. Meanwhile, Christian teaching developed and expanded.

Summary

Paul frequently mentioned the spirit of God in his letters written during his third missionary trip. The more the Romans raised questions about his negative view on the Law, the more frequently Paul answered them in connection with the spirit of God. It reached its peak in Rom(C). Then the frequency of mentioning the spirit was rapidly reduced in Rom(D) because the Romans were no longer willing to accept Paul's teachings. Then, Paul looked for a new way in the direction of referring to the spirit of Christ in Phil(B). A similar phenomenon also appeared during his second missionary trip. At any rate, his interpretation of the spirit was developed over time, having stayed away from the Jerusalem tradition. In the meantime, Christian teaching was expanded.

D. CONCLUSION

The spirit of God was an important factor to Paul. His interpretation of the spirit is divided into situations before and after he had been challenged by some Gentiles under the sponsorship of the apostles of Jerusalem. Before the challenge, Paul used the title "holy spirit" with a hope that the Gentiles would be the holy people of God. On the other hand, while having been challenged, Paul attributed to the spirit of God a role of convincing people of his teachings. In addition, he put the "spirit" in contrast with the "flesh" with a reference to human nature disobedient to God. Meanwhile, having been independent from the Jerusalem church, Christianity was born to the Gentiles. This kind of phenomenon appeared similarly in his relationship with the Romans during his third missionary trip. Paul presented his interpretation of the spirit of God taking into account the circumstances of the Romans. In the meantime, it varied according to his relationship with them and developed in the direction of broadening the range of the role of the spirit. In the meantime, Christian lessons were added in connection with the spirit of God.

8

The Church of God

PAUL OFTEN USED THE word "church" in his letters. Although its origin has not been known, it is not difficult to assume that "church" took after the synagogue of the Jews. Literally speaking, "church" [ἐκκλησία] refers to those who have been called out of the secular world. They are those who have been chosen by God, so that they might be distinguished from secular people. In other words, "church" is another term for the people of God. It seems that Paul understood the church from a Jewish perspective in the early days of his mission to the Gentiles. However, having faced the challenge of those sponsored by the apostles of Jerusalem in the middle of his second missionary trip, Paul began to understand the church of God in association with Christ. In this respect, Paul developed his view on the church of God in response to the changed relations to the Gentiles. Then, Christianity was born to them and began to grow.

A. THE FIRST MISSIONARY TRIP

Paul was changed from a persecutor of the church to her founder in the region of the Gentiles. His perspective on the church while he was persecuting the disciples of Jesus has not been known. However, after he had received the revelation about the Son of God, it seems that he learned an instruction on the church of God from Cephas in Jerusalem. After he had left there, he established churches in the region of the Gentiles during his first missionary trip. It seems that the church of God was brought about by taking after the synagogue, which had been the local center for the religious life of the Jews.

The church of God seems to have existed before Paul persecuted the disciples of Jesus. This is verified by the description that he persecuted the church of God when he had been a Pharisee (Phil 3:6; 1 Cor 15:9; Gal 1:13, 22–23). The specific reason that he persecuted the church of God has not been known; however, it has been believed to have been due to a different view on the Law (Phil 3:6; Q³ 11:39–42). Having received the revelation about the Son of God in Damascus around 35 CE, Paul stopped persecuting the church of God. Perhaps during the period between the death of Jesus and Paul's reception of revelation churches in Galilee were the targets of persecution. The description that Paul was personally unknown to the churches of Judea informs that his persecution had taken place before the disciples of Jesus advance to Judea, including Jerusalem (Gal 1:22–23).

Paul had a chance to learn about the church composed of the disciples of Jesus. Around 38 CE, three years after he had received the revelation, Paul met Cephas in Jerusalem (Gal 1:18). It seems that he learned from him about what Jesus had taught on the constitution of community based on the first three redactions of Q, which are supposed to have been complete in Galilee. First, according to Q, Jesus asked his followers to proclaim the kingdom of God and heal the sick (Q² 10:4–11). This indicates that they tried to expand the range of activity. Second, it is said that the contemporary Jews had persecuted the disciples of Jesus (Q³ 6:22–23b). This informs that there was a group of people persecuted by the contemporary Jews and that the instruction of Jesus had been to some extent known to them. It is likely that Paul was one of the persecutors mentioned in Q. Third, a teaching on the organization of community is reflected in the parable of stewardship (Q³ 12:42–46). The hierarchical ranks are reflected in the description of household, steward, and servants. Paul probably knew this kind of organization to some extent.

There were a number of disciples of Jesus in Jerusalem around 38 CE. This is known from the description that Paul met Cephas and James the Lord's brother there (Gal 1:19). At that time, it seems that Cephas was the leader of the Jerusalem church. This is revealed by the description that Paul met James by chance; in addition, Paul did not see the other apostles. This indicates either that the apostolate was not yet established or that the other apostles were out of Jerusalem. To my judgment, the former is preferred to the latter because it was not until the completion of the fourth redaction of Q around 41 CE that the twelve apostles were elected for the first time (Q^4 6:13–16). At any rate, it is definite that a number of disciples already advanced to Jerusalem between 35 and 38 CE. However, it seems that the church in Jerusalem was not well organized at that time. No other information about the Jerusalem church has been known.

It seems that there were several churches of Judea. This is detected from the saying that Paul heard of news about the churches of Judea during his first missionary trip (Gal 1:22–23). Some members of the churches of Judea said that they had not known Paul by face but heard about him proclaiming the faith he had formerly persecuted. This reflects the fact that many churches had already existed in Judea before Paul went on his first missionary trip. In other words, a certain number of Jesus' disciples established churches in Judea on their way to Jerusalem from Galilee. It seems that there were many members among the churches of Judea; however, they had not met Paul personally. Other information about the churches of Judea has not been known.

Paul established a certain number of churches in the region of the Gentiles by proclaiming the gospel during his first missionary trip. However, little has been known about the process of establishing them. Perhaps Paul participated in the synagogue of the Jews and preached the gospel to those he could reach. Some participants in the synagogue, especially the Gentile God-fearers, seem to have responded to his proclamation of the gospel. Then, they gathered together to form a church in the house of a person affluent enough to serve them. Having learned instructions on Jesus Christ the Son of God from Paul, they worshipped God. However, it is not clear whether the church followed the liturgical system of the synagogue at that time. It seems that the church was maintained even when Paul left for another region to proclaim the gospel. No other information about the churches established in the region of the Gentiles has been known.

It is important to learn about the formation of the apostolate. It seems that twelve apostles were appointed in the Jerusalem church while Paul was traveling the region of Gentiles. The list of twelve apostles is found in the fourth redaction of Q, which is supposed to have been complete around 41 CE. To them belong Peter Cephas, Andrew, James, John, Philip, Bartholomew, Matthew, Thomas, James the son of Alphaeus, Simon the Zealot, Judas the son of James, and Thaddaeus (Q^4 6:13–16). The number twelve was once mentioned by Paul as those to whom Christ had appeared after his resurrection (1 Cor 15:5).[1] In addition, the twelve apostles were given the authority to pass judgment on the twelve tribes of the Jews (Q⁴ 22:30). This is the highlight with regard to their authority. The twelve apostles seem to have been elected as the leaders of the Jerusalem church before the completion of the fourth redaction of Q. This shows the organization of the church in Jerusalem at that time.

Paul went up to Jerusalem a second time with great achievement after he had finished his first missionary trip around 49 CE. As written in Galatians, he was accompanied with Barnabas and took Titus a Greek at that time (Gal 2:1). This tells readers of what they had done during the mission to the Gentiles. First, Paul and Barnabas traveled all the way down to Corinth and met Titus there (cf. Acts 18:7). Second, they visited the Galatian church on their way back to Jerusalem. This informs the fact that they set up the Galatian church during the first missionary trip. If they had not visited Galatia on their way back to Jerusalem, Paul would not have mentioned the name "Titus" a Greek in Galatians. Third, they established churches in many places such as Galatia, Philippi, Thessalonica, Corinth, and etc. This is verified by the fact that letters were sent to the churches ahead of his visit during the second missionary trip. These are what Paul did with regard to the church during the first missionary trip.

The Jerusalem church had its own ministerial system at the time of Paul's second visit. This is revealed in Paul's description of those whom he had met at the apostolic meeting in Jerusalem. There were many members designated as "false bothers" who had taken the position that Gentiles should be circumcised (Gal 2:4). Then, there were some who had been "influential" among the members (2:6); probably, they were the twelve apostles of Jerusalem. In addition, there were leaders who were considered "like pillars" such as James the Lord's brother, Cephas, and John (2:9). At the time of the apostolic meeting, James seems to have taken on the primary authority. This is known from the fact that his name was mentioned ahead of Cephas and John. While Cephas had been the leader of the Jerusalem church at the time of Paul's first visit around 38 CE, James took the hegemony at the time of the apostolic meeting in

---

1. Then, it is definite that Judas Iscariot could not have belonged to the twelve apostles to whom the resurrected Christ had appeared (1 Cor 15:5). See Ra, Q, 196–97. It seems that later, around 70 CE, the author of Mark's Gospel substituted Judas Iscariot for Judas son of James (Mark 3:19; cf. Luke 6:16; John 14:22). MacDonald claims that the author created a narrative of Judas Iscariot modeled after Melantius in the *Odyssey* of Homer (*Homeric*, 38–39).

49 CE. It seems that there was a community large enough to select the twelve apostles among the members. The three types of status—those considered to be "like pillars," the "influential," and "brothers"—remind readers of three types of ranks written in the parable of stewardship (Q^3 12:42–46). Based on the previous discussion, it can be said that the Jerusalem church had its own ministerial system when Paul visited Jerusalem for the apostolic meeting.

Paul was subordinate to the authority of the apostles of Jerusalem. First, this is verified by the fact that he asked them to exempt the Gentiles from circumcision (Gal 2:3–4). If Paul had not recognized their authority, he would not have taken Titus, a Greek, there as an example for the uncircumcised Gentiles. Second, Paul was officially commissioned as a worker for the Gentiles by the apostles of Jerusalem (2:7–8). Had he not recognized their authority, he would not have made a comment on his appointment as a minister for the Gentiles. Third, Paul delivered the collected money for the poor saints of the Jerusalem church (2:10). This implies that Paul recognized the authority of the apostles of Jerusalem and regarded the Jerusalem church as a superior institution to the Gentile churches.

The Jerusalem church had an influence on the church in Antioch. This is reflected in the fact that Cephas came to Antioch (Gal 2:11). It seems that Barnabas invited him to Antioch in gratitude for the recognition of him as a minister to the Gentiles. However, when Cephas withdrew from the Gentile table upon hearing that the people from James the Lord's brother had arrived there, Barnabas joined him (2:12–13). Accordingly, Paul was forced to rebuke them; as a result, Cephas turned his back on him (2:14). If Barnabas had not been under the authority of the Jerusalem church, he would not have stood with Cephas. As a result, the Antiochene church remained under the authority of the Jerusalem church; on the other hand, Paul could not help but leave them.

Paul also lost relations with the apostles of Jerusalem. It seems that, having heard a report from Cephas, they were annoyed with Paul and turned their back on him. This meant the excommunication of Paul from the Jerusalem church. Subsequently, the apostles of Jerusalem decided to send representatives to the Gentile churches established by Paul. It seems that they wanted the Gentiles to be under their authority. This is supported by the fact that Cephas visited Corinth as a representative of the Jerusalem church (1 Cor 1:12; 9:5). Without doubt, having baptized some of the Corinthians, Cephas asked them to observe the Law as well as the instruction of Jesus. According to the apostles of Jerusalem, then, the gospel preached by Paul to the Gentiles "must be supplemented with observance of the Jewish law."[2] This can be said to be a return to the Jewish perspective. It seems that the only result was division among the Gentiles.

B. THE SECOND MISSIONARY TRIP

Without knowing what the apostles of Jerusalem had decided, Paul went on a second missionary trip to visit the Gentile churches. Until the middle of it, the church of God was often mentioned from a Jewish perspective. However, having faced the challenge of some Gentiles sponsored by the apostles of Jerusalem, Paul shifted focus to the connection of church with Christ. In this respect, his interpretation of the church changed in response to the changing circumstances of the recipients of his letters.

Thess(A)

Paul mentioned the word "church" for the first time in Thess(A). However, different expressions were used depending on what it referred to. It seems that Paul understood the church of God from a Jewish perspective.

The word "church" is closely related with the Thessalonians. This is revealed in the expression "the church of the Thessalonians in God the Father and the Lord Jesus Christ" (1 Thess 1:1). Paul connected the "church" to the Thessalonians more closely than God and Jesus Christ. The recipient of his letter is directly related to the church in the genitive form from a grammatical perspective. It was natural for Paul to show a friendly attitude toward the Thessalonians when he visited them again. This was probably his third visit to Thessalonica. The first visit took place when the gospel was preached to establish the church, and the second one was apparently done on his way back to Jerusalem from Corinth during his first missionary journey. There was no reason that Paul would not have had a friendly attitude toward Thessalonians at the time of his third visit in the early days of his second missionary trip.

Having referred to the church a second time, Paul associated it with God. This is revealed in the expression "the churches of God in Judea in Christ Jesus" (1 Thess 2:14). Paul connected the phrase "of God" to

---

2. Lüdemann, *Paul*, loc. 246 of 3299.

the churches located in Judea. The phrase "churches of God" appears for the first time here. This means that God is the master of the church, which would have been natural from a Jewish perspective. In addition, the phrase "in Christ Jesus" follows "in Judea" here. This implies that, having understood the churches in Judea closely with Christ Jesus, Paul had a friendly view on them at the time of writing Thess(A). It should be noted here that "Christ" is linked to the churches "in Judea" despite that they stood on the tradition of Jesus rather than that of Christ. This shows that Paul was seeking a combination of the Jerusalem tradition and the Damascus tradition at the time of writing Thess(A). It is definite that Paul had a good impression of the churches of Judea even in the early days of his second missionary trip.

It is necessary to take a look at Paul's posture for the interpretation of the church. While writing Thess(A), Paul did not know what the apostles of Jerusalem had decided. Had he known this, he would not have made a comment on the churches of God in Judea with favor. Without doubt, Paul approached the Thessalonian church with a friendly attitude from a Jewish perspective.

Cor(A)

Paul referred to the church in connection with the norm for all members in Cor(A). This reflects the fact that his adversarial relationship with the apostles of Jerusalem had not been formed yet. However, Paul did not specifically address the nature and system of the church.

The "churches of God" is mentioned in connection with a norm supposed to be observed by women. According to Paul, every woman had to have her head covered with long hair or a veil as practiced in the churches of God (1 Cor 11:16). It is necessary to excavate the range of the "churches of God." The "churches of God" was once used for those located in Judea in Thess(A) (1 Thess 2:14). Then, in Cor(A), the "churches of God" refer to all the churches in Judea, including the Jerusalem church. In other words, Paul argued that the Corinthians had to follow the customs practiced by all churches of the Jews. This shows Paul's thought that the Gentile churches should be run with the Jewish churches as their example. It turns out, then, that according to Paul the Corinthians were to follow the custom of Jewish women to cover their heads with a veil or long hair. This was practiced in order not to make a man have sexual desire for a woman, because a married woman belongs to her husband and an unmarried daughter belongs to her father.[3] Likewise, Paul taught the Corinthians to follow the Jewish tradition. In consequence, it can be said that Paul approached the church from a Jewish perspective even at the time of writing Cor(A).

Paul presented the phrase "all the churches" for the first time in connection with the norm to be observed by women. It is said that as in "all the churches" of the saints, women should remain silent in the churches (1 Cor 14:33b–34). Paul introduced "all the churches of the saints" as well as "the churches." It seems that the "all the churches of the saints" refers to the churches of God in Judea, including the Jerusalem church. This is supported by the fact that the churches in Judea were once presented as the model of Gentile churches as written in Thess(A). It is, therefore, reasonable to say that Paul had in mind the members of the churches in Judea, including the Jerusalem church, with the word "saints." If my argument is acceptable, it can be said that Paul taught the Corinthians to follow the Jewish customs in church. It seems that Paul's view of the church was from a Jewish point of view at the time of writing Cor(A).

No distinction was made between the churches of Judea and those in the Gentile region during the early days of Paul's second missionary trip. Paul seems to have applied the Jewish customs learned from the apostles of Jerusalem to the Gentile churches at the time of writing Cor(A). It seems that Paul did not know their decision to send representatives to the Gentile churches to ask for their observance of the Law. Thus, no negative stance toward the apostles of Jerusalem was taken yet. Rather, Paul taught the Corinthians an instruction on what should be observed in a church from a Jewish viewpoint.

Cor(B)

Paul showed great interest in the edification of the church in Cor(B). However, the Corinthian church was described as a group with many problems. This indicates that Paul came to know the reality of the Corinthians. Nevertheless, he did not reveal any negative attitude toward the Jerusalem church in specific, yet.

The word "church" is dealt with in connection with trial. According to Paul, the Corinthians were judged by someone who was not respected

---

3. Kim, *Paul*, 160–74.

in church (1 Cor 6:4). This means that there were unrespected persons in the church and they had passed judgment in a wrong way. This implies that while Paul was far away the Corinthians turned in a bad direction. It is not clear whether the unrespected judge was someone who heard the gospel preached by Paul and became a member of the Corinthian church. It is definite that there were many members who had joined the church while Paul had been absent. In other words, his fluency was diminished among the Corinthians at the time of writing Cor(B). In the end, it seems that Paul began to dismiss a friendly view on the Corinthians.

Paul mentioned "all the churches" again. It is said, "This is the rule I lay down in all the churches" (1 Cor 7:17). Paul stressed that the same lessons were taught in all the churches. This kind of statement appeared in Cor(A) with regard to the attitude that women should take in church (11:16; 14:33b). However, there is a difference in that while "all the churches" included the churches in Judea, especially the Jerusalem church in Cor(A), it seems to refer to the Gentile churches in Cor(B). This implies that Paul turned his eyes to the churches under his influence. However, this does not mean that Paul was trying to separate the Gentile churches from the Jerusalem church. Anyway, it is important that Paul tried to unite the Gentile churches when the apostles of Jerusalem wanted to keep the Corinthians under their influence by sending Cephas to them.

The church of God is set in contrast with Jews and Greeks. According to Paul, the Corinthians were not to cause anyone to stumble, whether Jews, Greeks, or the church of God (1 Cor 10:32). Paul tried to teach that the members of the church of God should be distinguished from Jews and Greeks. The phrase "church of God" was already used with a reference to the churches in Judea in Thess(A) (1 Thess 2:14) as well as "all the churches" in Cor(A) (1 Cor 11:16). They referred to the Jewish churches as the example of the Gentile churches. On the other hand, in Cor(B) the "church of God" seems to refer to the churches in Judea as well as in Gentile area. The church of God seems to be seen as a group of people separated in religious and social terms. This shows that Paul put the Gentile churches on the same level as the Jewish churches at the time of writing Cor(B).

The "church of God" and "church" are mentioned in connection with the issue of eating and drinking. They were used for the description of what happened at the supper after worship (1 Cor 11:18, 22). Paul pointed out the inequality and inadequacy resulting from the difference of economic levels in the church of God. This reveals the reality among the Corinthians. First, there was a ritual service called the "Lord's Supper" (11:20). Everyone had to bring their own food to eat and drink at the supper. Second, there were differences in economic level among the congregation. As a result, the rich made the poor ashamed of their insufficient food (11:22). Third, the difference in economic level resulted in division among the members of the church (11:18-19). Paul tried to solve the problem restraining the rich. Fourth, the interpretation of the Lord's Supper shows that Paul actively utilized the tradition initiated by Jesus and passed down through his disciples. The above descriptions make readers see the various aspects of the contemporary church from a ritual, economic, and social perspectives.

Paul mentioned the church with a sort of minister. This appears in the text that God has established various ministers in church (1 Cor 12:28). Above all, Paul introduced the offices of "apostle" and "prophet." They were the offices handed down through the disciples of Jesus as reflected in Q (Q^4 6:13-16; 13:34) and Thess(A) (1 Thess 2:15). In addition, those having gifts of healing remind readers of Jesus' command to heal the sick (Q^2 10:9). This indicates that Paul followed the ministerial office of the Jerusalem church. It is likely that Paul did not take an unfriendly attitude toward the apostles of Jerusalem at the time of writing Cor(B), even though he had known about the division resulting from Cephas's visit to Corinth. Paul has not yet expressed his objection to solidarity with the Jerusalem church.

The church was defined as a place to edify people. This is found in the description of edification in several places (1 Cor 14:4, 5, 12). Paul presented prophecy rather than tongues as a spiritual gift that edifies people (14:19, 23, 28). This gift has been given for the purpose of making people know the will of God. Paul put forth the edification of people with the expandability of the church in mind. This kind of interpretation appears for the first time; resultantly, this shows that Paul made a contribution to the interpretation of the church in terms of edifying people.

Paul referred to the "Galatian churches" in relation to collection. This is found in the description that they were presented as a model for the collection of money (1 Cor 16:1). Paul requested the Corinthians to collect money for the poor saints in Jerusalem. In this way, Paul formed a network between the Jerusalem church and the Gentile churches. Paul tried to collect money as much as possible among the Gentile churches.

This implies that Paul was willing to help the Jerusalem church at the time of writing Cor(B).

Descriptions of the church appear frequently in Cor(B). Paul basically taught that the Corinthian church should keep pace with other churches. In the meantime, the organization of the Gentile churches seems to have been attempted. On the other hand, Paul came up with solutions to many problems in the church. In spite of Cephas's visit to Corinth, which resulted in division among the Corinthians, Paul did not take a negative attitude toward the Jewish churches, including the Jerusalem church, yet. In any case, Paul wrote various things on the church over time.

Thess(B)

Paul did not mention "church" in Thess(B). Although the reason is not clear, it seems to be similar to how Paul did not mention the Law. Perhaps the main reason was because the representatives sent by the apostles of Jerusalem arrived at the Thessalonian church and made the Thessalonians confused with words.

The news that the apostles of Jerusalem had sent representatives to Thessalonica seems to have been shocking to Paul. When he sent Cor(B), he knew that Cephas had visited Corinth. However, Paul did not yet know how much Cephas had a significant influence on the Corinthians. This was probably because he thought he was able to cope because he was going to visit the Corinthian church soon. On the other hand, it was difficult for Paul to deal with the matter of the Thessalonians because he had recently visited the church and left. It was not possible for Paul to return to Thessalnica and fix the problematic matters. Anyway, Paul heard about the problematic matters from the Thessalonian church immediately after he had heard about the situation of the Corinthian church.

It seems that when he heard of news that the representatives came to Thessalonica and preached Jewish teachings to Thessalonians, Paul was shaken a lot. This probably made Paul take time to think about his relationship with the Jerusalem church. Then, he wanted to define the nature and role of the church. It seems that he could not think of the Jewish church as just ideal. In addition, there was a need to rearrange the connection between God and the church. Moreover, he had to clear up his relationship with the church he had established. Paul seems to have thought a lot about the church.

Paul did not mention "church" at all in Thess(B). However, a certain amount of information has been known out of silence. It seems that the challenge against the gospel of Christ made Paul think again about the nature and role of the church of God. Paul probably prepared to open a new chapter in connection with the church that he had established.

Phil(A)

Paul used the term "church" only once in Phil(A). The lack of explanation of "church" makes it difficult to trace its meaning. In the meantime, Paul implied the birth of Christianity by taking a negative stance against the Jerusalem church.

The word "church" is simply mentioned in connection with persecution. This is seen in the comment that Paul persecuted the church on account of zeal for the Law (Phil 3:6). Paul tried to show that the church he had persecuted was not worthy of keeping the provisions of the Law. In addition, the word "God" was not connected to the church that he had persecuted. Perhaps Paul was trying to reveal the view that the church he had persecuted had nothing to do with God at the time of writing Phil(A). This reveals Paul's unfavorable view on the church composed of the disciples of Jesus that he persecuted. It seems that the Jerusalem church belonged to that category.

There is a reason that Paul changed his attitude toward the church composed of the disciples of Jesus. This is because the apostles of Jerusalem sent representatives to Philippi and made the Philippians confused in their life of faith. Since they asked the Philippians to observe the Law and be circumcised, Paul was nervous with them. However, the Philippians decided to stay in the gospel that he had preached. As a result, having revealed his past of persecuting the church, he tried to say that those sent by the apostles of Jerusalem persecuted the Philippians in turn. This is why Paul did not connect the word "God" to the church that he had persecuted at least. In consequence, it can be said that Paul revealed his intention not to recognize the authority of the Jerusalem church any longer.

In Phil(A), Paul simply used the word "church" in connection with his persecution. It seems that due to being nervous with the apostles of Jerusalem, Paul did not want to use the word "church of God" for their community. Accordingly, Paul seems to have tried to re-establish the concept of "church." Therefore, Paul did not describe the nature of the church at all. It seems that having stayed away from the apostles of Jerusalem, Paul gave birth to Christianity from a ecclesiological viewpoint.

Cor(C)

Paul dealt with a variety of topics in association with the church in Cor(C). It seems that Paul tried to be independent from the Jewish tradition after the direct challenge of some Corinthians sponsored by the apostles of Jerusalem. On the other hand, there was an attempt to unite the Gentile churches.

Above all, Paul continued to use the phrase "church of God." This is found in the expression "the church of God in Corinth" (1 Cor 1:2). Paul resumed mentioning the church of God here. This is because Paul already used it in connection with the Corinthians in Cor (B) (11:22). In addition, the church of God is mentioned in close connection with those who had been sanctified in Christ Jesus in Cor(C). Whereas the word "saints" usually referred to the members of the Jewish churches in Cor(A) (11:33) and Cor(B) (16:1), it is applied to the Gentiles in Cor(C). It seems that the Gentile church was defined as the community of saints for the first time. It should be noted that the role of Christ Jesus in sanctification is emphasized here. It is of special significance because Paul tried to get the Gentile churches away from the influence of the Jerusalem church.

Paul seems to have looked for solidarity among the Gentile churches. This is detected in the description that Timothy would remind the Corinthians of Paul's way of life in Christ Jesus, which agreed with what he had taught in every church (1 Cor 4:17). Paul emphasized the fact that he had taught all the Gentile churches the same instruction. This is reminiscent of his saying that he had taught the same instruction in all the Gentile churches as written in Cor(B) (7:17). Accordingly, Paul could once again present the identity of the Gentile churches in Cor(C). This reveals Paul's intention to break away from the churches of the Jews, including the Jerusalem church, and to build solidarity among the Gentile churches after the experience of the direct challenge of some Corinthians.

The church of God is mentioned again in association with persecution. According to Paul, he could not be called an apostle because he had persecuted the church of God (1 Cor 15:9). Paul talked about his persecution of the church in the past. This makes readers think of his previous saying that he persecuted the church with great zeal for the Law in Phil(A) (Phil 3:6). Thus, in Cor(C) Paul mentioned that he had persecuted the church in his past when some Corinthians challenged him against the gospel. This was probably written to imply the fact that the Jerusalem church persecuted the Gentile churches at the time of writing Cor(C). In any case, Paul provided the Corinthians with a negative narrative of the church of God made up of the disciples of Jesus whom he had persecuted.

Finally, the church is mentioned at the ending of Cor(C). This appears in reference to the churches in Asia and of Aquila and Priscilla (1 Cor 16:19). Paul seems to have built many churches around Ephesus; in addition, there was a church located at the house of Aquila and Priscilla. It seems that they lived for a considerable period of time in Ephesus to form a church. This is the first case that Paul introduced communication among the Gentile churches. Although Paul had been upset after the severe challenge of some Corinthians, he did not want to give them up. Rather, it seems that Paul kept having communication with them. Paul seems to have concluded that he could not be with the apostles of Jerusalem any longer.

Paul tried to constitute solidarity among the Gentile churches at the time of writing Cor(C). For this, Paul claimed that the same teaching was delivered to all the Gentile churches and he tried to keep communicating with them. At the same time, he argued for his apostolate in spite of his previous persecution of the church. In this way, Paul tried to make the Gentile churches independent from the Jerusalem church.

Galatians

Paul mentioned the church a couple of times in Galatians. His account of it is presented as a platform for the Galatians to be independent from the Jerusalem church. Probably he did not have time to think deeply about the church because he had faced the severest challenge.

There were many churches in the region of Galatia. This is known from the expression "churches of Galatia" (Gal 1:2). Paul designated them as the recipient of Galatians. Paul once presented the Galatians as a model for the Corinthians with regard to collection in Cor(B) (1 Cor 16:1). However, Paul did not make any other comment on the nature of the Galatian church there. In addition, no adjective or phrase was applied to the church in Galatians, unlike the cases of Thess(A) (1 Thess 1:1) and Cor(C) (1 Cor 1:2). This means that Paul was uncomfortable with the Galatians at the time of writing Galatians. Nevertheless, the fact that there were several churches in the region of Galatia implies that the Galatians were zealous in their faith in God.

Paul mentioned the church in connection with persecution. This appears in his description of persecuting the church of God when he was in Judaism (Gal 1:13). Paul spoke of his active role by expressing the desire to persecute and destroy the church. This is a stronger expression than what Paul mentioned in Phil(A) (Phil 3:6) and Cor(C) (1 Cor 15:9). This means that Paul talked about the persecution of the church since he had faced the severest challenge of the Galatians sponsored by the apostles of Jerusalem. In this way, Paul emphasized the fact that the one who had persecuted the church of God had become a minister at the time of writing Galatians. In turn, this tells that the Jewish churches, which had previously been persecuted by fellow Jews, became the persecutor of Gentile churches. In this way, Paul showed a crack between the Jerusalem church and the Gentile churches.

The church in the region of Judea attracted attention. This is found in the expression "the churches of Judea in Christ" (Gal 1:22). Paul applied the phrase "in Christ" to the churches of Judea because he heard of news that the Jewish members praised him for preaching the faith that he had tried to destroy. This shows that even though the churches of Judea stood on the Jesus tradition represented by Q, Paul linked them to Christ. Of course, Paul heavily relied on the Jerusalem tradition when he heard of their praise of him during his first missionary trip. However, at the time of writing Galatians, Paul was more dependent on the gospel of Christ inherited from the Damascus tradition (1:6–9). Nevertheless, Paul linked the phrase "in Christ" to the "churches of Judea" with a wish to show that even the churches of Judea had been on his side. A similar expression was already used in Thess(A) (1 Thess 2:14). Having wanted the Galatians to accept the gospel of Christ, Paul tried to lead away from the instruction of those sent by the apostles of Jerusalem.

Paul referred to "church" three times in Galatians. However, it seems that he was not able to explain the nature of the church in detail while being challenged most seriously in regard to the Law. Having confessed that the persecutor of the church had become a preacher of the gospel, Paul tried to emphasize that the apostles of Jerusalem had persecuted the

Gentile churches. This is the reason that Paul asked the Galatians to stay away from the instruction of those sent by the apostles of Jerusalem and to be independent from the Jerusalem church.

Cor(D)

Paul referred to the church without significant explanation in Cor(D). It was mentioned in connection with collecting money for the saints of the Jerusalem church. However, he did not describe the nature of the church at all.

Paul mentioned the church in three places. First, the "church of God in Corinth" is mentioned at the beginning (2 Cor 1:1). Paul already used it to inform of the location of the Corinthian church in Cor(C) (1 Cor 1:1). However, no other information was given about the nature of the church. Second, Paul mentioned the churches of Macedonia in the narrative of collecting money (2 Cor 8:1). The churches of Macedonia were presented as the model for the Corinthians as the churches of Galatia were in Cor(B) (1 Cor 16:1). At any rate, the Macedonians worked hard on collecting money for the poor saints of the Jerusalem church. However, no other theological concept of church appears in this context. Third, Paul mentioned the church several times in connection with the person who would carry the collected money (2 Cor 8:18–24). Paul introduced a brother with the phrases "praised by all the churches for his service to the gospel" and "chosen by the churches" (8:18, 19). At the end, Paul praised Titus and his companions to be the representatives of various churches and an honor to Christ (8:23). Paul finally asked the Corinthians to show their love before the Macedonians (8:24). The above statements show that the recommendation system was valid among the Gentile churches. In addition, this shows that there was a certain kind of communication among the churches of Macedonia and Achaia. This implies that Paul was working on the effective network among the Gentile churches.

The phrase "all churches" seems to mean the Gentile churches in Cor(D). Paul tried to strengthen solidarity among the churches in terms of collection. Although Cephas as well as the apostles of Jerusalem turned their back on him, Paul steadily raised money to keep the promise to support the poor saints in Jerusalem (Gal 2:10). It is important that the word "all churches" was used for the Gentile churches independent from the

Jerusalem church. In the meantime, having established an organization of churches, Paul tried to expand Christianity among the Gentiles.

Cor(E)

Paul made no mention of the church in Cor(E). This is probably because he knew to some extent that the challenge against him did not disappear among the Corinthians at that time. This seems to have been a turning point for Paul in connection with the church.

No mention of the church appears in Cor(E). A similar phenomenon appeared in Thess(B) because Paul knew that there had been a challenge of those sent by the apostles of Jerusalem. Without doubt, the challenge against Paul did not disappear among the Corinthians at the time of writing Cor(E). He may have tried to rethink the meaning of the church. Whereas his office for the Gentiles was described in detail, the role of the church was not mentioned at all. This seems to reveal a skeptical view of whether the Corinthians were qualified to form a church.

It seems that Paul fell into a love-hate relationship with the Corinthians. They did not follow Paul's teachings; thus, they did not form a church properly. However, it seems that Paul was not able to give them up. Whatever he taught about the church, it seems that they did not accept it.

Cor(F)

Paul revealed a perspective of community on the church in Cor(F). This is to treat all the Gentile churches equally. In this way, Paul encouraged the Corinthians to join in the direction he was aiming for.

The term "church" is mentioned in connection with the issue of salary. This appears in the description that Paul received financial support from churches other than the Corinthian church (2 Cor 11:8). It seems that Paul asked the Gentile churches for it, except the Corinthians. According to Jesus, a preacher of the gospel should be compensated by their salary as written in Q (Q^2 10:7). However, Paul did not ask the Corinthians for it because he had already received grace from God (1 Cor 9:7–15). In reality, however, he could not ask them for financial assistance because they had challenged him against the gospel. Paul rebuked the

Corinthians by comparing them with the members of other churches. This shows Paul's effort to maintain fairness among the Gentiles.

Paul expressed his concern about all churches. This is seen in the assertion that he was more concerned about all the churches than the sufferings he had experienced during his missionary trips (2 Cor 11:28). Paul expressed his love for all the churches that he had established among the Gentiles. With this statement, Paul made it known that he had always been concerned about the church in Corinth. Likewise, all churches had to receive his spiritual care. It seems that, having shown his concern for all churches, Paul tried to put them under his spiritual authority.

Paul once again referred to "all churches" in the relationship with the Corinthians. This appears in the saying that he ministered diligently except that he did not ask them for salary in comparison with other churches (2 Cor 12:13). Paul argued that he did not ask for salary because of parental love. In doing so, he presented "all churches" as the object of comparison. This implies, in turn, that he received financial support from other churches that he had established. In this respect, Paul taught that as an apostle he deserved to receive the financial support from churches for the mission to the Gentiles.

In the end, Paul did not link the phrase "of God" to the church in Cor(F). This is because the Corinthians kept challenging him against the gospel and his authority. Nevertheless, in the middle of their severe challenge, Paul tried to improve relations with all the churches. Paul seems to have constituted a network among the Gentile churches that made Christianity grow.

Summary

Paul maintained the conviction that all the churches were under the sovereignty of God. So he made the Gentile churches imitate the Jewish churches, including the Jerusalem church, until the middle of his second missionary trip. Accordingly, Paul took the Jerusalem church as an example and let the Gentile churches learn from her. However, when those sent by the apostles of Jerusalem delivered the Jewish instruction to the Gentiles and asked them to keep the Law, Paul changed his view on the church. Thus, he sought for the Gentile churches to be independent from the Jewish churches, especially the Jerusalem church. In addition, Paul began to look for solidarity among the Gentile churches. In the meantime, they began to reveal the character of Christianity as a whole.

C. THE THIRD MISSIONARY TRIP

Paul mentioned the church several times in the letters written during his third missionary trip. It is, however, noteworthy that the nature and character of the church were rarely treated. Rather, he strengthened the solidarity among the Gentile churches and put them in close relationship with Christ.

Rom(A)

Paul presented a couple of churches in his greetings to the Romans in Rom(A). It seems that the communication among them came to the fore. In the meantime, Paul introduced the church "of Christ" for the first time. However, the nature of church was not treated much; rather, Paul repeated what he had already explained in the letters written earlier.

Paul referred to the Cenchrean church. This is mentioned for the introduction of Phoebe, who is supposed to have been the deliverer of Rom(A) (Rom 16:1). Paul did not hesitate to employ a woman as a messenger. She may have been one of the saints in the region of Achaia mentioned in Cor(D) (2 Cor 1:1). Her active role implies a communication among the churches in the region of the Gentiles. This is supported by the list of names found at the ending part of Rom(A) (Rom 16:3-15). Paul knew the names because he had communicated the members of the Roman church.

The expression "all the churches of the Gentiles" appears in connection with Aquila and Priscilla. According to Paul, the Gentiles should be grateful to them (Rom 16:4). This implies that Aquila and Priscilla had fellowship with the members of the Gentile churches. The couple had a fellowship with the Corinthians as mentioned in Cor(C) (1 Cor 16:19). Then, Paul heightened the solidarity among the Gentile churches with the expression "all the churches." This reminds readers of "all the churches" that included the churches of Judea as written in Cor(A) (1 Cor 14:33b) and Cor(B) (7:17). On the other hand, Paul used "all the churches" with a reference to the Gentile churches in Rom(A). This reflects the fact that Paul tried to make solidarity among the churches beyond the communication. The churches in the region of the Gentiles should be independent from the churches of Judea.

Paul presented the existence of a house church. This is found in the request to greet the church at the house of Aquila and Pricilla (Rom 16:5). Paul showed that a certain number of people gathered together in a house to form a church. This implies that the Roman church started at the house of Aquila and Priscilla. It seems that their house was big enough to accommodate a certain number of people to worship God. However, no detail is given with regard to the Roman church except the names of those who belonged to her as found in the list (16:5–15). It seems that the Roman church was well known to Paul.

The church was closely related with Christ. This is seen in the expression "all the churches of Christ" (Rom 16:16). Paul referred to the churches "of Christ" instead of those "of God" in Rom(A). Although Paul previously mentioned the churches "in Christ Jesus" in Thess(A) (1 Thess 2:14) and "in Christ" in Galatians (Gal 1:22), this is the first case referring to those "of Christ." As Paul did not link the phrase "of God" to the church in Cor(F), so did he not in Rom(A). In this way, Paul put an emphasis on Christ more as time passed. In addition, "all the churches of Christ" refers to those of the Gentiles (Rom 16:4). In this respect, Paul sought solidarity in Christ among the churches in the region of the Gentiles.

Paul mentioned the words "whole church." This appears to be what Gaius had cared for (Rom 16:23). Gaius was the one who had helped Tertius and the whole church. It seems that the "whole church" refers to the Corinthian church, to which Gaius and Tertius belonged. It is important to observe that Gaius dedicated himself for the Corinthian church in spite of division among its members. In this respect, he deserved the respect of the Corinthians. Paul made readers catch a glimpse of the situation of the Corinthian church at the time of writing Rom(A).

The word "church" appears four times in Rom(A). However, Paul did not say much about the nature and role of the church. It was not until the time of writing Rom(A) that the expression "church of Christ" appeared for the first time. Thus, as time passed, Paul emphasized Christ in relation to the church. It seems that Paul had close communication with the Romans. In addition, Paul tried to show the solidarity among the Gentile churches to be independent from the Jerusalem church.

Rom(B), Rom(C), and Rom(D)

Paul did not mention the word "church" in Rom(B), Rom(C), or Rom(D). This is probably because he was busy responding to the question and critique of the Romans with regard to his negative view on the Law. It seems that Paul could not afford to develop a theological interpretation of the church.

The Romans continued to demand that Paul clarify his negative views on the Law. Accordingly, Paul could not help but describe his position to the Romans, especially the Jewish members, in Rom(B), Rom(C), and Rom(D). Otherwise, he could not even talk about the funding for the mission to Spain. It seems that he did not have much room to describe the church. Since he prioritized building his relationship with the Romans, he seems to have focused on describing the answer to the question they posed.

It seems to have been disadvantageous for Paul that he had not established the Roman church. In other words, Paul could not lead the Romans in the direction he wanted. The Romans were already forming a church in their own way. Even if he had taught them about the nature of the church, they woul not have accepted it. Perhaps Aquila and Priscilla had run their own church based on the ecclesiastical view they learned from Paul in Ephesus. As Jews, they may have reflected much of the synagogue system. As Paul did not mention the Jewish church after being challenged by some Gentiles under the sponsorship of the apostles of Jerusalem, he stopped mentioning the church because the Roman church was mostly composed of Jews.

Paul did not deal much with the church in relation to the Romans. This is probably because they listened little to Paul's teachings. It seems that Paul did not mention this in detail because he was actually dealing with more important subjects than the church. Moreover, even though the Roman church was in a Gentile region, it seems to have not paid much attention to solidarity with other churches in the region of the Gentiles. This is because the Roman church was mainly composed of Jews.

Phil(B)

Paul introduced the Philippian church as the one giving him financial support in Phil(B). This informs that the Philippians did what they had to do for the servants of God. Thus, Paul took a friendly attitude toward the Philippians.

The word "church" is mentioned in a favorable mode. According to Paul, no one except the Philippian church helped him financially at the beginning of the gospel (Phil 4:15). Paul recalled having received financial support from the Philippians when he had left for the province of Achaia during his first missionary trip (2 Cor 11:9). Two more cases of financial support had been mentioned; in addition, they did one more time while he was in the prison of Rome (Phil 4:16–18). On account of their financial support, Paul was happy whenever he thought of the Philippians. This implies that they did well with Paul's teaching to treat the preachers of the gospel as written in Q, which had been taught at the time of establishing the Philippian church during his first missionary trip (Q^2 10:7). Thus, even when Paul was imprisoned in Rome, he maintained a good relationship with the Philippians.

Paul did not describe the nature and role of the church in Phil(B). It seems that the Philippian church was already functioning as a church. Therefore, the Philippians were doing their best to help Paul financially. Without faith in the gospel Paul had preached, they would not have supported him financially several times. Paul maintained the most ideal relationship with the Philippians. There was nothing to say about the nature and role of the church to the Philippians.

Philemon

Paul sent a personal letter to Philemon. It was written for Onesimus, whom he had possibly met in the prison of Rome. In the meantime, Paul mentioned the church that was formed in the house of Philemon.

Paul referred to the church to which Philemon had belonged. This appears in a reference to the church gathered together at a house (Phlm 2). Paul probably referred to the church in the house of Philemon. He seems to have been affluent enough to offer his house for a place to worship God. This reminds readers of Aquila and Priscilla, whose house was used as a church to worship God as written in Cor(C) (1 Cor 16:19) and Rom(A) (Rom 16:5). This shows that the churches in the region of the Gentiles started at private houses in general. Paul also mentioned those who worshiped together, such as Apphia and Archippus. Philemon was defined as Paul's dear friend and coworker. Archippus was a man whom

Paul regarded as "a fellow soldier" together. In this regard, Paul seems to have been familiar with those who were the members of the church located in the house of Philemon.

Paul did not give much information about the church to which Philemon had belonged. However, he made readers catch a glimpse of Gentile churches that started at a private house. Since Paul sent a personal letter to Philemon, it seems that the nature and role of church were not dealt with much.

Summary

Paul made a couple of comments about the Gentile churches in Rom(A), Phil(B), and Philemon, written during his third missionary trip. However, Paul did not mention the church at all in Rom(B), Rom(C), and Rom(D), written as a reply to the question and critique raised by the Romans. First of all, Paul put forth communication among the Gentile churches. In consequence, this seems to have aimed for solidarity among them to be independent from the Jerusalem church. In addition, the lordship of Christ over the church appears. In this way, the center of theological weight moved from God to Christ with regard to the matter of the church. Paul did not explain much about the nature and role of the church in the letters written during his third missionary trip. Nevertheless, it cannot be denied that Christian instruction on the church expanded.

D. CONCLUSION

Paul developed his theological interpretation of the church over time. It seems that Paul established churches in the region of the Gentiles during his first missionary trip and made them take after the churches of Judea, including the Jerusalem church. However, a different stance toward the church emerged during his second missionary trip. As some Gentiles sponsored by the apostles of Jerusalem began to challenge Paul, he led the Gentile churches away from their influence. In the meantime, Paul tried to build a network of communication and insisted in solidarity among the Gentile churches. This shows how Christianity was born among the Gentiles. However, during his third missionary trip, Paul did not give much interpretation on the church, except the new expression "church of Christ." Paul came up with his theological interpretation in response to the circumstances of the recipients of his letters. It is, however, to be noted that theological description of the church was relatively little compared to other topics.

Epilogue

PAUL IS THE PERSON most studied by New Testament scholars. However, research on him has not yet been complete and continues to this day. Nevertheless, there are many issues that have not yet been resolved. Thus, I am sure that a new interpretation should be come up with. While I pursued the nature of Christianity, I found that his theology went through a process of change and development. It is definite that Paul creatively interpreted Jesus Christ based on the many traditions he had inherited. So I came to the conclusion that I could not really understand Christianity without knowing his theology.

It is important to observe that Paul's theology developed gradually over time. For him, the first turning point was that he received a revelation about the Son of God around 35 CE. Then, he seems to have been exposed to the tradition about Christ handed down from the religious predecessors in Damascus. Three years later, around 38 CE, he went up to Jerusalem and learned from Cephas about Jesus and his instruction on the basis of the first three redactions of Q. He became a worker for Jesus after being one who had persecuted his disciples. After that, he set out on a missionary trip to the Gentiles under the leadership of Barnabas. They seem to have traveled through Syria and Cilicia to Galatia, Asia, Macedonia, and Achaia for eleven years. Finally, around 49 CE, they returned to Jerusalem and presented before some apostles what they had achieved among the Gentiles. Paul and Barnabas were recognized for their achievement and were appointed as ministers for the Gentiles. In addition, the Gentiles were exempted from circumcision. In the meantime, Paul had an opportunity to learn more about Jesus on the basis of the fourth redaction of Q, which is supposed to have been completed around 41 CE. This series of events may have enabled Paul to enhance his theological understanding of the Lord Jesus Christ Son of God.

There was an event for Paul that marked a turning point in his relationship with the apostles of Jerusalem. This was a theological controversy over the Gentile table in Antioch around 50 CE. As a result, Cephas and Barnabas turned their back on Paul. Thus, Paul could not rely on the Jerusalem church and the Antiochene church anymore, and he had no choice but to leave for the churches in the region of the Gentiles. In fact, they were the churches Paul had set up with Barnabas; thus, he was confident that they would welcome him. However, it seems that Paul did not yet abandon theological interpretation from a Jewish perspective.

Paul also had a turning point in his relations with the Gentile churches. There was a challenge from some Gentiles. This reflects the fact that the apostles of Jerusalem had decided to send representatives to the Gentile churches and ask them to refuse Paul and his gospel. While the Philippians and Thessalonians stayed in the gospel Paul had preached, the Corinthians and Galatians followed the instruction delivered by those sent by the apostles of Jerusalem. They tried to Judaize the Gentiles by asking them to observe the Law, to be circumcised, and to accept the lesson of Jesus represented by Q. In response to their challenge, Paul emphasized the Christ-centered gospel to make the Gentiles the people of God without Judaization. Eventually, having put them away from the Jewish instruction, Paul began to establish Christianity among the Gentiles.

Lots of letters were sent to the Gentiles during Paul's missionary trips. Among the epistles currently included in the New Testament, Romans, First Corinthians, Second Corinthians, Galatians, Philippians, First Thessalonians, and Philemon are supposed to have been written by Paul. However, except for Galatians and Philemon, they are most likely a combination of two or more short letters. They can be listed as follows according to the chronological order of composition: Thess(A), Cor(A), Cor(B), Thess(B), Phil(A), Cor(C), Galatians, Cor(D), Cor(E), Cor(F), Rom(A), Rom(B), Rom(C), Rom(D), Phil(B), and Philemon. It seems that, having argued for righteousness by faith, Paul began to reveal his own theological interpretation in Phil(A). It can be said that Christianity was born among the Gentiles at that time.

Paul developed his theological interpretation while having been challenged by some Gentiles. First, Jesus Christ was described as the savior, and his death was presented as the way for the redemption of people. Then, his crucifixion was introduced as the way of leading people to salvation. Paul began to show a negative view on the Law. In addition, apocalyptic eschatology was abandoned in response to the severest challenge at the time of writing Galatians. The spirit of God was emphasized in various ways. Paul sought solidarity among the Gentile churches. In this way, Paul made many theological changes as he responded to the challenges of some Gentiles sponsored by the apostles of Jerusalem. New teachings were even created. In consequence, it can be said that Paul tried to make the Gentiles in solidarity centered on Christ.

It is important to observe that the Lord Jesus Christ Son of God was the crucial factor in his theological interpretation. The theological interpretation of him is related to various topics such as soteriology, eschatology, the Law, pneumatology, and ecclesiology. However, Paul did not present the Lord Jesus Christ as an object of worship; rather, he was described as a figure that the Gentiles should set as the example in their life of faith. Although his transcendental character was mentioned, Paul presented only God as the object of worship. There was not yet a Trinitarian theology.

Of course, Paul did not seem to create a new religion from the beginning. However, when the apostles of Jerusalem turned their back on him and sent representatives to the Gentile churches to get them to deny his gospel, Paul tried to make them in solidarity based on the gospel of Christ he had preached. It seems that Paul thought it was the way to fulfill the mission of God given to him in connection with the revelation about his Son. Then, Paul seems to have been self-conscious in that God called him as an apostle for the Gentiles. Anyway, he conveyed instructions centered on Christ to make the Gentiles in solidarity and this resulted in the new religion of Christianity.

It is necessary to think about why Paul's sixteen letters were compiled into seven epistles and brought into the New Testament. First, we have to consider the problems that arise when listing the original letters in chronological order. They will result in inconsistency with the appearance of Paul described in the book of Acts. The harmony between Paul and Peter will be broken. This would be a shame for Christianity, which was prospering among the Gentiles in the second century CE. However, since the sixteen letters were compiled into seven epistles, those features are concealed. Therefore, we must understand the meaning of Paul's sixteen letters at the time they were originally written and distinguish the meaning of his seven epistles after the compilation.

As discussed earlier, I have dealt with Paul's epistles from a different point of view than other scholars have approached them. This made it possible to infer how Paul developed his theological interpretation on various topics as time went by. I believe that my research can resolve the contradictions previously shown by scholars engaged in the study of Paul's theology. I wish for my study to unlock the mystery of the birth of Christianity and play a valuable role in shaping today's Christianity. Of course, I do not think that my interpretation is completely correct. So, I am open to critiques against my research. I will continue to interpret Paul's theological topics that have not been treated in this book. In this way, I believe that I am fulfilling the mission God has given me. This is how I apply to myself what have I learned from Paul.

Bibliography

Allison, Dale C., Jr. *The Jesus Tradition in Q.* Harrisburg: Trinity, 1997.
Arnal, William E. *Jesus and Village Scribes: Galilean Conflict and the Setting of Q.* Minneapolis: Augsburg Fortress, 2001.
Barrett, C. K. *A Commentary on the First Letter to the Corinthians.* Peabody, MA: Hendrickson, 1987.
———. *The Second Epistle to the Corinthians.* Harper's New Testament Commentaries. Peabody, MA: Hendrickson, 1987.
Bauer, F. C. *Paul the Apostle of Jesus Christ: His Life and Work, His Epistles and Doctrine.* Translated by E. Zeller. 2 Vols. 2nd ed. London: Williams and Norgate, 1873.
Bauer, Walter. *A Greek-English Lexicon of the New Testament and Other Early Christian Literature.* Translated by W. F. Arndt and F. W. Gingrich. Chicago: University of Chicago Press, 1979.
Beare, F. W. *A Commentary on the Epistle to the Philippians.* London: A. & C. Black, 1959.
Beker, Johan Christiaan. *Paul and the Apostle: The Triumph of God in Life and Thought.* Philadelphia: Fortress, 1980.
Betz, Hans Dieter. *2 Corinthians 8 and 9: A Commentary of Two Administrative Letters of the Apostle Paul.* Philadelphia: Fortress, 1985.
———. *Galatians: A Commentary on Paul's Letter to the Churches in Galatia.* Philadelphia: Fortress, 1979.
Bornkamm, Günther. "The History of the Origin of the So-Called Second Letter to the Corinthians." *New Testament Studies* 8 (1962) 258–64.
———. "Die Vorgeschichte des sogennanten Zweiten Korintherbriefes." In *Gesammelte Aufsätze,* 4: 179–94. Beiträge zur evangelischen Theologie 53. Munich: Kaiser, 1971.
Brown, Raymond Edward. *An Introduction to the New Testament.* New Haven, CT: Yale University Press, 2010.
Cho, Jae Hyung. "Paul's Opponent in 2 Corinthians in Light of Gnostic Idea." *Korean New Testament Studies* 20 (2013) 443–78.
Conzelmann, Hans. *I Corinthians.* Hermeneia. Philadelphia: Fortress, 1975.
———. "On the Analysis of the Confessional Formula in I Corinthians 15:3–5." *Interpretation* 20 (1966) 15–25.
Dunn, James D. G. *Christology in the Making: A New Testament Inquiry into the Origins of the Doctrine of the Incarnation.* 2nd ed. London: SCM, 1989.

Fitzmyer, Joseph A. "Qumran and the Interpolated Paragraph in 2 Cor 6,14—7,1." *Catholic Biblical Quarterly* 23 (1961) 271–80.
Furnish, Victor Paul. *II Corinthians*. Anchor Bible 32A. Garden City, NY: Doubleday, 1984.
Garland, D. "The Composition and Unity of Philippians." *Novum Testamentum* 27 (1985) 141–73.
Hooker, Morna Dorothy. *Jesus and the Servant: The Influence of the Servant Concept of Deutero-Isaiah in the New Testament*. London: SPCK, 1959.
Hofius, O. *Der Christushymnus Philipper 2, 6–11*. Tübingen: Mohr, 1976.
Hurd, John C., Jr. *The Origin of I Corinthians*. London: SPCK, 1965.
Jeremias, Joachim. *The Eucharistic Words of Jesus*. Translated by Norman Perrin. New York: Scribner, 1966.
Jewett, Robert. "The Redaction of 1 Corinthians and the Trajectory of the Pauline School." *Journal of American Academic of Religion Supplementary* 46 (1978) 388–444.
Kim, Panim. *Paul and the Corinthian Church*. Seoul: Dongyun, 2014.
Kim, Seyoon. *The Origin of Paul's Gospel*. Tübingen: Mohr, 1981.
Kloppenborg, John S. *The Formation of Q: Trajectories in Ancient Wisdom Collections*. Philadelphia: Fortress, 1987.
Knox, John. "Chapters in a Life of Paul." In *Colloquy on New Testament Studies: A Time for Reappraisal and Fresh Approaches*, edited by Bruce Corley. Macon, GA: Mercer University Press, 1983.
Lietzmann, Hans. *The Beginning of the Christian Church*. Rev. ed. New York: Scribner, 1949.
Lovejoy, Arthur O. *The Great Chain of Being: A Study of the History of an Idea*. New York: Evanston, 1960.
Lüdemann, Gerd. *Paul, the Founder of Christianity*. Amherst, NY: Prometheus, 2002. Kindle.
———. "Paul, the Founder of Christianity." http://wwwuser.gwdg.de/~gluedem/eng.
MacDonald, Dennis R. *The Homeric Epics and the Gospel of Mark*. New Haven, CT: Yale University Press, 2000.
Mack, Burton L. *The Lost Gospel: The Book of Q and Christian Origin*. New York: HarperCollins, 1993.
Marxsen, Willi. *Introduction to the New Testament: An Approach to Its Problems*. Philadelphia: Fortress, 1970.
Osiek, Carolyn. *Philippians, Philemon*. Abingdon New Testament Commentaries. Nashville: Abingdon, 2000.
Patte, Daniel. *Paul's Faith and the Power of the Gospel: A Structural Introduction to the Pauline Letters*. Philadelphia: Fortress, 1983.
Ra, Yoseop. *A Commentary on Galatians: The Gospel of Cross*. Seoul: Hahndle, 1998.
———. *The Origin and Formation of the Gospel*. Eugene, OR: Wipf & Stock, 2015.
———. *Paul's Six Letters for the Corinthians*. Seoul: Pubple, 2018.
———. *Paul's Four Letters for the Romans*. Seoul: Pubple, 2018.
———. *Q, the First Writing about Jesus*. Eugene, OR: Wipf & Stock, 2016.
Reuman, John Henry Paul. *Philippians*. Anchor Yale Bible 33B. New Haven, CT: Yale University Press, 2008.
Richard, Earl. *Jesus, One and Many: Christological Concepts of New Testament Authors*. Wilmington, DE: Glazier, 1988.

Robinson, James M., Paul Hoffmann, and John S. Kloppenborg. *The Critical Edition of Q*. Hermeneia. Minneapolis: Augsburg Fortress, 2000.

Schmithals, Walter. "The Historical Situation of the Thessalonian Epistles." In *Paul and the Gnostics*, translated by John E. Steely, 123–218. Nashville: Abingdon, 1972.

Schnelle, Udo. *History and Theology of the New Testament Writing*. Translated by M. Eugene Boring. Minneapolis: Fortress, 1998.

Scroggs, Robin. *The Last Adam*. Philadelphia: Fortress, 1966.

Seeley, David. "The Background of the Philippians Hymn (2:6–11)." *The Journal of Higher Criticism* 1 (1994) 49–72.

Standhartinger, Angela. "'Join in Imitating Me' (Philippians 3:17)." *New Testament Studies* 54 (2008) 418–26.

Steck, Odil Hannes. *Israel und das gewaltsame Geschick der Propheten: Untersuchung zur Überlieferung des deuteronomistischen Geschichtsbildes im Alten Testament, Spätjudentum und Urchristentum*. WMANT 23. Neukirchen-Vluyn: Neukirchener, 1967.

Strack, H. L., and P. Billerbeck. *Kommentar zum Neuen Testament aus Talmud und Midrasch*. 1922–1961.

Theissen, Gerd. *The Gospels in Context: Social and Political History in the Synoptic Tradition*. Translated by L. M. Malony. Minneapolis: Fortress, 1991.

Thrall, Margaret E. "The Problem of 2 Cor 6:14—7:1 in Some Recent Discussion." *New Testament Studies* 24 (1977) 132–48.

Vielhauer, Phillip. "Paul and the Cephas Party in Corinth." *The Journal of Higher Criticism* 1 (1994) 129–42.

Welborn, L. L. "On the Discourse in Corinth: 1 Corinthians 1–4 and Ancient Politics." *Journal of Biblical Literature* 106 (1987) 86–111.

Westermann, Claus. *Genesis 1–11*. Translated by John Scullion. Minneapolis: Augsburg, 1984.

Wilkens, U. *Weisheit und Torheit: Einie Exegetischereligionsgeschichtliche Untersuchung zu 1Kor 1 und 2*. BHT 26. Tübingen: Mohr-Siebeck, 1959.

Wright, N. T. "Adam in Pauline Christology." In *Society of Biblical Literature Seminar Papers 1983*, edited by K. H. Richards, 359–89. Chico, CA: Scholars, 1983.

Yeo, Khiok-Khng. *Rhetorical Interaction in 1 Corinthians 8 and 10: A Formal Analysis with Preliminary Suggestions for a Chinese, Cross-Cultural Hermeneutic*. Biblical Interpretation Series 9. Leiden: Brill, 1995.

Ancient Document Index

GENESIS

1:2	200, 201
1:27	82
3:1–6	83
3:15	80, 83
3:16	157
21:8–21	213

EXODUS

13:21	68
14:21–30	68
17:6	68
20:14	130
25:17	118

LEVITICUS

2:3	159
4:1—5:19	87
19:18	98, 163

DEUTERONOMY

5:18	130
6:13	155
6:16	155
8:3	155
32:11	201

2 SAMUEL

7:11–14	85

PSALM

2:7	85
110:1	86

PROVERB

8:22–31	64, 70, 76

ISAIAH

2:12	180
28:11	156
40:3	62
49:8	142
53:10	17, 87, 99

JEREMIAH

1:5	58

EZEKIEL

30:3	180

DANIEL

7:13	62, 175

HOSEA

6:2	17

JOEL

2:1	180

JONAH

1:2	201
3:4	201

MICAH

4:1–2	175, 176

ZECHARIAH

14:14	176

WISDOM OF SOLOMON

3:9	65
7:25	65

4 MACCABEES

17:2–4	65

1 ENOCH

42:1	64

TESTAMENT OF LEVI

18:1–9	16

Q

3:2–4	19
3:3	126
3:4	62
3:7	66, 128, 179, 195
3:7–8a	19
3:8	109, 126
3:8a	
3:8bc	27, 28, 63, 79
3:9	19, 176
3:16	200, 210
3:16–17	19
3:17	176
3:21	202, 205, 210
3:21–22	19, 61, 68, 77, 200, 213, 218
3:22	21, 68, 85
4:1–2	28, 68, 202, 205
4:1–10	
4:1–13	27, 28, 63, 68, 77, 100, 160
4:3	69
4:4	155
4:8	155
4:9	69
4:12	155
6:12–16	27
6:13–16	28, 63, 67, 229, 236
6:20a	27
6:20b	19
6:21	19
6:22–23b	19, 22, 228
6:23c	27, 28, 100, 102
6:27	19, 98, 126
6:28	19
6:29–30	126
6:29–31	98
6:29–38	19
6:39–42	19
6:43–45	19
6:46	23
6:46–47	62, 66

ANCIENT DOCUMENT INDEX

6:46–49	19, 137	11:39–46	20, 22
6:48–49	76	11:47	102
7:1–10	20, 201	11:47–51	27, 28, 100, 102
7:6–7	23, 62, 66	11:49	63
7:18–27	20	11:52	20, 22
7:24	19	12:2–3	20, 187, 190
7:28	27	12:4–5	27
7:29–30	20	12:5	177
7:31–34	20	12:6–7	21
7:33–34	69, 71	12:8–9	21, 22
7:35	27, 63, 70, 76	12:10	27, 28, 63, 68, 127, 202, 203, 205
9:57–58	20		
9:59–60a	27	12:11–12	27
10:2	20, 70	12:12	204
10:3	27	12:22–31	21
10:4–11	70, 228	12:29	69, 71
10:4–12	20	12:33–34	21
10:7	159, 243, 248	12:39–40	21, 175, 181, 185
10:9	236	12:42–46	21, 180, 181, 184, 194, 228, 231
10:13–14	201		
10:13–16	20	12:49	27
10:16	70, 76	12:49–53	100
10:21–24	20	12:51–56	28
10:22	21, 62, 210	12:58–59	28
10:24	102	13:18–21	21, 185
11:2–4	20	13:24–27	21
11:4	110, 126, 132	13:28–29	28
11:9–10	20	13:28–30	28, 177
11:11–13	20	13:29	28
11:14–15	20	13:30	28
11:16	20	13:34	76, 102, 236
11:17–20	20	13:34–35	28, 100, 102
11:21–23	20, 22	14:5	28, 100, 155, 160
11:24–26	27	14:11	28
11:29–30	20	14:16–24	28
11:31–32	20, 176, 185	14:23–25	185
11:32	102	14:24	28
11:33–35	20	14:26–27	27
11:39–42	154, 228	14:27	99, 104

(Q continued)

14:34–35	28
15:4–7	28
16:13	27
16:16	27
16:16–17	27, 155
16:16–18	28, 100, 160
16:18	155
17:1–2	28
17:3–4	21
17:4	110, 126
17:6	28
17:23–24	21, 176, 178, 184, 187, 188
17:24	62, 66, 72, 74, 128, 182
17:24–26	71
17:26	62, 66
17:26–27	21, 176, 185
17:27	69, 71
17:30	21, 184
17:33	27
17:34–35	21, 182, 185
17:37c	28
19:12–26	28, 177, 184, 194
22:30	28, 63, 177, 191, 193, 230

LUKE

3:21–22	15
22:47–23:49	52

ACTS

1:12–15	14
7:54–60	13
9:1–2	15
9:1–19	14, 15
9:3	15
9:5	96
9:10–19a	17
9:19–22	16
9:23–25	17, 60
9:23–27	18
9:23–30	24
9:27	22
11:25–26	24
13:1–15:5	24
15:1–21	15
15:35–41	24, 25
15:40	25
16:1	25
16:6	24
18:1–2	25, 41
18:7	230
18:18–23	47
19:1	48
19:21–22	48
20:1–2	48
20:3–6	48
20:13–16	48
21:27–28:15	52
22:3	13, 24
22:8	96
22:14	96
22:20	13
26:4	13
26:5	13
26:15	96
28:16	54
28:23	54
28:30	54

ROMANS

1:1–7	6, 49
1:1–17	5

ANCIENT DOCUMENT INDEX

1:4	61, 85, 97, 116, 218, 221	5:20	168
		6:3	119
1:5	92	6:6	119
1:8–15	49	6:10–12	119
1:16	144	6:14	168
1:16–17	49	7:1–25	51
1:18–2:11	50, 166	7:4	119
1:18–3:31	5, 6	7:5	168
2:5	194	7:6	220
2:12–3:18	50	7:8	168
2:12–3:31	166	7:11	168
2:17–19	166	7:12–20	169
3:19–31	50	7:21–25	169
3:20	147, 148, 167, 168, 196, 220, 221	8:1–30	52
		8:2	169, 221
3:22	86	8:2–3	88
3:22–24	146	8:3	91
3:24	87, 148	8:3–6	147
3:25	87, 118, 146	8:4	169
3:31	167, 169	8:9	221, 224
4:1–15	87	8:9–10	221
4:1–25	49	8:11	119, 195, 221
4:1–5:11	5, 6	8:13–14	221
4:13	165	8:16	223
4:15	50, 118, 146, 165, 166, 168, 195	8:23	222
		8:23–24	148
5:1–11	49	8:26–27	222
5:5	219, 220	8:31–39	5, 6, 49
5:6	85, 116	8:34	86, 92, 117, 121
5:8	116, 144, 219	9:1–2	223
5:8–10	88, 144, 146	9:1–5	53
5:9	85, 87, 144, 146	9:1–11:36	5
5:9–10	117	9:1–12:2	6
5:10	145, 149	9:4	170
5:12–19	147	9:6–29	53
5:12–21	88	9:25–26	149
5:12–6:23	51	9:30—10:1	149
5:12–8:30	5, 6	9:30–10:21	53
5:14	168	10:4	88, 149, 171

(Romans continued)		16:3	85
10:9	93, 120	16:3–16	49, 166
10:9–10	90, 149	16:4	245, 246
10:13	92	16:5	246, 248
11:1–36	52	16:5–15	246
11:11–14	150	16:16	246
11:20	150	16:17–20	6, 52
11:26	150	16:21–27	6, 49
12:1–2	52	16:23	49, 246
12:1–16:27	5		
12:3–13	6, 49		
12:14–13:7	6, 50		

1 CORINTHIANS

12:19	195	1:1	40, 242
13:8	170	1:1–3	5, 40, 75
13:8–10	6, 52	1:2	92, 239, 241
13:10	170	1:4–9	5, 33
13:11–14	6, 53	1:7	67, 103
14:1–12	6, 49	1:7–9	67
14:9	117	1:8	67, 130, 131, 180, 181, 196
14:12	194		
14:13–23	6, 50	1:9	61, 68
14:17	219	1:10	69
15:1–13	6, 52	1:10–12	40
15:9	92, 228	1:10–17	3, 5, 35
15:13	222	1:11	34
15:14–21	6, 53	1:11–12	107, 157
15:16	224	1:12	30, 36, 40, 70, 74, 183, 231
15:19	46, 47		
15:20	92	1:12–13	70
15:22–29	6, 49	1:12–17	104, 107, 210
15:25–26	47	1:13	71, 104, 111
15:26	48	1:14	49
15:30	220	1:17	40, 70, 71, 104, 108, 112
15:30–32	47		
15:30–33	6, 50	1:17–4:21	40
15:31	51	1:18	91, 108, 112, 136, 141, 144
16:1	245		
16:1–2	49	1:18–25	85
16:1–16	6	1:18–31	3

1:18–3:15	5, 40	6:9–11	34, 219
1:22	76	6:9–20	5, 33
1:23	108, 136	6:11	68, 70, 76, 92, 205
1:23–24	75, 108	6:14	72, 103, 105, 113, 180, 182, 183, 191
1:24	114		
1:30	76, 87, 108, 136, 137, 146, 148	6:15	130
		6:18	130, 131
2:2	91, 108, 112	6:19	34, 205, 211, 215, 221
2:3	39		
2:4	211, 212, 218, 222	6:19–20	130
2:8	108	6:20	137, 139
2:8–10	108	7:1	37
2:10	222	7:1–17	5, 35
2:10–13	210	7:12–16	132
3:1–3	212, 221	7:16	135
3:10–11	76	7:17	132, 235, 239, 245
3:10–14	137	7:18–24	5, 40
3:16	205	7:23	137, 139
3:16–17	5, 33, 34, 40, 221	7:25	37
3:18–23	40	7:25–40	5, 35
3:18–4:21	5	7:26	181
3:23	76	7:28	132
4:1–21	40	7:29	181
4:5	187, 190	7:31	181
4:17	40, 239	7:36	132
5:1–5	5, 35	7:40	206, 214
5:3	217	8:1	37
5:4	92	8:1–13	3, 5, 35
5:5	131, 135, 181, 209, 221, 230	8:6	70, 76, 82, 91
		8:11	79, 104, 106, 109, 114, 116
5:6–8	5, 40		
5:7	77	8:12	132
5:9	33	9:1	15
5:9–13	5, 33, 35	9:1–15	40
5:10–11	22	9:1–27	3, 5, 40
5:11	33	9:5	231
6:1–8	5, 35	9:6	25
6:4	235	9:7–15	243
6:5	71	9:8–9	159

(*1 Corinthians continued*)

Reference	Pages
9:13–14	159
9:15	39
9:15–18	159
9:20–21	159
9:21	163
10:1–4	68
10:1–22	3, 5, 33
10:3–4,	71
10:4	77
10:16	69
10:16–17	23, 71
10:16–22	71
10:21	69
10:23—11:1	3, 5, 35
10:32	235
10:33	133
11:2–16	5, 33
11:3	82
11:7	82
11:16	233, 235
11:17–29	5, 35
11:18	235
11:18–19	236
11:20	236
11:22	235, 236, 239
11:23	23
11:23–26	23, 105
11:24	106
11:24–26	71, 109
11:26	119
11:30–32	5, 40
11:33	239
11:33–34	5, 35
12:1	5, 35, 37
12:2–3	4, 5, 40
12:3	90, 93, 149, 210, 214
12:4	206
12:4–12	5, 35
12:7	207
12:8–11	207
12:12	71
12:13	5, 40, 210
12:14–27	71
12:14–31a	5, 35
12:28	236
12:31b–14:1a	5, 33
13:1–13	34
13:3	111
14:1b–19	5, 35
14:4	236
14:5	236
14:12	236
14:18–19	4
14:19	236
14:20–22	4, 5, 33
14:21	34, 156
14:23	236
14:23–25	4
14:23–33a	5, 35
14:26–33a	4
14:28	236
14:33b	235, 245
14:33b–34	234
14:33b–36	33
14:33b–38	4, 5
14:34	34, 156
14:37	34
14:37–38	33
14:39–40	4, 5, 35
15:1–2	90
15:1–3	61
15:1–5	15, 77, 97, 120, 138, 144
15:1–11	3, 5, 40

15:3	41, 79, 80, 87, 88, 109, 111, 112, 116, 138, 141, 144	16:10	34
		16:10–11	5, 33, 34
		16:11	34
15:3–5	16, 17, 21, 77, 125	16:12	36, 37, 40
15:4	16, 175	16:13–14	5, 34
15:5	16, 230	16:15	36
15:7	41	16:15–18	5, 35
15:8	15	16:17	36
15:9	13, 58, 239, 241	16:19	39, 41, 85, 144, 160, 166, 240, 245, 248
15:12	105, 110, 114, 116		
15:12–19	182	16:19–24	5, 40
15:12–28	3, 5, 35, 183	16:22	188, 197
15:12–24	191		
15:17	133	## 2 CORINTHIANS	
15:20–23	71		
15:20–28	182	1:1	242, 245
15:21–22	77, 88	1:1–2	44
15:22	72, 147	1:1–2:13	4, 5
15:23	72, 86, 148, 222	1:3–7	44
15:23–28	182	1:5	81
15:24	183	1:6	140
15:29	119	1:8	39, 55
15:29–58	3, 5, 40	1:8–9	42
15:44	77	1:8–2:4	44
15:45	77, 88, 147	1:9–10	113
15:45–47	82	1:14	190, 197
15:46	77	1:16	47
15:51–52	188	1:16–17	39
15:52	196	1:19	25
15:53	74, 191	1:22	124, 215, 223
15:56	50, 160, 161, 166	2:4	39, 109
16:1	37, 45, 236, 239, 240, 242	2:5–13	44
		2:12–13	41, 44
16:1–4	5, 36	2:13	45, 47
16:5–6	4, 5, 34	2:14–17	45
16:6	34	2:14–6:13	5
16:7–9	4, 5, 39, 40	2:14–7:4	4
16:8	41, 41, 109	2:15	141
16:8–9	42	2:16	141

(*2 Corinthians continued*)

2:17	46
3:1	46
3:1–4:6	45
3:3	215
3:6	215, 220, 221
3:6–7	164
3:6–8	224
3:13–14	81
3:17	216, 224
4:2	45
4:4	82
4:6	15
4:7–5:10	45
4:10	113
4:14	113, 191
5:1	191
5:2	191
5:4	191
5:10	191, 193, 194
5:11–6:13	45
5:14	114
5:17	82
5:18–19	145
5:18–21	145
5:21	141, 147
6:2	142
6:6	216, 219
6:14–7:1	4, 5, 33, 34
7:2–4	5, 45
7:4	197
7:5–6	41
7:5–7	45
7:5–16	4, 44
7:5–8:24	5
7:6–7	25, 83
7:10	140, 141
8:1	242
8:1–24	44
8:2	46
8:9	81
8:10	45
8:16–18	45
8:18	242
8:18–24	242
8:19	242
8:23	45, 242
8:24	242
9:1–15	5, 46
9:2	46
9:3	46
9:5	46
10:1–11	47
10:1–13:10	5
10:2	47
10:12–12:13	47
11:2	83
11:3	83
11:5	31, 47
11:8	243
11:9	248
11:13–15	47
11:13	31
11:15	192
11:22	13
11:28	244
11:32–33	17, 60
12:13	244
12:14	47
12:14–13:10	47
12:18	46, 217
13:1	47
13:4	114
13:11–13	5, 45
13:13	214, 219, 225

GALATIANS

1:1	42, 43, 110, 114, 116
1:1–4	85
1:1–5	42
1:2	240
1:4	78, 79, 80, 88, 110, 111, 112, 114, 116, 138, 141, 144, 189
1:6–9	241
1:6–10	42
1:6–2:14	42
1:11–24	42
1:13	13, 18, 228, 241
1:14	13, 154
1:15–16	58
1:16	14, 21, 58, 59, 67, 96, 125, 175, 180, 201
1:16–17	60
1:16–18	175
1:16–19	154
1:17	14, 15, 16, 18, 21, 59
1:17a	59
1:18	15, 18, 228
1:18–19	61
1:19	18, 228
1:21	23
1:22	14, 18, 241, 246
1:22–23	22, 96, 228, 229
1:23	58
2:1	8, 15, 24, 230
2:1–2	24, 26
2:1–3	25
2:1–4	176
2:1–10	42, 43
2:1–14	6
2:2	26
2:2–3	24
2:3	25, 154
2:3–4	231
2:3–6	26
2:4	230
2:6	230
2:7	26
2:7–8	231
2:8–9	26
2:9	28, 230
2:10	231, 242
2:11	231
2:11–14	24, 25, 29, 42, 43, 64, 177
2:12–13	155, 231
2:14	127, 231
2:15–21	43
2:16	49, 87, 141, 144, 161
2:16–17	139
2:19	161
2:19–20	111
2:20	61, 79, 85, 97, 111, 114, 116, 119, 163
3:1	43, 92
3:1–6:10	43
3:2	161, 165, 167, 169, 211, 212, 221
3:2–5	43
3:5	161, 167, 169, 212, 219, 221, 223
3:6–15	87
3:6–5:12	43
3:10	161
3:13	79, 80, 91, 111, 161
3:14	212
3:16	79
3:17–18	162, 165

(*Galatians continued*)

3:19	43, 50, 162, 165, 168
3:21–22	168
4:4	89, 91
4:4–5	80, 83, 139, 148, 162
4:4–6	222
4:5	139
4:6	212
4:17	43
4:25	60
4:29	213
5:2–24	222
5:4–5	161
5:9	43
5:11	112
5:12	30, 43
5:13–6:10	43
5:14	163, 170
5:16–18	213
5:16–24	219
5:18	221
5:19–23	213
5:25	213
6:2	89, 163, 167, 169, 170, 171
6:8	196, 213
6:11–18	43
6:12	112
6:13	43
6:14	112

PHILIPPIANS

1:1–2	53
1:1–3:1a	5
1:3–11	53
1:10	196
1:12–17	54
1:12–26	54
1:13	54
1:18–19	150
1:19	224, 225
1:27–28	151
1:27–2:18	54
1:28	54
2:1–2	225
2:5–11	90
2:6	90
2:7	91
2:8	151
2:8–9	121
2:9	92
2:10–11	93
2:12	151
2:16	197
2:19–24	39
2:19–30	54
2:25	54
3:1	2
3:1a	53
3:1b–16	38
3:1b–4:3	5
3:2	30, 38, 74
3:2–3	107
3:3	208, 209, 212, 222
3:5	13
3:5–6	13, 154
3:6	13, 58, 96, 158, 228, 238, 241
3:8a	15
3:9	38, 49, 73, 76, 135, 139, 141, 144, 158, 161
3:17–4:1	38
3:18	38, 108, 112, 136
3:18–20	75, 85

3:19	107
3:20	74, 86, 107, 135, 136, 186
3:21	186, 188, 191, 196
4:1	39
4:2–3	38
4:4–7	5, 53
4:5	197
4:8	2
4:8–9	5, 38
4:10–19	54
4:10–23	5
4:15	248
4:16–18	248
4:18	54

COLOSSIANS

4:9	55

1 THESSALONIANS

1:1	33, 65, 232, 241
1:3	65
1:1–2:16	5
1:2–10	32
1:5	203, 210, 211, 218
1:5–6	204
1:6	202, 203
1:8	66
1:9–10	33
1:10	66, 68, 71, 72, 73, 74, 85, 86, 97, 101, 103, 105, 106, 110, 114, 116, 128, 130, 131, 134, 139, 178, 179, 195
2:1–12	32
2:7	32, 67
2:11–12	32
2:13–16	32
2:14	14, 232, 233, 235, 241, 246
2:15	98, 102, 104, 106, 236
2:15–16	129
2:16	134, 179
2:17–20	36
2:17–3:13	5
2:19	72, 74, 184
3:1	38
3:1–5	36
3:2–3	38
3:4–5	37, 134
3:5	30, 38, 72, 75, 106, 157
3:5–6	208
3:6	38
3:6–7	37, 134
3:8–10	37
3:11–13	37
3:13	72, 74, 183, 184, 208
4:1	2
4:1–8	5, 32
4:1–5:28	2
4:2	32, 34
4:3–5	33
4:3–7	204
4:8	204, 211
4:9	37
4:9–12	37
4:9–5:25	5
4:13	37
4:13–18	37
4:14	106, 110, 114, 116
4:14–16	72, 74
4:14–17	134

(*1 Thessalonians continued*)

4:14–18	185
4:16	86, 188
5:1	37
5:1–11	37
5:2–3	185
5:4–5	134
5:8	134, 135
5:9	74, 106, 114, 134, 135
5:9–10	73, 75, 85, 116, 136
5:10	79, 106, 109, 134, 138
5:12–25	37
5:17	188
5:19	207, 208
5:23	72, 74, 183, 207, 208
5:26–27	5, 32
5:28	5, 37

PHILEMON

1–3	54
2	248
4–7	55
8–10	55
11–13	55
14	55
15–16	55
17–19	55
20–22	55
23–25	55

www.ingramcontent.com/pod-product-compliance
Lightning Source LLC
Chambersburg PA
CBHW050842230426
43667CB00012B/2107